*Motivating People in Lean Organizations*

# Motivating People in Lean Organizations

Linda Holbeche

Butterworth-Heinemann
Linacre House, Jordan Hill, Oxford OX2 8DP
225 Wildwood Avenue, Woburn, MA 01801-2041
A division of Reed Educational and Professional Publishing Ltd

ℛ A member of the Reed Elsevier plc group

OXFORD    BOSTON    JOHANNESBURG
MELBOURNE    NEW DELHI    SINGAPORE

First published 1998
Reprinted 1998

**British Library Cataloguing in Publication Data**
Holbeche, Linda
    Motivating people in lean organizations
    1. Employee motivation
    I. Title
    658.3´14

ISBN 0 7506 3375 1

Typeset by Harper Phototypesetters, Northampton, England

Printed and bound in Great Britain by
Biddles Ltd, Guildford and King's Lynn

FOR EVERY TITLE THAT WE PUBLISH, BUTTERWORTH-HEINEMANN
WILL PAY FOR BTCV TO PLANT AND CARE FOR A TREE.

# Contents

## 3  Communications

## 4  Developing the organization through teamworking and leadership

## 5 Introducing structure change – a strategic approach

## 6 The Operations Development Project at Thresher

## 7 Introducing lean organizations: cross-cultural experiences

## 8 Motivating and retaining people – the roles of the line manager and the Human Resource professional

## 9  Changing roles

## 10 The new employee

## 11 Should organizations care about career management?

## 12 (Changing) great expectations

## 17 Conclusion

# *Figures*

# Foreword

In the late 1990s, there are very few organizations left in the UK which have not felt forced either by competitive pressures or by government policies to become 'leaner'. Even extremely successful and enviably profitable companies in their field, such as Shell and British Airways at the time of writing, introduce yet further efficiency and restructuring initiatives to safeguard their competitive advantages. The comfort of arrival at one's goal seems gone for ever, as even greater heights of growth, profitability, quality, productivity, market share, Economic Value Added, or league table position are immediately set. The forces of global competition are powerful, and as long as nations (or their companies) continue to compete in economic warfare they show no signs of going away or diminishing.

Accepted truisms of life in large organizations particularly (many smaller organizations still have a combination of loyalty and shared risk) have been shaken to their foundations, and especially in terms of career expectations. Although the reality in many may not be nearly as harsh as the rhetoric, the latter has been fuelled by prevailing philosophies, gurus, and over-enthusiastic HR people. It is not surprising that confusion and insecurity are widespread. The mental switch, let alone the needed practical know-how, from 'the system will look after me' to 'personal ownership of career development' is very demanding for most people. Of course a proportion of high-flyers have always looked after themselves, though they represent only a small minority of employees. Most have relied on steady, or maybe just occasional, progress through a complex grading system that from time to time yields a jump in benefits or some real extra responsibility. With a bit of luck too, the ever more frequent reorganizations can be relied on to justify re-evaluation and another grade up. A system based on a hierarchy or grades is one that enables everyone to know where they stand, what they can aspire to, and gives a sense of order and fairness.

Now organizations are reducing hierarchical steps, abandoning multiple grade systems, reducing managerial roles, and asking people to take a stronger role in looking after themselves. Is this but a perverse and fashion-driven blip in the history of organizational progress, that will be submerged back into normal accepted ways of organizing people and work? In some organizations maybe so – for hierarchy, complex administrative systems, pressure for consistency and uniformity, and other established symptoms of bureaucracies are natural human tendencies. (Are not some replacing the inflexible parameters of job evaluation with equally complex and universalist approaches to competencies? And is it not natural for staff departments to retain their power through the systems they design, albeit in the name of progress?) But for organizations with their eyes on the next century, these are not reversible changes.

For organizations to be flexible and responsive to the forces that beset them, they need flexible and responsive workforces. Those that win will be those that can replace for ever the gods of neatness, consistency, complexity and hierarchy with a new model. This model is one where individuals are valued for their total ability to contribute (not the job they happen to be doing today), where project teams are more important than positions on organization charts, and where continuous learning at every level is embedded into the culture. Can a person have a career in this type of organization? It depends on the mental map that one holds of the concept of a career. If it is seen as the continuous growth of personal capability (rather than rungs on a ladder) – assuredly so! But if my organization persists in making it painful reward-wise for me to move laterally or even downwards in hierarchical terms, then I am not going to believe that *their* understanding of career progress has changed at all.

Structural change has forced many individuals to consider new alternatives. Perhaps it has meant leaving the womb of the organization they hoped to retire from; perhaps starting a completely new career; perhaps being unceremoniously outsourced to a new employer. Some, like myself, have voluntarily chosen the role of 'portfolio manager', and many have become consultants in the field of what they know best. I suspect, nevertheless, that the majority of people prefer to belong to a community, to an organization, to be identified with something bigger than themselves. The question for them is the extent to which they can see employment, within or beyond their current organizational context, as variable and not bounded by a particular job or even single profession.

This is a whole new world, and it is a revolutionary one in terms of how organizations can, and indeed must, work in the future. Linda Holbeche has already made acclaimed research studies of the effects of de-layering on career development and in this book she brings together many aspects of this revolution. Here she puts it in the full context of changing organizational models and approaches to personal development. Liberally illustrated with case material, she paints a contemporary picture that gives us reality rather than rhetoric.

*Andrew Mayo*

*Andrew Mayo is a consultant, speaker, writer and facilitator in international Human Resources management, with a specialism in people and organization development. He is a Director of ShareFair Networks Ltd and of Mayo Learning International Ltd, and is a Visiting Professor at Middlesex University.*

*He worked for nearly thirty years in major international organizations, most recently as Director of Human Resource Development for the ICL Group.*

*He is the author of two books,* Managing Careers – Strategies for Organizations *and (with Elizabeth Lank)* The Power of Learning, *both published by the Institute of Personnel and Development.*

# *Acknowledgements*

I would like to express my thanks to my husband, Barney and my parents Elsie and Bill, without whose ongoing support and encouragement this book would not have been written. I would also like to thank those who have contributed to the book – Laurence Jackson and Michel Syret; Andrew Mayo for his foreword, and all the organizational representatives who have helped me to prepare the cases described. Thanks are also due to the team at Roffey Park – Christina, Caroline, Pauline and Valerie who have helped in the data gathering, and to Jacquie Shanahan of Butterworth-Heinemann whose cheery encouragement has been an inspiration.

# 1   *Introduction*

## What is a lean organization?

In recent years there has been much talk of 'lean organizations'. Lean organizations are those that trim their internal costs to produce the highest possible margins on whatever goods or services they are providing. When the organization is operating like a well-oiled machine, with every part interconnecting effectively with other parts in order to provide superb goods and services for the customer, economic survival and growth seem assured. The logic is impeccable. No wonder that management gurus have recommended them!

Lean organizations are generally considered to be 'a good thing' since they appear to make sound business sense. In theory they enable an organization to reap the benefits of flexibility and innovation while facilitating such useful practices as teamworking. In business process terms, the aim is to reduce the cost of supplying the input whilst at the same time maximizing the value of the output to the customer. In some cases organizations have attempted to do this by improving or re-engineering their internal processes, introducing quality initiatives and making better use of technology.

The impetus for change may be the introduction of Total Quality, or may simply be the urgent need to shed costs. Some organizations have attempted to cut costs of production by slicing out those parts of the workforce that appear to be redundant. In many cases, a combination of both approaches has been used. In the macho 1980s, being 'lean and mean' was considered to be commercially desirable. By the late 1980s, for the first time in living memory, downsizing had started to affect white-collar workers on a big scale, producing shock-waves within society as a whole.

Becoming lean usually involves reshaping organization structures to enable business goals to be achieved more effectively. Consequently, employees have become familiar with apparently continuous rounds of re-engineering and restructurings which reflect the current needs or fads of the organization. Thus structures have been set up which operate along process lines, as a matrix, as project structures, as federations. As they internationalize, businesses have decentralized, recentralized, become 'virtual' with global centres of production and customer service. Change has become the norm.

## Flat structures

One of the most fundamental forms of restructuring has been the inexorable trend towards flatter organization structures, which remove selected layers of the management hierarchy. For organizations in the West, flatter structures represent a radical shift in thinking. They are more closely linked to the Japanese model of organization. Whereas for Japanese organizations, influenced by the works of W. Edwards Deming, flatter structures are a familiar way of operating, in the West they are relatively new, except in certain types of organization such as partnerships and consultancies. We are used to more hierarchical structures.

In many cases, delayering has involved removing several layers of the organization hierarchy, reducing the number of levels between the 'front line' staff and the head of the organization from twelve, for example, to four. In other cases, the amount of delayering has been negligible yet the organization still describes itself as 'flat'. Why should this be? It perhaps relates to the mindset and working practices which relate to flat structures, rather than to the number of management levels. Organizations want the benefits of flatter structures perhaps more than they want the flat structures themselves.

### Potential benefits of flat structures

Flatter structures should enable organizations to get the best out of their employees. An empowered workforce should be able to achieve more than in more hierarchical structures where the power of individual contributions is more limited. As one CEO said: 'We're having to empower people because we've disempowered them'. Flat structures should enable organization-wide quality movements to be carried out by cross-functional teams. This should mean that fewer and more flexible roles are called for, which brings potential cost-savings, with peripheral services outsourced.

The creation of a multi-skilled core workforce operating across previously rigid functional barriers should enable the organization to adapt and flex to market conditions. Taken to its logical conclusion, this could eventually lead to the 'virtual' organization in which completely flexible teams are brought together for specific purposes and times. Given the competitive environment within which organizations operate, the need for flexibility, core strengths and speed of response has perhaps never been greater.

## Lean organizations and the competitive environment

Organizations are going through massive shifts as they face the new global business environment. Some of the features of that environment are so fundamental that they are likely to drive greater change in future than we have already seen. One of the biggest change drivers is the rapid advance of new technologies.

### Technology

Technology is having a major impact on work, with many formerly labour-intensive processes now being automated. Consequently whole groups of mainly semi-skilled jobs have disappeared, while other forms of work have been created. The era of the 'knowledge worker' is upon us. Technology has also brought changes in information and communications. The development of cell phones, laptops and modems means that employees are expected to be accessible anywhere, at almost any time. Distinctions between work and home life are blurring. The possibilities of accessing information via the Internet appear almost boundless; we are yet to see the full implications of such technology on our work and personal lives.

Technology is helping established organizations to reinvent themselves. One major financial services organization recognized that increased competition in its financial products was making sustained profitability difficult to achieve. Senior management realized that the company's huge databank of customer details was in itself a major resource, and they reinvented themselves as being in the information business ahead of their competitors.

Technology has also led to the development of new kinds of business, such as home banking, new forms of organization and occupations. It has made possible the development of global teams, virtual teams and other groups who can be based in different geographical areas but are able to provide a seamless and cost-effective service to the customer, wherever the customer is. Teleworking is not only a possibility but a reality for many. Technology has helped many organizations to expand their horizons from national or regional boundaries to become global players. Through the use of technology unexpected competitors are suddenly able to challenge long-established businesses on their home ground. Technological advance provides a short-term competitive edge, but any advance can be easily replicated. It is increasingly recognized that the best form of competitive edge comes not only from having the best product but also from the quality of customer service the organization provides.

### The customer service revolution

Relative affluence in the West over the past three decades has meant that most people have acquired a wide range of goods and products. By the nature of things, what were regarded as luxuries yesterday are today's necessities. In terms of products, customers are becoming ever more discriminating and demanding. What the customer wants is innovative, higher quality, cheaper goods – by yesterday! Lean organizations seem to offer an ideal way of keeping costs low, since when employees are working to their full potential and teamwork ensures maximum leverage of human skill, there is less need to employ a huge workforce or to pass on such costs to the customer. Similarly, innovation is easier to 'design in' to processes which have fewer layers of bureaucracy to overcome before they are approved.

It seems that customers are looking nowadays not only for a quality product, but also for the element of pampering or individual attention known as customer service. Getting the material goods right, therefore, is only part of the answer. Good customer service involves the human touch. Customer service can be outstanding when employees are 'empowered' to use their initiative in dealing with customer needs. Flatter structures can facilitate this, allowing ideas to flow, since there are fewer communication barriers, and innovation to flourish. All in all, flatter structures seem an ideal way of organizing work.

# Lean organizations and society

The term 'lean organizations' encompasses an increasingly bewildering range of organizational types that have emerged in the past few years as organizations try to ensure that they are competitive. Whether these are management 'fads' which will be replaced by other fashions in their turn or whether they represent part of a bigger shift in the way in which work is organised is not easy to see. What is evident is that there are a number of sea-changes under way which will fundamentally affect the world of work as it has been known in the West for the past forty years.

### The changing nature of employment

Lean organizations challenge some of the basic suppositions on which the so-called 'psychological contract' between employers and employees is based. One of these presuppositions is that having a career means being employed full-time in a secure job.

Organizations have taken the opportunity during the long recession of the late 1980s and 1990s to concentrate on their core business and outsource peripheral activities. Downsizing has cut workforces to the bone, reducing to a nonsense the idea that a job can be for life. Whether these workers will be reintegrated into the main business as growth returns remains to be seen.

Core workforces are shrinking. It is estimated that by the year 2001, 41 per cent of work patterns will be non-traditional (*ISR: Labour Market and Skill Trends 1996/1997*). The growth of flexible working in its many forms – contract work, part-time work, teleworking, 'hot desking' – is already obvious. In the retail trade in particular, the impact of customer choice has led to shops being open seven days a week, and in some cases round the clock. Shift working, so often in the past the preserve of semi-skilled workers, is increasingly applying to office workers and managers. There has therefore been an increasing trend towards generalism amongst members of the 'core' workforce as people are expected to be adaptable and multi-skilled.

New types of work and more fluid working patterns require new skills, behaviours and types of performance. Economic changes which have led large numbers of workers to shift to new forms of employment look set to continue. For many people whose skills are perceived to be obsolete this can mean redundancy, or at least the fear of losing their job. In the West as a whole unemployment has become a familiar spectre, and people are being thrown back much more on their own resources. Although flattening organization structures does not automatically involve downsizing or job losses, the combined effect of changes usually does involve some job loss. The implications of the changing nature of the employment market have as yet barely started to be understood. As Mark Hastings (1996) of the UK's Institute of Management states:

> Employers, government and individuals must now look to the future and grasp the opportunities this new (employment) market represents.

For many people in the ever-changing workplace, self-employment has become a viable alternative to full-time employment with one employer. Yet the full-time employment model continues to dominate our thinking. There is still some stigma attached to flexible working. Many self-employed people find it important to transfer over to their new form of employment symbols and status from their employed life. Consequently, 'independent consultants' and 'freelancers' become 'company directors' in no time. This is hardly surprising since, in the UK in particular, the economic infrastructure of society is to a large extent still geared to a conventional employment model.

Flatter structures in particular challenge the presupposition that having a career means being promoted. In a vertical hierarchy, with many levels through which people can progress, career development has usually involved acquiring experience and seniority gradually, with clear levels of accountability at each stage. Flatter structures reduce the number of opportunities for vertical promotion and as yet there is no clear alternative career model which seems to be gaining ground. The main alternative model involves the gradual acquisition of skills through increasingly developmental responsibilities, at the same organizational level, yet in practice this model is often difficult to implement. There are often seemingly insuperable difficulties to be overcome by the individual who wishes to develop a lateral career path. Moreover, alternative careers, including self-employment, are seen as the risky option.

**Cultural shifts**

In the UK, the trend towards lean organizations is also driven by ideological and political beliefs. In recent years organizations in public ownership have been privatized to bring about, in theory, the benefits of increased customer care and efficiencies achieved by the private sector. These changes have been accompanied by increased regulatory pressures, and new forms of management have emerged. Such cultural shifts are not without their costs. Employees who were attracted to a career in the public sector because of its vocational nature may now find the organizational values in operation to be at odds with their own.

# What are the implications of lean organizations for employees?

For employees lean organizations have a number of implications. First there is the nature of the work itself. In a hierarchical structure decision-making responsibility is carefully restricted to certain management layers. Work is normally functionally organized and career development usually takes place up functional 'silos' (Figure 1.1).

By contrast, in a flatter structure work normally takes place across functions, often in process teams. Decision-making is devolved to each level in the hierarchy. Career development in principle takes place at the same level and involves growing skills and experience (Figure 1.2).

New working practices call for new skills, behaviours and management styles. In a hierarchical structure in which roles are clearly segmented and responsibilities often narrowly defined, a command and control management style may be appropriate. If things go wrong it is the manager who takes on the role of fire-fighter and problem-solver. In times of relative stability hierarchical structures are useful since they minimize the need for crisis management and make for easy standardization of procedures. In lean organizations, with fewer employees who are called upon to carry out more complex tasks, the manager is no longer the sole decision-maker. 'Empowered' employees who have the skills, resources and training for their tasks need support and guidance from their managers rather than control. This implies that participative and enabling styles of management are more appropriate.

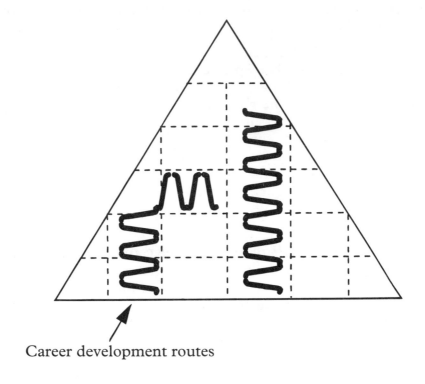

Career development routes

**Figure 1.1** *Traditional hierarchy*

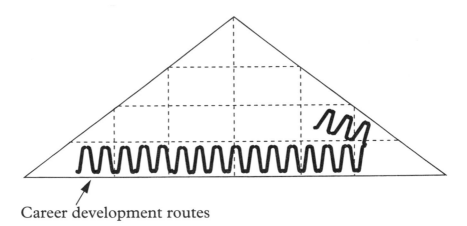

Career development routes

**Figure 1.2** *Flatter structure*

Lean organizations therefore require different types of working relationship. Whereas in a hierarchical structure relationships between management levels might be described as parent–child, flatter structures call on people to be able to interact on a more adult–adult basis. This implies that if accountability and responsibility are to be shared, so also must authority. Similarly, if problem-solving is to be shared, so also must support and resources. Working in any sort of team is different from working in a work group. For many people these shifts represent a massive change, and we will be looking in more detail at different reactions to change in Chapter two.

The biggest changes of all have affected people's careers in lean organizations. The effects of on-going restructuring include insecurity and increasing work loads (Holbeche, L., 1994). Delayering has exploded the myth of onwards and upwards, yet there are no clear career alternatives. People are being told to manage their own careers. All of these changes are having an impact on people's morale, motivation and willingness to deliver 150 per cent performance when there seems to be no end to the pressure and little to be gained other than continued employment.

## The challenge is how to make flat structures deliver on their promise

This is where the logic of lean organizations breaks down. There is one vital factor that the economic argument for leanness fails to take into account – people. In fact, many organizations have made a virtue out of becoming 'lean and mean'. In almost every industry the real key to competitiveness lies in developing and supporting innovative products or services with excellent customer service. Technology can help but, in the final analysis, these can only be provided by people. The quality and motivation of the people working within the organization as well as the active use of the potential of the workforce are therefore directly related to business results. The financial equation suggests that returns to shareholders or other stakeholders are dependent on business results, which in turn are dependent on individual results.

The 'people' side of the equation needs to be addressed. In tough times for businesses, people issues often take a back seat to more pressing problems. Organizational needs take priority over employee needs every time, and short-termism rules. However, there is real evidence that it is not tenable in the long term simply to expect higher outputs from people in terms of performance with fewer inputs in terms of resources, people, training, time and support. Things have got out of kilter.

It is becoming increasingly obvious that employees are not adjusting as well or as quickly to the changing workplace as businesses might hope. Even where positive business results are being achieved, it is questionable how sustainable these are in the long term if the people producing them are unable or unwilling to deliver to ever higher targets. Even some of the original advocates of lean organizations, such as Stephen Roach, are now suggesting that downsizing has gone too far. Other cultures too are experiencing the 'worm turning'. In South Korea, the end of guaranteed employment has provoked serious and widespread strikes. In France, government attempts to reduce workers' employment rights resulted in strikes and government backdowns.

Many organizations are waking up to the need to address issues of employee motivation, but managers often express a sense of impotence about how to deal with them. If lean organizations and flatter structures are here to stay, the challenge is to make these structures work. The key question now is how to make them work from the point of view of meeting employee needs, so that in turn organizational needs are met. This calls for a strategic, long-term perspective which is uncharacteristic of many organizations, for whom investing in people is a mere act of faith.

## Do organizations understand what people find motivating?

More than any other 'asset' of an organization, people are perhaps the most volatile and easily damaged. Well-motivated people, especially when they are also competent, are the key to outstanding performance. When people are really 'firing on all cylinders' there is usually a complex set of factors at work which enable them to be motivated. These can include loving their work and being stimulated by it, feeling loyal to and valued by their employer, believing that they have a positive future and that their work helps contribute towards securing that. Lean organization structures can have very strong effects on employees' morale because they hit directly at what many people find most motivating.

Indeed, it is arguable that rather than being motivated by others, most people can motivate themselves given the right conditions. This is the equivalent of making the horse thirsty before you take it to drink. There is at least one school of thought that suggests that it is better to concentrate less on finding ways to motivate people and more on finding ways to eliminate what is known to demotivate people. Trying to motivate people can be a fool's errand if based on mistaken assumptions. Employers, for instance, often misunderstand what the majority of employees find motivating, especially in times of change. In one survey of employers and employees, 89 per cent of employers believed their staff worked mainly for money and only 11 per cent thought job satisfaction was an important factor. Employees, on the other hand, thought that the most important sources of motivation, in rank order, were: interest and enjoyment, security, sense of achievement, basic pay. Perhaps listening to what employees say they want can lead to a better understanding of what needs to change in order to motivate them.

Thus 'intrinsic' rewards were much more important sources of motivation than 'extrinsic' rewards. Trying to deliver new forms of extrinsic motivators such as reward systems is hard enough. Many of the 'intrinsic' motivators are badly affected in lean organizations, since many of the internal processes are at odds with what the organization is trying to achieve and what employees need. Judging by much of the research evidence, if extrinsic and intrinsic motivators are to flourish in flatter structures, a wide range of organizational factors need to be brought into line with what the organization is trying to achieve. Even then, individual needs and aspirations need to be taken into account in a way that centralized, inflexible systems do not always allow for. There is increasing evidence that unless the balance of motivating factors is right, people are starting to vote with their feet.

So in this book we shall be looking at a range of factors which are known to have a bearing on people's motivation. We shall be looking at both the positive and negative effects of lean organizations on employees, and considering how these organizations change people's roles, skill requirements and career options. We shall examine some new ways of thinking about careers and explore some examples of effective career management in lean organizations. We shall also be looking at people within organizations who have a special responsibility with regard to addressing issues of motivation – line managers and Human Resource professionals. We shall consider how the very process of introducing change can be a key ingredient in activating people's motivation. We shall also address some of the real challenges of reconciling what the organization needs with what employees need. This book is about redressing the balance.

# 2 The effect of lean organizations on employees

The ongoing relentless nature of change appears to be taking its toll, according to Stephen Drew (1994):

> People in organisations appear to be suffering from a disabling form of future shock. Individuals are often stressed from having to cope simultaneously with increased workloads and technological change.

No employee can escape the impact of such wide-ranging changes. Research carried out at Roffey Park and elsewhere has been looking at the impact of lean organization structures, in particular on employees. In this chapter we will explore a few of the effects on employees of flatter structures.

The story begins back in 1994 when I first started to research the effect of flat structures on people's careers. My interest was sparked by a number of observations and conversations with line managers from a range of organizations which had recently delayered. I was struck in particular by the case of a senior manager in a financial services organization whose job had recently been regraded as 'team leader', some four steps down the previous hierarchy than his old job title had been. He had joined the company as a young man and gradually worked his way up the multi-level hierarchy, getting a promotion roughly every two years. Then, in his early forties, the next step would have been to become a director. He was loyal to the company and indeed, as his entire career had been spent successfully with one employer, he had no thoughts of looking for other roles. Indeed, he considered that his experience to date was so company-specific that finding a job in another company would probably be difficult.

As manager he was responsible for the output from part of a division employing 200 staff. He had six direct reports. After the delayering exercise his direct span of control went up to twenty direct reports. Though his salary was not reduced it was effectively frozen for three years. The company informed him that they were buying back the entitlement to a company car. The chances of becoming director receded overnight. Not surprisingly, he was unhappy and demotivated by what had happened, yet he was expected to be the implementer of new processes in his area which would produce higher productivity from his team. I wondered what the chances of him achieving these targets were in the circumstances.

The research project was set up to explore issues relating to the effect of delayering on employees' careers, to establish whether the apparently negative effects were just short-term or more far-reaching, whether the effect on people's morale had any connection with their performance or output, and whether therefore organizations needed to do something to address the issues. We wanted to know why organizations had chosen to delayer, what were the effects on roles and individuals, and whether organizations were taking morale and career issues seriously.

We worked with 200 organizations and asked four groups of people in each the same questions. The groups consisted of senior line managers and senior Human Resource (HR) professionals (who might be expected to be involved in decisions to delayer) and more junior line and HR professionals who might be expected to be on the receiving end of such decisions. These were people who were working in the organization at the time of the delayering, since we reasoned that people who had chosen to work in a flat structure might feel differently about it than people whose experience of the organization was of a more hierarchical structure.

## What seems to increase the negative effects of change on employees?

In broad terms we found that the new structures had produced wide-ranging effects, some positive but mainly negative, on employees. We found interesting differences of reaction from different groups, which led us to wonder how much the strength of reaction is linked with the amount of control over the situation the individuals feel they have. There seemed to be a direct connection between being on the receiving end of someone else's decision, especially when one does not know the reasons for that decision, and with feeling negative about the effect of the decision.

When we asked, for instance, why the organizations had delayered, there was a wide discrepancy between junior and senior employees about the reasons. Senior people were much more likely to give a 'strategic' sounding reason such as 'we're going global', 'refocusing our markets' or 're-engineering'. More junior people were less likely to highlight such reasons. For them the overriding reason was cost-cutting. This seemed to colour how they perceived they were affected.

We found that the majority of employees who took part in our research considered the effects on them to be negative. If people thought that the reason for the change was just cost-cutting they reported having lower morale, more staff leaving, fewer promotion prospects and less responsibility. They were more likely to think of themselves as victims of other people's incompetence than were other people who could see a more strategic reason for the change. Sometimes there were other reasons, apart from cost-cutting, for the changes. However, people often did not know about them since communications were poor, and in other cases people did not believe their company rhetoric.

Some of the other common factors that increase the negative effects of change on employee morale are listed below.

- An external requirement for change. Morale was perhaps worse in UK government departments and public sector bodies where the changes were on the whole being externally imposed by government policy.
- A constrained, unsupportive environment.
- Change that is extensive in scope and apparently never-ending.
- Change does not appear to be controlled or backed by the head of the organization.
- There is a radical shift in the organizational mission. Where there was once a fit at the values level between organization and employees, there is now a discord if employees are unable or unwilling to adapt their values. This is particularly noticeable in newly privatized organizations or where public bodies seek to adopt more commercial values and practices.
- Change is introduced purely to reduce headcount.

# The effects of change over time

When we started our research, we expected many organizations to be experiencing the traumas of undergoing the change process. We were curious to find out what would happen as time moved on. Would people have adjusted to the new situation and all would be well, or would the effects of change still be working through? When we revisited the same research groups after a gap of two years to see what, if anything, had changed, there were some strong themes, which appeared to be the same as those found by our earlier research.

## Positive effects

Of course, over time many organizations are experiencing some of the benefits of flatter structures, notably on their bottom line. Many employees, too, are experiencing benefits.

### *Empowerment culture*

Some of the main benefits are in working conditions. For people who are ready to respond to the challenge of empowerment, flatter structures provide an ideal environment. In particular, the shorter lines of command, reduced bureaucracy and sharper focus provide people with direct access to key information that they need to do their job effectively. This in turn can help people to achieve tasks which would previously have been the preserve of another rank. Success can breed confidence, which in turn can encourage people to use their initiative and challenge the status quo. Since individual performance is more apparent, 'dead wood' is usually removed, which leads to higher levels of performance all round. There is usually an increase in teamwork since work processes often call for crossfunctional co-operation.

### *Opportunities*

All of these shifts represent opportunities for some people. Many people talk of appreciating the chance to broaden their skills and experience in the new structures. In many cases this has allowed them to break out of a rut in which they had felt trapped for years. In some cases their current role has expanded, increasing the scope of their responsibilities. This job enrichment often gives people access to resources and opportunities which would previously have been beyond their role. In other cases people have moved into other roles or taken part in projects that have widened their understanding of their business. Increased skills often lead to increased employability, and many people reported having been head-hunted. In most cases where roles had broadened, people helping us with our research reported having increased job satisfaction, which in turn had positive effects on their motivation.

The flatter structures also seem to offer a form of status to people who have greater access to working with senior managers than in the old hierarchy. Working in project teams on an important organizational issue can be stimulating in itself. In such cases, the loss of status stigma means that people are able to contribute their skills and experience more directly and thus have influence on the course of business decisions in a way which may have been denied them in the old structure.

## Negative effects

Going back to our research, though, we found that most employees experienced more negative effects than positive effects from the new structures. Most people reported having lower morale, fewer promotion prospects and more work to do than in the old structures. In lean organizations, every employee's contribution becomes more important and the effect of low morale more evident. The biggest sources of dissatisfaction were lack of job security and lack of career opportunities. There was still a strong impression that most of the benefits of new structures were being reaped by the organization rather than being shared with employees.

### *Why the changes appear to have such negative effects – a look at motivation theory*

Before looking in more detail at some of the apparently negative effects of lean organizations on employees, it may be useful to look at some well-known theories of motivation for possible explanations of the many negative perceptions. One set of theories talks of expectancy and takes into account that people have different needs. An example is the so-called '**motivation calculus**', which assumes that when an individual experiences a need he or she is usually ready to perform in order to satisfy that need. However, before expending the energy and effort required to do this, the individual makes an (unconscious) calculation based on the expected outcome or reward for the effort made. If the reward is not likely to satisfy the need, it is unlikely that the individual will make the effort required. If the reward is great but the effort required to achieve it is too great, the need remains but the task can seem hopeless and demoralization can set in. For a virtuous cycle of need–performance–reward to be established, the balance has to be geared to the individual's circumstances, competencies and expectations on the one hand and to what the organization needs and can offer employees on the other.

In other words, the theory suggests that people have to believe that they have the capacity to improve performance. Yet in a lean organization, how clear are the skills, competencies and experiences required for success, and do people generally have a good level of self-awareness of their own skill levels? People also have to believe that improved performance will not be unduly costly in terms of energy, effort or social cost. In a lean organization, how clearly are work levels defined and processes clarified so that people are able to work smarter, not harder? People have to know that improved performance will result in demonstrably good results – measurable and perceived as improved. However, how often do people make extra effort which is taken for granted and becomes expected as the norm? How much feedback is given about performance, both positive and negative? People also have to know that results will be seen as a positive contribution, that results will be rewarded and that the reward will be relevant and equitable. Yet how often are organizations and managers unclear about what really constitutes a good performance and unable to reward employees flexibly? In a lean organization, with ongoing change and few clear markers on which the motivation calculus can be based, poor motivation, overwork and failure to deliver superlative performance may all be symptoms of the breakdown of that balance of needs.

Another set of theories looks at the satisfaction of needs. Abraham Maslow's famous '**Hierarchy of needs**' suggests that human needs are organized in a series of levels, a hierarchy of importance, starting with physiological and safety/security needs, followed by social needs (Maslow, 1943). Higher level needs relate to the self, both for self-esteem and self-fulfilment. Consequently, the satisfaction of certain higher levels of need, such as having the opportunity for self-actualization or self-fulfilment, is interdependent with lower needs, though the higher level need may emerge before the lower need has been completely satisfied. Applying the theory to lean organizations, which typically are characterized by lack of job security and promotion opportunities, the interplay between different levels of need may perhaps be seen in the continuing aspiration for promotion when there are few or no opportunities available. Promotion may be linked for many people with satisfying their higher-level needs. Even when there is continuing employment uncertainty, some people may still aspire to promotion. On the other hand, for some people their job represents basic security and they are keen to retain their job no matter what. Taking on extra work may be a means of self-protection rather than a means of satisfying other ambitions. If security is threatened, interesting work in itself may not be considered satisfying.

**Herzberg** also describes motivation in terms of satisfaction, and his theory assumes that a satisfied employee will be a productive employee (Herzberg, 1966). Herzberg argues that the factors which produce satisfaction for people at work are different from the factors which cause dissatisfaction. Extrinsic factors, such as company administration, management, relationships with peers, bosses and subordinates, are more likely to result in dissatisfaction and are known as 'hygiene' factors. Intrinsic factors, such as achievement, growth, recognition, responsibility, the challenge of the work itself, are more likely to produce satisfaction and are therefore called 'motivators'. From an organizational standpoint, the theory suggests that manipulating intrinsic factors into job design is more likely to increase job satisfaction. Manipulating extrinsic factors will not lead to satisfaction, but merely the absence of dissatisfaction. Applying this theory to lean organizations, the balance between the possible negative effects on motivation of extrinsic factors and the strongly motivating effects of intrinsic factors may be out of kilter for many people. It would therefore not be surprising if people who are not experiencing the satisfaction of intrinsic needs, such as the opportunity for growth, should complain about their company's pay system or management.

The debate about the so-called motivational value of 'intrinsic' factors, such as a sense of personal mission, and 'extrinsic' factors is often reflected in organizational pay schemes. Incentive theories are based on reinforcement or the 'carrot and stick' principle. Conventional pay schemes for salespeople usually contain an element of bonus as an extrinsic motivator. This is variable according to individual performance, on the assumption that higher levels of performance are unlikely unless people are incentivized to make the effort. Incentive approaches can work when increased reward is seen as worth the extra effort, performance is measured and attributed to the individual who wants the reward which is available and increased performance does not become a new minimum standard. As we shall see in Chapter 16, which discusses Reward and Recognition, organizations increasingly rely on extrinsic forms of motivation, whether or not people find these motivating.

## *Job insecurity*

The first of these negative effects on employees, job insecurity, may have its roots in fear. Few people expect to have a job for life these days, yet do not find it easy to deal with ongoing uncertainty about jobs. The effect of insecurity can be seen in the way in which people take on huge workloads without demur. Few organizations have studied workflow to the extent that they are able to eliminate unnecessary processes altogether. Consequently many people are having to do work that was previously carried out by others on top of their own workload, which itself requires them to do new things. This adds to employees' stress levels. In many organizations, appearing unable to cope with the workload is seen as a mark of weakness and puts the individual's job at risk. Very often people are able to improve their personal organization and thus produce higher outputs, but this may not be sustainable in the long term.

Similarly, many senior managers complained about the lack of accountability lower down the organization. They were often disappointed that people did not show more initiative in sorting out key issues. Often the reasons for this lie as much in the organization's culture and leadership style as with the individuals concerned. In strongly achievement-driven cultures, being personally successful appears to count for more than the whole team or organization winning. Consequently, passing the buck if things go wrong becomes the norm. In other cases people are asked to take on responsibility for making decisions for which they have neither the training nor the support. If they also get into trouble if things go wrong, it is unlikely that many people will stick their necks out when jobs are still at stake.

Lack of security is a major contributor to stress, which is little wonder when for most people loss of a job is nothing short of personal disaster. In the UK any form of employment other than full-time is often considered a risk by conventional sources of finance. Even people who are self-employed and earning a reasonable income often find it difficult to obtain a house mortgage, for instance, let alone capital for a start-up venture. People in certain age groups are especially vulnerable to job insecurity since many companies take the soft option of reducing headcount amongst older employees. Unless one has particular skills and marketability, obtaining a new job over the age of fifty can be difficult. People in this age bracket are often still supporting children in higher education or looking after dependants. With the prospect of less state pension support and their own company pension reduced in value, the chances of a comfortable old age diminish.

## Loss of job satisfaction

Some people helping us with our research have experienced a loss of job satisfaction. Senior managers in particular talked of a sense of loss brought about by the need to delegate areas of responsibility which they considered their own. The shrinking areas of responsibility reduced their level of interest in the work. Similarly, people in specialist roles are often under pressure to broaden their areas of work or move to a more useful specialism for the business. If the individual has a strong personal interest in their work, such a shift can be demotivating.

In many cases, the new regime operating in their organizations had a profound effect on people's job satisfaction. This was particularly true in public sector organizations which were now operating under a stronger commercial imperative. In the British National Health Service there were numerous examples of clinicians bitterly resenting what they saw as interference in patient care brought about by greater management control of decision-making. Similarly, in Germany, in a public health laboratory which was experiencing similar pressures for change, subject experts were reluctant to take on the multi-skilled approaches and shorter-term perspectives required of them by management.

## Confusion

Another common issue is ongoing confusion. In some cases this is most evident at the top, with senior managers unable to agree on a clear direction for the organization. This then has consequences lower down the organization. In some cases operational units are called on to interact with each other in new ways. Often lack of process leads to chaos and a negative effect on quality and project control. One of our respondents stated that motivating his team was proving very difficult in such circumstances: 'My biggest challenge is attempting to maintain staff interest in quality service delivery with our unknown structure.'

Confusion is also obvious in the ways in which some organizations seem to suffer from 'layering syndrome'. This peculiar phenomenon is evident when organizations experiment with different numbers of levels in parts of their organizations and revert to the original before any part of the new structure has had time to stabilize. Typically this occurs when 'high-flyer' employees threaten to leave unless they are promoted and new levels have to be introduced. Even the use of ambiguous titles such as 'head of ...' does not disguise the fact that promotions take place. They simply cause confusion over who has what level of authority.

At the individual job level, there are frequently overlaps between jobs that leave people unclear where their job ends and another begins. This then makes saying 'no' to unnecessary work very difficult. Lack of training often compounds the problem, with people not really sure how to tackle particular work issues. Of course, few people wish to admit to having a problem with their own work, but many look for some organizational solution to the problems they are experiencing.

Often managers have such wide spans of control that they are unable to provide the kind of support many employees would like in order to be effective. Typically, the lean organization has few problem-solvers waiting in the wings to sort out major issues. The trouble with bringing in external consultants is that usually by the time a problem has been acknowledged, it is already deeply entrenched and has become part of the new way of doing things. Furthermore, depending on a whole range of factors, the 'solutions' identified may not actually graft on to the organization's culture in a way that sticks.

Confusion also exists about how to succeed in the new structures. People are often told that they are responsible for managing their career, and yet there are examples of people in almost every organization who receive special opportunities provided by their employer. Judgements are often made about who is capable of developing some of the new skills and behaviours required in the organization. Those who are perceived to have potential are given the opportunities; it was ever thus. The difficulty is that since few people are told that they are unlikely to progress in the new organization, they continue to aspire to having a career managed in partnership with their employer.

### Lack of career development

Some of the greatest effects of flatter organization structures are being felt on individual careers. Whilst most people are aware that objective career patterns which include job security and promotion on seniority are a thing of the past, their own expectations and reactions to this situation (their subjective career) may not have accepted the change. Our research suggests that many people still aspire to remaining with their current employers for many years and most hope to be promoted. This is even more marked in people who are described as 'high-flyers'. Very few expect to develop their career sideways, even if their experience to date has included periods of lateral development.

Typically people felt that opportunities for advancement were not there, or were only there for the privileged few. For those aspiring to reach the next level there was a common perception that the gaps between levels had widened, making it very difficult for people to acquire the necessary skills and experience to bridge them.

### Status

Traditional hierarchies have always had clear and distinct marks of privilege attached to rank. In the military, uniforms, saluting and officers' messes are visible symbols of superior rank. In an office environment, such symbols are perhaps more discreet but are none the less obvious. Marks of privilege include such precious commodities as cars, parking spaces, more money, bigger desks, more space, even an office. Perhaps most precious of all, there is usually more interesting work, greater choice and influence and prestige within the organization. Is it any wonder that so much of what people have been encouraged to aspire to is available only through vertical promotion?

Status is a particularly sensitive issue. People have always sought to have their marks of distinction noted by others and to achieve the physical trappings of success. The notion of hierarchy goes down deep and there are many cultural variations on this. In Britain, hierarchy has been reflected in all forms of employment and institutional life for generations. In Victorian times, the status of employed women was generally low, with employment opportunities often restricted to service in wealthy households. In terms of status, women's employment was rated much lower than men's. Yet even the lowly housemaid could aspire to becoming the head housekeeper one day, together with the material trappings of success such as having her own parlour. Aspirations such as these and attitudes towards what 'success' means are unlikely to disappear overnight.

## Age

We have seen that promotion remains a key focus of people's aspirations, even though the small numbers of opportunities mean that there is far greater competition for each role. This is where age as a distinguishing factor becomes apparent. Perhaps the people hardest hit by flatter structures are those in their mid-thirties to late forties who are hoping to make further career progress. They are typically competing now with people who are in their early thirties or late twenties. There seems to be a new breed of 'super executive' emerging who is likely to have managed several businesses by the age of forty. People who were patiently making their way up the old career ladder are now finding themselves being overtaken by people who can more easily step over the missing rungs. There is also still a strong tendency for people to be pensioned off early, often before they are ready emotionally or financially.

## Inappropriate leadership

A common cause of dissatisfaction in changing organizations is inappropriate leadership. Indeed, people who feel most unhappy about their own lack of career opportunities are usually most likely to say that they have poor managers. Flatter structures require team members and their leaders to interact in ways which are very different from the command and control styles often evident in more hierarchical structures. Typically, managers have large spans of control and fewer intervening layers between themselves and the front-line team. In theory, team members who are empowered to make decisions themselves and have the relevant training and experience for what they are expected to do should be capable of taking on some of the responsibilities that were once the sole preserve of managers.

The reality is often different. Many managers complain about team members being unwilling to take on additional responsibility without pay and many team members complain that their managers are unsupportive and unwilling to delegate. Others complain that their managers delegate everything, effectively abdicating responsibility and leaving their teams to carry the can if things go wrong. These continuations of hierarchical attitudes with their 'parent–child' relationships seem at odds with the need for 'adult–adult' relationships implicit in an empowerment culture.

*Reward and recognition*

A common issue in flatter structures is the inappropriate nature of the reward system. Indeed, this is such a key issue that Chapter 16 looks into it in more detail. Broadly speaking, it seems that people feel unhappy about the way they are paid if they are also unhappy about other things. Typically, if people are dissatisfied with their current role and also with their career prospects they are likely to be dissatisfied with their pay and with the way they are managed. People who are reasonably happy with their current role and with their job prospects are less likely to complain about their pay. In flatter structures individual performance should become more apparent, but few reward systems are flexible enough to meet individual needs. Just as importantly, few people who helped with our research felt that their contribution was even noticed by their managers. When people did receive recognition, this had a positive effect on their motivation.

# Winners and losers – or how people react to change

Why is it that some people find working in flatter structures so demotivating while others see plenty of opportunities for themselves? Why do some people consider themselves 'winners' in the new contexts, whilst others act like victims or 'losers'? Is it simply that some people are lucky and have better breaks than others? Do some people relish change while others find adjusting to any change very difficult? Do people experience the same event in the same way? It is of course pointless to generalize since everyone's situation, reactions and motivation are different.

Psychologists have numerous theories to explain why people react as they do. Some describe the effects of typical responses to change, such as catatonic non-responsiveness, suspicion and secrecy, psychological manipulation, denial and pathological rigidity, as leading to Kafka-like circuits of work, delay and error. Indeed, philosophers too have wrestled with aspects of the human condition such as these for generations. As the stoic philosopher Epictetus said, 'It is not what happens to a man which marks him; it is what a man thinks about what happens to him which does'. Yet there is increasing evidence that some people are able to react positively to change and adjust quickly to new circumstances. These people are generally considered to be more effective in these new organization structures and better able to become 'winners' than those who are unable to adjust to ongoing change.

To understand why some people may adjust better to change than others it may be useful to borrow from counselling theory. In the well-known 'transition curve', people experiencing change, especially traumatic change such as bereavement, pass through certain clear stages before they are able to resume 'normal' life, focusing positively on the present and future rather than hankering after the past (Figure 2.1). In the curve, the areas in which energy is focused on reacting to the change are often full of negative emotions and behaviours. Some people find moving out of this phase difficult, especially if they see no clear or desirable alternative future route other than that they have lost. Taking career issues as an example, they prefer to 'hold on' to old attitudes, aspirations and expectations since they see no viable alternative. This is all the more difficult when the world is patently unfair in the eyes of the individual since other people are enjoying what they have been denied. The tendency then is to blame the system and refuse to accept that the world has changed.

In this phase, the role of the manager may best be that of a counsellor, supporter and listener. As the individual starts to let go of the past and experiment with new ways of thinking and behaving, the manager can usefully encourage and coach people in new ways of working. In particular it may be useful to have some open discussions about the changes and their impact on employees. Often people find that just talking frankly about how their career prospects have been affected is part of coming to terms with the new order. Giving employees the chance to gain a realistic assessment of their skills and an understanding of the skills needed for the future can help. Similarly, when people understand what is

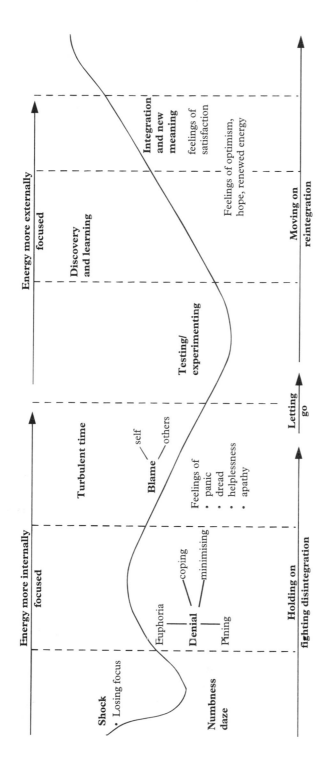

**Figure 2.1** *The transition curve (based on the work of Elizabeth Kubler-Rosse)*

really important and motivating to them they often realize that their former aspirations were not what they really value now.

When the person is ready to 'move on' in their thinking they have usually been able to integrate the best of the past with the new ways of operating so that they are to a large extent operating under their own steam. At this point the manager needs to supply ongoing encouragement and recognition of their improved attitudes and enhanced performance. Of course, any theory is an over-simplification of reality, especially since people rarely experience just one major change at a time. However, the theory suggests that support can be useful in helping people move through the phases of change to the more forward focused stage. Perhaps the 'winners' are those people who need less support and are able to adjust rapidly to new situations. People who are able to embrace change positively and make opportunities for themselves in times of ambiguity are more likely to thrive in changing organizations than people who wait for normal service to be resumed.

## The search for balance

Pressures, both business and personal, can cause some employees to work extremely long hours. The UK is ahead of all other European Countries in the average number of hours worked. According to a survey in *Personnel Today*, one in eight managers regularly clocks up over sixty hours a week, while 40 per cent work over fifty hours. Other surveys have found that over a third of junior managers regularly take work home at weekends. Long hours and heavy workloads in themselves need not be stress-inducing. Some people genuinely thrive in such circumstances. We have found that where business results improve as a result of the effort made by individuals and teams, morale can be high despite the long hours worked. Conventional wisdom suggests that stress is experienced as negative if the person feels that they are unable to control the sources of pressure.

There are consistent reports that many employees are experiencing increased stress levels and are developing 'change programme weariness'. The flattening of structures often increases the range of pressures on people, causing them to respond to the pressures rather than feeling in control. Greatly increased workloads, the loss of key personnel, unreasonable deadlines and office politics are experienced by many people. New structures call for new working patterns, but these usually consist of adding new procedures to existing ones, increasing employee overload. So great is the pressure on time that few people take the opportunity to make space for themselves on a regular basis.

Conflict between work and being a good parent is a contributory factor towards stress, with few managers claiming to be able to juggle different responsibilities well. The question of home/work balance is increasingly being debated, with few examples currently available of employee-friendly policies such as discouraging workaholism. Long hours and the ever-increasing demands on employees tend to blur the distinction between different parts of life, and in some organizations, evidence that the job comes first is seen as a sign of commitment. Some managers openly describe how they deliberately separate out different aspects of their personalities between their private lives and work, and see this as a means of managing boundaries.

## Downshifters

There are numerous examples, mainly from the United States, of the phenomenon known as 'downshifting'. This is where people who are often in highly paid professional work voluntarily opt out of the rat-race and prefer instead to adopt a less lucrative but more satisfying lifestyle. They are looking for a better balance between business and personal life. Often work has become so all-consuming in its demands that other important aspects of life have suffered. In other cases people have developed coping mechanisms, bringing only certain aspects of their personality to work in order to keep some part of their life which has nothing to do with work.

Mark B wanted to become a head teacher in the private education system in the UK. He was short-listed for a prestigious school in the south of England. An important qualification for the job was fulfilling an 'ideal' role; being married, having two children, being a pillar of the community. When he actually obtained a headship, Mark found that in reality he was expected to act as if his home life did not exist and that all his (spare) time was to be spent supporting the school, especially with its community involvement. So Mark spent every Saturday watching pupils play rugby, went on school trips, attended innumerable evening meetings. He was not surprised when his marriage finally suffered. For him, his marriage was too high a price to pay for his work and he took the decision to take on a part-time teaching post at a much lower salary.

I have encountered many similar examples during the course of my research. It seems that when people know what is really important to them they eventually realize that work, if uncontrolled, will exert too great a pressure on them at the expense of other important things. The triggers for stepping out of the workplace often seem to be important family or personal milestones, or when morale hits rock bottom. The fact that people are becoming more aware of other options for earning a living than full-time employment increases their sense of having a choice. When people also know their own worth and have no fear of being unable to earn money, they will tolerate negative work situations for only a relatively short time. They will not allow themselves to be turned into victims. The irony is that these are often the very people that organizations want to retain, but do not have a clue how to give them the opportunities to satisfy really important needs. Throwing money at the problem may not be the answer.

## The paradoxes of flatter structures

Laurence Jackson, Senior Consultant with MSL International, has long been actively interested in the effects of flatter structures on organizations and employees, since in his business, the importance of effective adjustment to changing requirements is very obvious. The following interview sets out what Laurence perceives to be the ten paradoxes of flatter structures.

*Question: The business imperative for introducing lean organization structures seems very strong. In your view, do lean organization structures work?*

*Laurence Jackson*: Although there is a powerful business argument for making these changes, the sad fact is that between two-thirds and three-quarters of change initiatives fail. There is a simple reason for this. Although the measures taken are **right for the business** – in terms of sharpening quality or customer focus, improving cost efficiency, streamlining processes and optimum utilization of resources – in most cases these are **not right for the people within them** – who feel threatened, overworked and disillusioned.

Extensive research has shown that such exercises result in low morale, increased workload, and a perception that opportunities for advancement are limited or cut off altogether (Holbeche, 1994).

Suddenly, there is discontinuity in people's assumptions about their own career, their relationship with their employer and their self-worth. This response has been summed up thus: 'It is hard to carry on believing that you are the company's most valuable resource, when you see clearly that you are also the most disposable.'

*Question: Yet it might be argued that people should be glad that they have a job. Why should flatter structures in particular have such apparently negative effects on employees?*

*Laurence Jackson*: In analysing the outcomes of these exercises, it is possible to identify recurrent themes that typify the breakdown in commitment and understanding between employees and their companies. The ten 'paradoxes of flatter structures' go a long way towards explaining what triggers the negative reactions and to pointing up strategies that businesses need to adopt to re-establish trust.

### Business strategies lack people dimension

The first point is that **business strategies,** that is, the technical and systems-related issues, are in the vast majority of cases much better thought through than the **people strategies.** Once key decisions have been taken the damage is done, but expectations are generally that people will accept and come to terms with the new realities. Sadly very little consideration is given to the impact on people of changes, and the best approaches to minimize the anxieties and discomfort as the organization adapts to the changes and learns new ways of working.

Working with one client, we found that the major considerations of the implementation team centred around establishing an integrated data base, replacing core systems without disrupting operational continuity, standardizing software and hardware, etc. When asked about relationships, they felt that suppliers and business partners took a higher priority than those relating to staff within the business. It was only when they recognized that a detailed training and communication strategy was necessary that the deep level of internal concern and mistrust could be addressed so that progress could start on implementation.

As business's whole approach to customers changes and new working patterns are introduced, organizations expect their people to develop a whole new set of behaviours, but what has emerged is a series of contradictory and hostile responses. Instead of being grateful for keeping their jobs after cutbacks, those remaining display negative attitudes towards the business, and rather than reinforcing improvements in productivity, cost-effectiveness, team working, etc., we witness in fact a series of negative outcomes. I am calling these the 'ten paradoxes'.

## Paradox 1: The ideal is usually wrong

What has been designed as a perfect solution in organizational terms for one particular part of the business tends to be imposed on the whole organization – or even worse, a solution that may be right for one business is transposed without thought to a completely different type of business.

In many cases, concepts that prove valid in some circumstances are just not appropriate in others; for example, the idea that one can suddenly become a 'status-free organization' is clearly not feasible and leads to much cynicism. Reducing grading structures dramatically quite often results in a regrowth of the old structure through the creation of sub-grades. The reward policy is generally not reviewed to take account of the new behaviours required and formal and informal rewards tend to reinforce the old values. In short, an elegant design concept is soon proved to be inadequate in its implications for the detailed practicalities of organizational existence.

## Paradox 2: Survivors bite back

Initially, following a job-cutting exercise, fear for their jobs tends to result in a flurry of more productive activity on the part of the survivors. Indeed, a new term 'presentee' has been coined (Cooper, 1994) to describe those survivors who, motivated by fear, work long hours simply to be seen at the work place to avoid being in the next round of cuts. Genuine commitment and loyalty to the organization have been replaced by a more calculative response towards the company, and productivity drops. There have also recently been several instances of fraud by managers in falsifying internal accounts and recharges to other departments in order to make their departments appear to meet increasingly demanding targets (MORI, 1995).

*Paradox 3: Services decline*

While the idea of outsourcing non-core activities is initially attractive, the experience is that these are actually harder to manage. Reductions in numbers mean that short-term absences cause major crises in service delivery, and from the customer perception the reassurance of dealing with the same people on a regular basis and people who have time to talk and take an interest is replaced with a bewildering succession of different contacts as a range of direct or indirect services are used to meet customer needs.

*Paradox 4: Draining the life blood*

The impact of removing layers of middle management has been to take away the very people who have discretionary time to nurture and support the business, and to reflect on strategic issues; hence it is increasingly difficult to find mentors, and requests for members of project teams are met with 'I'd love to but ... .' As businesses focus on short-term results, this also sends a message about investing for the future – there is already a disturbing trend towards reducing investment in training as apprenticeships have all but disappeared and succession programmes are severely threatened as logical career moves are blocked.

*Paradox 5: Zeal quashes debate*

A business that is undergoing rapid change needs to involve its people and seek out their thoughts and feelings along the way. However, when the master plan for the future is unveiled, it takes a bold individual indeed to pipe up and suggest that there may be some merit in reconsidering some aspects of the approach. Such people are generally thought to be 'wimps' and certainly not 'part of the future.'

*Paradox 6: Society expects*

Humans are social animals and build up a way of relating to fellow humans which gives them both a feeling of purpose and an external identity. Indeed, the most common form of introductory question is 'What do you do?' In the exciting new age, our social paradigms are breaking down. We hear of the death of the job, which is replaced by clusters of tasks. But our value systems and life planning are built around obtaining a mortgage (generally predicated over a lengthy period of reliable income generation), starting a family and other assumptions which centre around the concept of stable, gainful employment.

### Paradox 7: Granny expects

Even if the individual comes to terms with the new realities, it is often difficult to go home to relatives and face the question 'What job do you do now?' and certainly it would not be helpful to reply, 'I don't have a job as such, actually I carry out a cluster of tasks in a variety of leaderless teams.'

### Paradox 8: Clash of values

This has been summed up as 'many middle managers are feeling angry and deceived – they thought they had a deal with their organization.' They find it hard to keep believing that the organization really does value its people when they see a steady stream of their colleagues leaving, and the traditional notions of a decent employer are destroyed. We were brought up to believe that in return for hard work and loyalty, employers would provide a stable and secure work environment. That form of 'psychological contract' has now largely disappeared, and companies are groping to establish new understandings.

### Paradox 9: Duty of care

Recent case law has established that employers imposing unrealistic demands are not only unfair, but they are also now acting illegally. In a well-known High Court Action, *Walker* vs *Northumberland County Council*, an employer who saw symptoms of stress and failed to give effective help has been adjudged to be in breach of an implicit duty of care and was fined accordingly.

### Paradox 10: Virtual people

Taking all this to its logical conclusion, the role of people in organizations can be reduced to a more mechanistic model. Hence we have 'hot desking', which may reduce costs by up to 30 per cent but which generates the angry response: 'I like my desk and the muddle around it – it is one of the few things I can rely on.' In sum, whilst the organization seeks high productivity, flexibility and impermanence, its people crave a sense of belonging, stability and some long-term commitment from the business and an opportunity to progress within it.

The feelings of frustration and anger are heightened when exhortations to change, to become more productive and so on are accompanied by a reassuring statement that 'there is no need for any change at the top of the organization.'

*Question: How much is talk of 'survivor syndrome' common in boardrooms? In your view, are employers aware of the consequences of not addressing the paradoxes you have highlighted?*

*Laurence Jackson*: Interesting research has been carried out into the extent to which employers are aware of and actively plan to cope with the feelings and concerns of their people and the implications of these (Doherty and Horsted, 1995). Whereas 80 per cent of employers provide outplacement for leavers (and generally provide very caring and helpful support), very few 'inplacement' programmes are set up. Where they are, the approach tends to be short-term (mainly focusing on technical skills, counselling or help lines). Strategies for retention or motivation concern straightforward issues on rewards and training rather than career development and career management.

Survivors suffer a sense of loss as well as guilt, and whilst their commitment to their colleagues increases, their loyalty to the business diminishes. In this, there are strong analogies to post-traumatic stress disorder, which results in a detachment and lack of interest and a tendency to avoid anything that reminds people of unpleasant past events.

Rather than giving their people an opportunity to air their feelings and providing them with strong support and encouragement to overcome these, most organizations assume that once the new systems and structures are in place, people will soon come to terms and forget. This is a dangerous assumption.

*Question: What do you see as the way ahead?*

*Laurence Jackson*: There is strong evidence that high-performing organizations, and ones that can become stronger through change, are characterized by clear leadership and direction, allied to a conscious strategy of regular involvement of staff in issues affecting them (Wickens, 1996). In the more traditional 'command and control' type organizations, people will wait to be told what to do and expect to be punished for mistakes; in such cultures militant trade unions flourish as disenfranchised workers use their skills and creativity against the business. Such responses are heightened in circumstances of transition, where there are added uncertainty and anxiety.

If the critical factor is the ability of the organization to absorb and adapt to massive changes and become stronger, organizations must put as much effort into working with survivors as they do with the casualties. This long-term investment involves first understanding what people are going through so that the business leaders can:

- relate the changes in structures, roles, systems, etc. to a genuine business imperative;
- define future roles in terms that staff can relate to – and specify the new skills and behaviours required;
- reassure and support people in adapting and learning the new skills;
- excite and enthuse everyone about opportunities (whilst not getting too carried away!); and ... **most importantly:**
- involve everyone in designing their future.

In short, the challenge is to replace the understandable fear of change, of each other and of failure with a fear of what customers might do if they become dissatisfied, a fear of what competitors are already doing to try to steal business advantage, and a fear of what might happen if we just sit back and reflect on yesterday's achievements.

# 3 Communications

Far from thriving on chaos, organisations are reeling from progressive impacts of successive change programmes.

Stephen Drew (1994)

*Projecting the feel-good factor: communicating your organization's system of values in a manner that allows employees to easily identify with, and reflect, the organization's culture.*

What role can communications play in the development of lean organizations? Are good communications vitally important at some times and less so at others? What do we mean by good communications and what effect do they have on employee motivation? These are some of the questions we shall be looking at in this chapter.

Good communications are arguably the most important tool in the creation and implementation of a new organization. It is often thought that lean organizations are simply the same organizations as before, but with fewer staff. In truth, however, when organizations are delayered, downsized, decentralized, recentralized, have different products, competitors and markets they are actually different organizations from those in the days of the monolithic single-focused corporation. Often the main point of continuity with the past is that there is a body of employees from the previous organization who may be bewildered and uncommitted to the new. This is likely to be even more the case with mergers and acquisitions when the 'victorious' side is likely to expect to impose its ways onto the 'losing' side. Good communications are critical in helping to create a new organizational culture of which employees feel part and to which they want to commit.

By good communications I am not talking just about company newsletters and attitude surveys. After all, how can a few communications initiatives used in isolation redress one of the biggest consequences of organizational change, namely low morale? We have already seen that one of the commonest symptoms of low morale is stress caused by ongoing uncertainty, insecurity and overwork. Communications certainly play a part in helping people to understand the need for change. The absence of good communications can add to employee stress levels. We have also already seen that when people do not understand or believe that there is a strategic reason for organizational change, they are likely to respond with cynicism and lack of commitment to the 'new' organization. Unless people really buy into the strategic purpose behind change, they are likely to believe that they are being asked to pay the price for incompetent management, often with their own careers. That is not to say that people who perceive a clear strategic purpose, such as going global, refocusing markets or becoming a customer-focused organization, will be ecstatic about the change. They are simply more likely to bring their intellectual capital to the problem or issue that the organization is trying to address.

## Communications and the change process

Communications have specific roles to play at all stages leading up to, during and following the implementation of the new structure. In the period leading up to change they help create a climate for change and an awareness of the need for change – that staying as we are is not an option. Periods of change can challenge people to rethink the way they work. Some resistance to change is only to be expected. Communications help people understand why they must change and how the change will affect them. They are important in stabilizing the organization as it undergoes some of the human trauma experienced during times of change. They are vital in refocusing employees and gaining their support for the change. They are critical in informing, educating and encouraging people to adopt new behaviours, in developing the new 'way we do things around here'. They are essential in reinforcing the best aspects of the new organization and creating a positive focus on the future.

A sign of good communications is when employees at all levels know and understand what is happening from each other's perspectives. In large organizations, it is often assumed that communications specialists, sometimes called 'employee relations managers' or some off-shoot of Human Resources, are responsible for making good communications happen. In practice, effective two-way communication rarely happens as a result of the interventions of a specialist department unless they succeed in gaining support from the whole organization.

*The shadow system of communication*

More often than not the formal communications system in an organization will reflect the preferred management style of senior managers. This may mean that communications are often 'top-down', with lots of well-meaning attempts to keep employees informed of what is going on to the extent that is considered appropriate. It often comes as a great surprise to managers who have conscientiously carried out team briefings, taken part in the management roadshow and in other ways tried to convey the message, how little is understood or, perhaps more importantly, believed by employees about what is going on.

Conversely, information which is meant to be disseminated on a just-in-time or need-to-know basis is often widely known weeks before it is officially released. Many senior managers underestimate the power of the grapevine. This is not so much the formal communication as the informal or 'shadow' system which tends to thrive when the 'mushroom' principle of communications is applied (i.e. keep them in the dark, buried in farmyard organic matter and just watch them grow). In the absence of real consultation, fears about what the change might mean for individual employees might become exaggerated.

## Creating a climate for change

Of course, this might be just what is needed to create a climate for change. One of the lessons John Kotter of Harvard (1995) draws from his extensive studies of organizational change, both successful and unsuccessful, is the importance of creating a sense of urgency. Most successful change efforts begin when some individuals or groups take a long hard look at an organization's competitive position, its market position for instance, and find ways to communicate this information broadly and dramatically, in a way that gets attention.

One managing director of a UK-based engineering company despaired of the workforce agreeing to abandon some restrictive practices which were gradually eroding his organization's competitive position. Knowing that the grapevine was infinitely more effective than his previous formal attempts to persuade employees of the need for change, he created a rumour of the imminent takeover of the company by a rival company, with inevitable job losses. Though the rumour was not true, it had sufficient credence amongst employees that it created the solidarity and willingness to improve processes in the short term which the MD was looking for. This is not a tactic I would recommend, but other means of creating a sense of imminent crisis or of great opportunity may produce a similar willingness on the part of the workforce to question the status quo.

## Attitudes to change

Why is it that so many people are resistant to change? One explanation comes from the work of Kurt Lewin (1958) who talked about the status quo as a steady or 'frozen' state. In times of relative stability, methods of doing things, the use of power and 'comfort zones' become established. These may make change threatening to people who perceive the present state to be preferable to an unknown and untested future state in which their own status could be in jeopardy.

In particular, change may cut across familiar mental models for decision-making, for instance, or may even call into question long held values. One example of this is the widespread trend towards making processes more commercially focused in the British National Health Service, Europe's largest employer. Many clinicians enter their medical field with a strong vocation and decision-making practices within the NHS have long favoured the 'right' of the medical practitioner to make key medical decisions. In recent times, the introduction of more obvious 'management' of hospitals and health authorities has led to a shift of decision-making to managers. Their concern for bottom-line considerations may lead them to suggest different courses of action from those that medical staff would prefer. The resulting frustration of many clinicians has been widely written about.

Not everyone sees change in that light, or indeed considers every change a threat. If you were told that you had just won a fortune on your national lottery, or that an elderly, very distant relative had just bequeathed all their vast wealth to you, this change may present a different kind of challenge. At any rate, the initial response to this kind of change may be different from that to news of an impending organizational restructuring.

Indeed, some people seem positively to thrive on change and find stable states suffocating. Using the familiar metaphor of the pioneer in the American Wild West of the nineteenth century, the people who set off into the unknown to discover 'gold in them thar hills' were often courageous loners who were driven by a clear objective. The settlers who came in their wake would often group together for defensive purposes, arranging their wagons in circles with guns pointing out at night and with sentries posted. The settlers would often prefer the prospect of cultivating some rich farmland discovered en route to continuing their quest for gold. For them, comfort meant relative safety, the opportunity to farm with reasonable chances of success and a predictable future for their children.

Applying the metaphor to modern organizations has its limitations except in so far as it indicates different kinds of mindsets in response to change. In times of change both sorts of mentality are called for: a willingness to challenge the status quo in the face of as yet unachieved visions as well as a pragmatic realization of the current opportunities; a desire to move forward and a willingness to stabilize the change with effective processes. Too much of either set of attitudes may result in undue turbulence with little real achievement or else complacency and the missing of commercial opportunities.

## Creating a sense of urgency

The unfreezing process described by Lewin may be harder to achieve without a real sense of urgency. Creating a sense of urgency in a large bureaucratic organization, such as a government department, may involve challenging decades of inertia. In 1978, Charles Handy described bureaucratic organizations as typically having a role culture which works by logic and rationality. Procedures and rules are of key importance in terms of getting things done. In this type of culture, position power is the major power source, with personal power being frowned upon and expert power being tolerated in its place. Even a highly charismatic chief executive would find it difficult to create a sense of urgency in such an organization, and often the requirement for change is imposed on such organizations from outside, usually, in the context of functionaries, by the government. Our research suggests that when the need for change is imposed from outside the organizations, especially when job losses are likely, loss of staff morale is inevitable.

In France, the power of interests in maintaining the status quo was demonstrated vividly in the 1995 General Strike, during which the Chirac government's stand on reducing social security benefits provoked long and bitter organized resistance. In the UK, the gradual effect of government policy has led to a significant reshaping of the public sector, with relatively little organized resistance. In this case, the powerlessness of the public bodies to do other than respond to central government directives produces an anxiety about imposed change.

Ironically, it is often easier to create the sense of urgency when prospects for the organization are really bad, than when things are going reasonably well. Bad results of one sort or another get people's attention and provide an impetus for change. The difficulty is that bad results often reduce the amount of room for manoeuvre. The danger of introducing change only when there is an obvious need to do so is that any remedy may come too late. According to the Japanese principle of *kaizen*, continuous improvement of products and processes is essential for keeping ahead of the competition, and for providing the quality leadership demanded by discerning customers. As Figure 3.1 shows, the average life-cycle of a product or organization is fairly predictable. The point at which processes need to be improved is early in the product life-cycle, before the product's performance has started to level out or decline (point A). Unfortunately, human nature being what it is, the temptation to leave things as they are and cream off profits is very real.

The process improvement strategy alone, however, may not be sufficient to maintain a product's success. At some point, it will be necessary to take a long hard look at the product and decide if it is still appropriate to its market. If not, it will be necessary to change it, kill it off or do something different with it. The theory has been borne out in practice many times. The problem is that the point at which organizations take that long hard look at their core businesses and products often comes later in the life-cycle (point B)

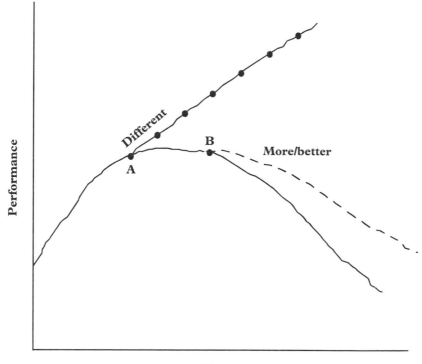

**Figure 3.1** *The failure curve*

when persistent competition and market forces are setting the pace on what the organization or its products can achieve. At that point, introducing continuous process improvement usually merely slows down the rate of decline rather than sending the product into a new upward trajectory. The time to be re-engineering products, processes or businesses is ideally when they are still on the upward curve (point A). If an organization is simultaneously improving its processes and finding new and better ways to please their customers, it is likely to remain in business, but change is likely to be an ongoing feature of organizational life.

Indeed, according to James A. Unruh (1993), Chairman and Chief Executive of Unisys:

> All restructurings ought to be ongoing. If they're not, they're no more than a process for catching up and catching up means paying a price.

Noticing that something needs to be done when the figures start to show the decline may lead to the sorts of reactive, fire-fighting changes introduced out of desperation or fashion. Even with the best forecasting it can be difficult to predict when to introduce change since the best time to do this is before the decline has started. This is where relying on economic forecasts is only part of the strategic equation. Old-fashioned intuition is also involved in the best decisions. While products are profitable and things are going well there can be a great temptation to milk the cash cow for as long as possible, but the evidence of organizational failure throughout the 1990s suggests that this may be a short-term policy. The best time to introduce change, therefore, is when things are going well and figures are on the up. What is needed is a frank discussion of potential dangers such as the growth of new competition, or increased customer demands, so that maintaining the status quo seems more dangerous than launching into the unknown.

### Champions of change

The next stage is to ensure that the change is not seen to be the responsibility of one person, even if this is the chief executive. Often, responsibility for change is delegated to a 'change agent', often a head of quality or business process re-engineering (BPR). Unless these are exceptional individuals or are seen to exercise great power, this approach often results in vested interests within the organization undermining the change effort. What is needed is a powerful enough group of people committed to the change that the impetus for change grows.

The group should include people with a blend of information, expertise, titles and relationships. It is hard to be specific about the size of such a group, but anything up to a fifth of the workforce is not unrealistic. It must include senior managers and it should also include political sources, including for example a union leader or staff representative. Since changing anything means acting outside the normal boundaries, it helps to have a powerful group developing a shared assessment of what formal boundaries and expectations might be. This can be difficult if there is no history of team work at the top, or there are poor industrial relations; in these circumstances, the value of a coalition approach can be underestimated. However, our research suggests that without a coalition approach, opposition to the change can prevent the change from working.

# Creating a compelling vision

An organization which can't figure out where it's headed will have a devil of a time developing the talent to get it there.

M. McCall et al. (1988)

Also critical to creating a climate for change is developing a sense of purpose and direction. This not only provides a reason for changing the way things are, but also gives employees a sense that the organization has a future, even though they may themselves not be part of it. The sense of purpose, expressed as a vision, needs to be easy to communicate and appealing to customers and other stakeholders, such as employees. It is not just about numbers; it is about clarifying a direction in which the organization needs to move.

Often the process of developing a vision takes time, sometimes up to twelve months or longer. This is the danger time, when employees and other stakeholders begin to doubt the rationale for change. The more stakeholders are meaningfully involved in developing the vision the better. Involving people implies that communication is more than one-way and that consultation is genuine. Visions which are simply a forecast of future growth based on previous business performance are hardly inspirational.

Ideally a vision should be a clear, compelling statement which simply inspires all who hear it. A few years ago, one photocopier giant (Company A) created a vision of becoming the world number one in this product despite being the world number two. They faced severe competition from several organizations including Company B, then number one. They developed a clear vision, a short-term mission statement 'Beat Company B', which became the motto used throughout Company A. It appeared on all internal memos, regular updates on progress were published and the staff had no difficulty remembering what their targets were. Needless to say, they achieved their mission in record time.

In a real sense, leaders can become the creators of legends and stories which teach employees what is valued within the organization. Some executives use metaphor to convey, even in an apocryphal way, what is required. Take, for instance, the well-known story that has circulated for years in a major computer company. It concerns a bright young executive, highly trained and fresh from completing his MBA, who was offered the chance to run the operation in a European subsidiary. Within a matter of months the operation was in difficulties and, thanks to a bad business decision, losses amounted to $10 million. The executive, believing that he had better do the honourable thing, presented himself before the chairman of the board and tendered his resignation. The chairman replied: 'Don't you think of resigning. We've just spent $10 million training you!' Needless to say, within that organization, the message that it was possible to learn and recover from mistakes reached staff as a whole, who were more inclined to be innovative in their search for business solutions. Such messages help to create and consolidate the new culture.

## Communicating the vision

This is where the communication of the vision is critical and where organizations typically underestimate the need for reinforcement. Where a vision has not been created, because the change process is being imposed from outside, a local or team vision helps direct efforts. Typically the vision is set out and publicized just before or after a delayering exercise. Often people rely on communicating using one of three methods. First they will implement the change and then hold a meeting to explain it. Used in isolation this is one of the least effective ways of communicating the vision, especially if people do not see the need for change.

Usually people find it hard to take in the message this way. They may be feeling guilty or relieved to still have a job, if the delayering process has included some redundancies. They may believe what they heard on the grapevine more than what they are being told, and in any case, the short-term memory of many people is very short indeed. People do not get the message in one meeting. Also, some people respond better to the written or electronic word than to the spoken word. Others may prefer visual information such as graphics, flowcharts or videos.

A second approach is for the Chief Executive to launch a road-show and make lots of speeches. Often these act as a showcase for the new direction but fail to win commitment from employees if they do not have the chance really to debate the issues. One American tobacco company head took the issue of bringing the vision to life so seriously that he set up a 'hotline' and promised to respond personally to messages from employees during the restructuring. While staff hesitated initially, the demand grew to the point that the CEO had to establish a single point of communication, with his original undertaking being maintained to a lesser degree; he continued to respond personally selectively. Having this single point of communications allowed him and his team to 'take the pulse' of the organization.

A third method is to produce lots of newsletters detailing the vision, but the printed messages are very different from employees' everyday experience of the organization. When senior managers, for instance, do not 'walk the talk', there tends to be cynicism about how seriously the messages are to be believed. Typically, these 'credibility gaps' mean that the written statements do not convey real meaning. In terms of change, people need to be willing to make short-term sacrifices. Employees are usually not willing to do this, even if they are unhappy with the status quo, unless they believe that useful change is possible. Without credible communication, and a lot of it, the hearts and minds of the troops are never captured.

It is vital that a vision spells out what growth possibilities there might be for survivors and demonstrates a commitment to treating fairly people who are about to be laid off. 'The survivor syndrome' is now a familiar phrase. It describes the negative effects on employees who are apparently the lucky ones in times of redundancies. Often, the survivors perceive themselves to be the victims of a repressive organization and over time they come to envy those people who, having lost their jobs, have made a fresh start elsewhere. A vision, underpinned by values, needs to remind people of the potential of the organization, but words alone do not make the difference. They need to be acted upon.

One American financial services giant suffered a number of waves of redundancy during the late 1980s. The company published some statements of values, including their ambition to 'treat people with respect and dignity.' Initially employees could not reconcile this statement with the practice of cutting jobs. What changed as a result of this statement was the way in which people whose jobs were going were treated. Earlier practices, such as informing people that their job had gone by cancelling their car park swipe card, were replaced by a more considerate approach, with counselling and outplacement services available to all departing employees. The surviving staff could see the difference and were somewhat reassured by the new approach.

## Reinforcing the vision

Perhaps the most effective way of reinforcing the vision is for executives genuinely to incorporate the messages about the vision into their daily activities and to take every opportunity to remind others of the link. For example, if managers are having a quarterly performance review for their particular operating unit, they should take the opportunity to show how the results of the unit are contributing to the vision, as well as to the bottom-line goals. They should use all available communication channels to broadcast the vision, like writing lively articles in organizational newsletters, being positive about change in management meetings, putting a special emphasis in training programmes on business problems and the new vision. Most of all, executives must be prepared to walk the talk and be open to feedback from peers and subordinates.

Brian Wisdom, Operations Director of Thresher, a UK drinks retailer which forms part of Whitbread plc, is a good example of an executive who takes the communication of the vision seriously. Wisdom is one of the prime movers behind the Operations Development Project (ODP), a major change project which will be described in a later chapter. Wisdom and the Human Resource Controller, Chris Johnson, have been personally involved in every stage of the project, which has involved extensive consultation with the workforce, the trialling and evaluation of new working practices and the implementation of successful approaches.

Wisdom has used every opportunity to reinforce the ODP vision when working with operations staff, including giving ODP teams the responsibility and the opportunity of communicating the vision themselves in sales conferences. One of the immediate benefits of the ODP was the discovery that each area sales manager received on average three and a half kilos of paperwork each week. By rationalizing what was needed to enable employees to do their jobs, the Thresher team were able to draw the vital distinction between deluging employees with data and providing them with valuable information.

At British Airways Engineering's Material Maintenance and Components Operation (MMCO), two-way communication is given a high priority. Team briefings are useful and are held regularly. Other communication channels such as management meetings, company newsletters and training programmes reinforce the vision. A key ingredient in successfully restructuring an organization is the climate of open and honest communication from the top down, throughout the workforce. It takes time for trust to be established, but without a free flow of information the benefits of the flatter structure may not be realized.

## Creating a new culture

Creating a climate for change is one thing, but changing from what to what? 'The way we do things around here' defines the organization's culture. It comprises values and beliefs which may be very deep-rooted and hard to shift. It is also evident in attitudes and behaviours which may also be resistant to change. How strong these are will depend to some extent on the nature of leadership exercised. Employees quickly learn which behaviour is acceptable and rewarded by leaders. Long-standing employees will be more firmly attuned to the corporate culture than newcomers, who may only discover how things are done when they make mistakes. Interaction with colleagues in work and social contexts is a key means of perpetuating the corporate culture.

Going back to Lewin's model, the stage after 'unfreezing' is 'moving on'. This involves clarifying the way we are going to do things in the new organization created by the flatter structure. It is important to define the kind of culture which is appropriate to a flatter, leaner organization. To be able to adapt to ongoing change requires a flexible, innovative and responsive culture. This is likely to be a far cry from some of the other types of corporate culture, which tend to be more resistant to change. These include bureaucratic role cultures in which people have carefully delineated responsibilities, control cultures in which decision-making is in the hands of the privileged few, and competitive cultures in which employees are rewarded only for individual achievement rather than collaboration.

### Visible signs of corporate culture

Culture includes all the small visible things which mark out one organization from another: the dress codes, the layout and appearance of offices, how customers are greeted. These are relatively simple to change and relatively minor changes can produce significant changes in the way people behave. A British government department recently abandoned its separate offices in favour of open-plan. The result was an increase in communication and sharing of information across previously separate functions.

In a US financial services organization, the Friday 'dress down' day on which employees were allowed to wear anything they liked within reason produced a more relaxed but business-like atmosphere. Customers appreciated the difference and the number of telephone complaints received on Fridays dropped significantly. There was also an increase in creativity with clear benefits to the customer. The company is now planning to extend 'dress down' to the entire week for office-based staff.

In another example from the same organization, the customer services operations consisted of over a thousand employees, many of whom were based in one open-plan office block. Directors had separate, roomy offices, usually attractively laid out and private. When the customer services operations were delayered in 1994, the directors decided that retaining their privilege of private offices was not in keeping with the messages they were sending to their staff. They opted to move into the open-plan context, leaving their former offices to be used as meeting rooms. The attempt was short-lived for all of the directors but one, who remained in the open-plan context. The others felt unable to concentrate when surrounded by their staff. The teamwork and energy levels in the area where the director continued to work amongst his team were noticeably higher, with predictably beneficial business results.

*Power structure and hierarchy*

This visible manifestation of the director's desire to 'walk the talk' reflects some of the deeper levels of organizational culture. The attitudes underpinning the way people behave may take longer to shift than changing the company logo. The way in which power is exercised in the organization is another manifestation of the culture at work. Often this has little to do with the official organization chart, which represents how power is supposed to be distributed through roles. As Figure 3.2 demonstrates, power may be distributed a little differently in reality.

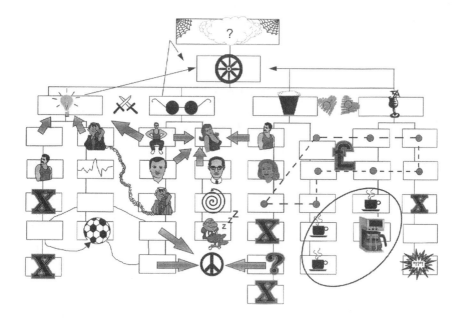

**Figure 3.2** *Organizational micropolitics*

Typically, power and influence are exercised through political processes. These include use of the grapevine and deliberate networking. Power also protects vested interests. Power battles are typically fought out over resource allocation, status protection and decisions about who gets promoted. Typically, change can threaten power distribution and in the case of flatter structures may call for redistribution of decision-making processes to different people. Cultural norms can be fairly resistant to change, although lip-service may be paid to the change effort.

### Values and beliefs

More deep-seated still are the long-held assumptions, beliefs and values about the nature of the organization. These are usually known, but not articulated. Values in particular are often evident in recruitment practices, where organizations often recruit people in their own image. This can lead employees to become cynical about change initiatives, for instance. The underpinning belief may be that employees are expendable but that the organization will go on for ever. As the Chief Executive of a small consultancy business put it:

> Consultants come and go but there's something about the nature of this place which stays the same ... it must be something in the woodwork!

In theory, a flat structure lends itself to providing excellent customer service since unnecessary parts of processes are eliminated. The principle of horizontal operations is underpinned by cross-organizational teamwork and good communications. Unfortunately, the reality is often different, with work practices continuing much as before, with fewer staff and resources and little benefit to customers or employees. Working out the implications of the new structures on the existing culture takes some doing, because so much is hidden in time-honoured practices which may be so familiar that they become invisible. Yet some of the biggest barriers to effective change are embedded in the culture. Unless they are dealt with, the change process may be undermined.

## Changing the way we work – the implications

A few basic questions can help pinpoint some of the ways in which we may have to work differently:

- Are we going to work horizontally, following through processes from customer to customer?
- What will this mean for the way in which work is currently handled? Who will win or lose? How will we handle this?
- How will this affect the way employees will interact? Will the customer actually benefit; if so, in what way? Will this require training for employees?
- How well equipped are we for new ways of working? Are we flexible, willing and able to work in teams? What will we do to encourage employees to behave differently, if change is needed?
- Are there contradictions in the way we currently operate compared with what we need to do? Are we encouraging employees to get a better balance between work and home but continuing to approve of the people who work until eight o'clock each evening? What do we value and currently reward? How will this change in the new organization we are creating?

## Developing a learning culture

Questions such as these are being addressed in a large international pharmaceutical company with a base in the UK. Following their takeover of an American pharmaceutical company in 1995, a number of new working practices are being introduced, including team work. One initiative involved appointing a number of line managers to the role of team coach. The coach's role is to look at the skills needed across the team and decide how these should be developed.

After extensive training, the coach had to address a number of the cultural challenges which affect performance. One such issue was performance management. Individuals were encouraged to think about their career, their fears and personal development needs in the short, middle and longer term. One team coach found a strong level of unrealistic expectations from previous appraisals. In the earlier culture, it was not usual for managers to confront poor performance. The norm was to pass the mediocre performer onto another department. Sackings, except for ethical issues, were unusual.

In the new environment, there was no room to hide. This coach took the decision to develop the skills of the individual as far as possible rather than hiring in new staff. She created an environment, especially in meetings, where people were given time to reflect on what was happening. Team members were encouraged not to assign blame when things went wrong. Instead everyone involved was asked to look at what they could do differently in the future to improve. This is starting to create a learning culture rather than a blame culture.

### Encouraging innovation

In a major software company, the previous operating norm has been a 'zero-defect' culture. Though this has had major advantages in maintaining the quality of existing products, the company itself was beginning to suffer from a lack of innovation and experimentation. Its products were increasingly becoming obsolete. When the chief executive looked into the probable reasons for this, he found that his own 'don't bring me any surprises' style of management reduced the willingness of his immediate team to encourage risk-taking, however minor.

The chief executive decided that since his own style represented a powerful role model he would deliberately use this to his organization's advantage. Accordingly, he has revised his dictat to read: 'Bring me surprises; don't bring me shocks.' He set up multidisciplinary project teams, with budgets to develop new products, and shielded them from interference by other parts of the organization. Employees now realize that innovation is valued and recognized as a positive contribution to the business. As you can imagine, creativity is starting to flow.

*Modelling equality*

In Honda UK Cars, the general manager places a heavy emphasis on maintaining the climate of equality which exists and is reflected in the layout of offices. All employees have the same kind of desk and office equipment. At the manufacturing plants, all employees, including the general manager, wear 'whites' and take part in the morning exercise routine which is intended to focus minds positively on the day ahead. The easy access by employees to senior managers means that there are few hierarchical barriers to hide behind, and senior managers are obliged to consult widely before making major change.

*Re-freezing*

If change is to succeed it needs to become the new 'way we do things around here.' The final stage of Lewin's model suggests that change should lead to benefits which need to be stabilized. The 're-freezing' stage involves institutionalizing the changes into the organization's culture. A conscious effort needs to be made to show people how the new approaches and behaviours result in improved performance and productivity. It also involves pointing out that the changes were not accidental.

So good communication is vital for people to make that connection. You need to discuss why performance is improving and productivity is increasing. You also need to make sure that as personnel change over the years, the next generation of senior management embodies the new approach, otherwise the change effort will result in a lot of disruption with little gain.

Trifast, a UK-based engineering company, produces nuts and bolts for the electrical industry. They have a market share of 14 per cent and sites around the UK and in Singapore. They employ 490 people across these sites. About a quarter of the staff work in manufacturing; the rest are in marketing and sales. John Wilson, the MD, says:

> Nuts and bolts are boring and to give ourselves the edge, we need to make our customer service the hottest thing around. To do that, we need training.

Trifast is a company which applies total quality management to its processes and has a strong belief that happy staff give them an edge over their competitors. The emphasis is on fun and empowerment.

Trifast have had a policy of encouraging staff to feel free to talk since the 1970s. They actively develop this through their quarterly staff appraisals and by sending staff on assertiveness training courses, actively encouraging them to speak up with their own opinions. They are also introducing training aimed at increasing staff motivation and confidence. One example of this is the 'Make a difference' (MAD) campaign in which people are expected to come up with new ideas for doing things and to put those ideas into practice. This is a culture where the 'way we do things around here' produces real business benefits and vice versa.

## Attitude surveys

Many organizations make use of attitude surveys to identify what needs to be changed or to provide year-on-year indicators of employee morale and links with business performance. Typically, attitude surveys can increase employee dissatisfaction, rather than simply identify it. This happens if there is no feedback about what the survey revealed or where no action appears to be taken as a result of the survey.

One US financial services organization held annual attitude surveys and published the results. However, as far as employees were concerned, nothing was ever done to address some of the most glaring sources of employee dissatisfaction. A new chief executive decided to address some of these issues and challenged his senior management team and Human Resources executive to do something about the most urgent. When only small steps were taken and the next attitude survey results showed no improvement in staff morale, the chief executive cut the bonuses of senior managers until there were measurable improvements in survey findings.

Another American organization employs highly skilled software engineers who are much in demand and are frequently 'poached' by the competition. The company aims to become the worldwide employer of choice in its field. To support this aim, quarterly surveys of all staff take place. The survey asks a few simple, but telling, questions, such as: 'Do you have a meaningful job?' The findings are reported to the worldwide executive and actions are put in place to address employee concerns. Internal benchmarks are set on a number of human resource practices and targets are set on closing gaps between actual and desired practice. This has led to the development of new appraisal and reward systems as well as revised career development processes.

## A forum for communication

Often the issue is not so much that communication is not taking place, but that employees feel they have no regular forum for communicating their views. In one UK-based engineering company, under their previous Managing Director, the forty members of the management team were used to meeting regularly as they were training together to achieve a National Vocational Qualification. After the training ended and with the arrival of a new MD, there were no other formal opportunities for the group to meet together and share information, problems and opportunities across the business. Nobody realized at the time that the value of the training was less in the content of the course, and more in the way it provided a regular opportunity for people to increase their understanding of the changing needs of the business.

The need to meet was not openly expressed until the new MD showed his dissatisfaction at the lack of initiative shown by the management team. Meeting together to address the issue, the team and MD realized that it was lack of information about the company linked with ever-growing pressures to be operationally effective that were preventing senior managers from acting strategically. By reinstating regular 'learning' workshops, the team was again able to make a significant contribution to the running of the business.

In the British Airways MMCO department, with 2300 employees, staff notice-boards are used to convey timely information for team members, for advertising job opportunities and general updates on progress against targets. Team or 'cell' managers hold weekly team meetings to talk about general areas of progress. In addition there are separate meetings where team members can report back to their colleagues about specific issues. These examples of a range of established meeting patterns allow employees to understand the organization's strategy, to have input and to receive recognition for moves in the right direction. The meetings provide an important forum in which employees can have input to the development of the organization.

## Use of information technology

In theory, IT can be very helpful in ensuring good communication. E-mail and other electronic communication systems are widely available, but there are a number of drawbacks which mean that they are perhaps not used as widely as possible. Often organizations have acquired information technology in a piecemeal way, resulting in inconsistent hardware and software as well as lack of training for employees. Another difficulty/drawback is that in organizations where E-mail is in use, there can be an ill-disciplined approach to overloading people with dozens of messages each day. The availability of modems means that there is no escape from dealing with such messages even when travelling on business. In other cases, part of the workforce fails to use E-mail regularly, with the result that they gradually become out of touch since paper messages are no longer sent. Worse still, paper and electronic duplicates add to the amount of information to be processed by employees.

To avoid this, some organizations develop policies about the use of electronic media and provide training in their use. In other cases, the hardware exists but thanks to the lack of an overall strategy there are different buying patterns in parts of an organization, so that various systems are unable to talk to each other without the need for duplication. Again, this often requires courageous reinvestment to ensure that consistency is achieved. In some organizations, the use of voice mail has become an art form. Again, in principle this should aid communication but in many cases, voice mail has come to be used as an effective filter of phone calls to the exasperation of customers – internal or external – who may begin to doubt whether the person they are ringing actually exists.

However, when used appropriately, the benefits of such tools are clear. They should make for better use of time and enable more to be done by fewer people with less effort. The team coach in the pharmaceutical company uses E-mail to transmit the action points arising from team meetings to all interested parties as the meeting ends. There are no bureaucratic delays or excuses. Speed can also be advantageous when conveying important company information, market intelligence and customer news. It is making possible so-called virtual teamwork, enabling colleagues who work remote from one another to have ongoing contact. IT is therefore a valuable tool in creating a global corporate culture. In one global fast moving consumer goods organization, all employees are equipped with laptops and are able to communicate with colleagues anywhere in the world via their Intranet using Lotus Notes. As a result, people receive quick responses to their information requests. There is a real sense of the company acting globally and the use of IT is facilitating such complex activities as international career planning.

IT can also challenge cultural norms about who should receive what information. In organizations that are encouraging two-way communication, the benefits of sharing business information more widely include a more empowered workforce and greater involvement by all employees in growing the business. IT is also useful in providing public recognition of good performance and an ideal forum for sharing suggestions and for open job posting. There can be few excuses for not knowing.

## Meetings

Flat structures seem to give rise to meetings, meetings, meetings: departmental, cross-departmental, project team meetings, to name but a few. So often, meetings appear to lead to poor communication when their purpose is not clear, the wrong people attend or there is an undisciplined approach to the use of time. Similarly, decisions taken at meetings are frequently not implemented or followed up.

Basic training in meetings skills can prevent a lot of the problems. Training can help employees plan for the effective use of meetings, contribute effectively during the meeting and follow-up as appropriate. In the planning phase, team members are encouraged to decide the purpose of the meeting, what needs to be achieved and therefore who needs to be there. Typically, agendas are prepared on the basis of the type of item, such as seeking or giving information, decision-making and approximate timings allocated for each item. Team members are trained to address some of the 'process' issues which can interfere with the business of the meeting. They learn, for example, to disagree constructively and reconcile conflict.

Team meetings can lead to opportunities for greater involvement. They can be useful for creating a sense of team spirit, ensuring that everyone is working towards the same goals, jointly addressing problems and saving time by communicating the same message to everyone at the same time. When they work well, team meetings can be a useful piece of the communications jigsaw, and can help to create the positive work climate needed in the flatter structure.

## A positive work climate checklist

Corporate cultures where change can thrive have certain common features. A critical aspect is trust. People are likely to resist change if they doubt the motives of those introducing it, especially if they perceive themselves to be on the losing end of the change process. Open and honest communications are essential in building trust and belief in the necessity for change. Another key feature is support. Change on the scale implicit in flatter structures calls on people to perform in new ways that will often involve a steep learning curve.

The style of management needed will provide clear direction but also enable people to deliver what is required. This will involve challenge and stretch for everyone in the organization. After all, what is being created is a new organization with change for all. Similarly, the new culture will call for strong follow-through of the change process if the new structures are to work effectively. Just changing targets without thinking about the resources needed and the reward for accomplishing them is unlikely to be successful. This will require careful and determined reworking of internal systems to support what the organization is trying to achieve.

### 1   Understand your current culture

A first step in changing organizational culture is understanding your current culture, looking at the kind of change you want to make, and thinking about how to make the change in such a way that what you do is aligned with the organization's aims.

How ready is your organization for a flatter structure? Would you describe your situation as one which has the following:

- an open problem-solving atmosphere?
- trust among staff members and between staff members and their manager?
- a clear sense of purpose and direction?
- a sense of ownership of goals and targets?
- participation of staff members in decision-making and problem-solving?
- an 'enabling' management style?
- a high level of responsibility amongst individual team members?
- effective use of both the formal and informal channels of communication?
- skills in giving and receiving feedback?
- the ability to deal with conflict constructively?
- managerial commitment to change?

If not, do not despair, but if your goal is to establish a work climate that is both effective for the carrying out of business as well as satisfying to employees, you may need to address any big gaps in this list.

### 2    Work out how to break established patterns of working

This may involve removing management layers and practices which reinforce old ways of doing things.

### 3    Set new standards

This involves defining the behaviours which will be valued in the new organization, such as people using their initiative. Make sure that these new behaviours are recognized formally, through award schemes, and informally, through training managers in the skills of feedback and coaching. Revise compensation schemes so that enhanced performance is rewarded. Create new 'myths' and 'heroes' within the company who demonstrate the new behaviours.

### 4    Give people the opportunity to exercise the new skills and behaviours

Give them the support they need to do their jobs. Eliminate obstacles to the new way of doing things.

## 5 Involve employees

Research consistently suggests that involving people in things which affect them leads to higher commitment and motivation. If you do not trust your workforce, how ready are you for an empowerment culture?

## 6 Challenge sacred cows

Encourage people to challenge the status quo. It is easy for new behaviours to become debased or for complacency to set in.

## 7 Stabilize and revitalize

It is important to notice what is working and to turn that into part of the new way of doing things. If it then becomes set in stone, this too will cease to be effective. Introduce the notion of continuous organization improvement – and celebrate successes!

# 4

# Developing the organization through teamworking and leadership

*How can teamworking and leadership contribute to the creation of an effective lean organization?*

## Why teamwork?

One of the biggest advantages of lean organizations is that they should make it easier for people to work in teams. Teamwork should enable the individual contributors to achieve a collective output which is much greater than the sum of the parts. Team 'synergy' should lead to cost savings, through avoiding duplication of effort. It should also lead to greater innovation and customer satisfaction. Working in teams should increase people's skills, job satisfaction and motivation. This is the theory.

Sometimes the theory holds true. Effective teamwork really can result from simply identifying the right individuals from different work groups to achieve a clear set of objectives which they could not accomplish on their own. In one major government department in the UK, multidisciplinary teams (MDTs) are being formed which cut across previous functional boundaries. These MDTs are made up of individuals who have usually had some military training and who are familiar with the notion of teamwork. For them, the new teamwork structure provides greater opportunities to use initiative.

The problem is, this seems to be the exception rather than the rule.

One difficulty is that teamwork does not happen automatically just by putting together a group of employees with a common goal. Often there are political rivalries or a resistance to giving up individual spheres of influence which may make it hard for people to really share in the group task or in making the team work. Sometimes groups tend to develop a common approach to the extent that they reject new ideas or 'outsiders'. The resulting 'group think' can lead to mediocre rather than superb performance.

Of course, teamworking can produce remarkable results and cross-functional teamworking is increasingly being introduced. At the Rover Group, for instance, the cross-functional team set up to develop and launch the Land Rover Discovery was extremely successful in saving two years of the usual product development cycle time. Indeed, for individuals, successful teamworking can offer a new form of status as a member of an 'elite' team. However, Rob Lummis, personnel director at Land Rover Vehicles, speaking at the Economist Conference in 1995, warned of the potential danger of bringing a team together which may be perceived this way by others, in organizations where teamwork is not yet well established. Such groups can become remote from other parts of the organization because they filter the information coming in to achieve their own targets and can effectively cut themselves off from others, becoming potentially disruptive. Rob Lummis believes that being aware of the possible difficulties this would cause is key to avoiding falling into the trap. He suggests that good communication about and within the project team can 'normalize' the situation, since if project teams start to be seen as a way of life, there is less danger of their being considered an elite.

In some organizations, the prevalence of the teamwork culture means that individual activity can be frowned upon, yet not all work is performed more effectively in teams. In one organization which specializes in diamond sorting, the craftsmen sit at individual booths, sorting diamonds by category and value. To carry out their tasks effectively they need concentration and quiet. When a craftsman is in doubt about a particular stone, he or she consults a more experienced craftsman. The system has worked well for decades. Attempts by a new managing director to introduce 'teamwork', involving production meetings and mentoring arrangements, met with some puzzlement. As far as the craftsmen are concerned they have always operated as a team and they do not see what is to be gained by working differently.

So one of the first questions to be asked in designing a new organization is: What are the work processes that need to be carried out and what might be the best way of doing this? If teamworking is needed, what sort of teams are appropriate and why?

## Types of teams

Teamwork can take different forms according to the needs of the organization. A few examples follow.

### Senior management teams

As a minimum, teamwork at senior levels may involve putting the needs of the overall business ahead of the interests of any one department or function. One major financial services organization experienced internal difficulties because of extreme rivalry and lack of co-operation amongst its executives. This was seriously interfering with the effective flow of operations, so the CEO decided that his 'senior management team' should start to act like a team.

When they failed to do this, the CEO caused a few heads to roll. After the painful lesson had been learnt, the surviving executives were at pains to demonstrate, at least in public, that they were a real team. The effect on the organization initially was minimal because employees were cynical about how long the new approach would last. Eventually, however, persistence and a few demonstrations of active teamwork at the top led to an improved strategic focus and better business results.

Without teamwork at the top, greater collaboration lower down the hierarchy is more difficult to achieve, yet instances of poor senior management teamwork are widespread. Often this poses a dilemma for the organization. The symptoms of poor teamwork at the top may be apparent to others within the organization but, by definition, more junior staff may not have sufficient influence to persuade the senior managers to address the problem. Often, too, senior managers are aware of the problem but feel too vulnerable, exposed or are simply unwilling to deal with the issues. Frequently, external consultants are called in to provide management consultancy or to run 'strategic' workshops which allow top teams to look at the problem from the business perspective.

## Process teams

In some organizations, Business Process Re-engineering (BPR) has led to greater collaboration between departments as they handle different parts of a process. Usually the biggest difficulty in managing processes is the 'handover' point at which the work of one department is dependent on another. Often this is caused by a lack of appreciation of the needs of the other department and quality errors can occur, causing delays and unnecessary duplication or correction of errors. Training can help. Typically people learn to act as internal consultants, developing an understanding of each others' needs and problem-solving skills. In many cases, employees are being encouraged to think of each other as 'internal customers'.

## Project teams

Other types of teams include project teams that are brought together for specific business projects, which may have a short duration. Often these teams work in a matrix structure where functional expertise is theoretically more accessible than in a conventional functional structure. Team members continue to report through their regular reporting lines and usually return to 'normal' duties on completion of the project. Normally, project teams need to co-ordinate their work with that of other teams; the danger can be that having large numbers of projects under way at any one time can lead to confusion and dissipation of effort.

Typically such teams are given specific types of training relevant to the task at hand. These may include process mapping and continuous process improvement techniques or other technical requirements. In the oil and construction industries there are conscious attempts made at 'partnering' with clients in order to produce mutual benefits. This may call on both parties in the project team to learn to communicate in ways which reflect both sets of needs rather than acting as customer and supplier.

## Self-directed teams

In some organizations, with the gradual reduction in the number of managers, there are attempts to create so-called 'self-managed' or 'self-directed' teams. Typically these are groups of three to ten people who work without any direct supervision. As the terms imply, these teams tend to have a longer duration and to be responsible for managing all the processes of the team, from the control of absenteeism to recruitment and reward. Half the self-managed work teams in Rank Xerox distributed their own salaries budget completely in 1994. Self-directed teams make decisions on the tasks of the day, take responsibility for quality control, set their own goals and learn all the jobs that fall within their team's area of responsibility. According to Robert Waterman (1994), the idea is straightforward:

> Organise employees into teams that can cut across old boundaries. Train them. Put them into jobs that challenge their abilities. Give them the information they need. Tell them what they need to accomplish. Then turn them loose.

The reality is not so simple, and self-directed teams meet with varying degrees of success. Typically problems can arise when the manager's role is phased out rapidly, before the team has had time to understand how it will work together. Alternatively, the manager's role is retained but the team is given the mandate to be self-directing. If the manager is unable or unwilling to take on a supportive role, preferring a command and control style, the team soon learns that their decisions will be countermanded and performance suffers. The semi-autonomous team can experience confusing messages about what is required of them.

## Introducing teamworking

In many organizations people recognize that some help may be necessary to enable teams to develop the 'process' skills they need to work effectively together. There are many variations on the way support is offered. In a financial services organization's customer service department, delayering removed supervisor positions and increased managers' direct span of control from six people to nearly thirty. Some of the surviving managers were unwilling to take on a more supportive role to their teams and wanted the opportunity to be involved in more strategic projects themselves.

These were some of the reasons for wanting to encourage teams to be more 'self-directing'.

## The team developer

Following a successful experiment at their parent organization in the US, the company borrowed the notion of the 'team developer'. This role, carried out by former line managers who had a particular interest in people development, was essentially a temporary one. It involved training the team over a period of months to take on the responsibilities previously carried out by their managers and essentially to manage themselves.

According to the 'natural' learning needs of the team, the team developer provided on the spot training and coaching as required. These included training in quality techniques, decision-making and problem-solving as well as process skills such as holding effective meetings and giving each other feedback. In order to be able to help the team in this way, the developer required extensive training and a willingness to abandon 'direct' power over the team. As the team became more skilful and independent, the developer's role gradually became superfluous.

## The team coach

A similar approach used at Glaxo Wellcome in the UK involves using a 'Team Coach'. These are usually former line managers or training and development professionals whose qualifications include being sufficiently high performers that they can act as role models, and seeing people development as a high priority. The coach role was introduced in a sales division following an extensive re-engineering programme in which decision-making was brought closer to the customer. With the decentralization of support services such as administration and marketing, people's job roles grew. One difficulty during the period of change was that people were uncertain about how empowerment would work. The size of the team was expanded on average from eight to twenty-seven.

Each team was asked what it would choose to be measured on. One of the twenty-nine teams decided as follows:

| | |
|---|---|
| • sales | 50 per cent |
| • business plan | 15 per cent |
| • team development, self-development, customer focus | 35 per cent |

The team, with help from the coach, looked at ways in which this could be measured. They decided how they should be appraised, suggesting that the whole team should be involved in the process rather than just the manager, who they felt could not have a total picture of what each individual was doing. This meant that there had to be a high level of trust amongst team members. This has to be an ongoing process otherwise people are reluctant to be honest if they feel they might get a team member into trouble. The coach enabled the team to confront performance issues, on some occasions acting as a facilitator, on others as an interested observer.

An important issue arising out of the emphasis on the team was that some high-performing individuals were very cynical. Previously they had received large individual bonuses for their work but now everyone in the team had the opportunity to earn the bonuses. They therefore felt that they were not getting the recognition they deserved. The coach was able to address this issue by finding new ways of rewarding people, usually through stretching their roles considerably. The team coach is seen as vital in making 'empowerment' possible.

Often difficulties arise in teams simply because people lack a basic understanding of team processes. In many organizations training involves helping teams gain insight into the stages of team-building and an understanding of the different types of contribution required in teams. Instruments used include Dr Meredith Belbin's Team Roles, which describes the different kinds of behaviours required by successful teams. Others are intended to help team members appreciate diversity and work on the basis that difference may indicate a strength needed in the team. Such instruments include the Strengths Deployment Inventory (SDI) and Life Orientations (LIFO). Others include psychometric instruments such as the Myers Briggs Type Indicator (MBTI).

Research carried out by Roffey Park into flatter organization structures indicates that there is an increase in teamwork in European organizations, if only because in many cases time and resources are stretched so thinly that managers have no choice but to encourage teamwork as a way of 'working smarter, not harder'. As structures continue to change, teamworking and the qualities of team members are likely to become more important.

Our stereotyped views about the roles of leaders and team members, or followers, are becoming inappropriate to flatter organizational structures. Instead of thinking of the leadership role as being more active and superior to that of the follower, it is perhaps more relevant to think of them as different but equal. Many employees are now recognizing that developing effective team skills – both team membership and team leadership – is a key ingredient in making them more employable, both inside and beyond the organization. A short self-assessment checklist can help to clarify any areas which may be helpful in deciding whether teamwork is for you.

# A team member's checklist

*How ready are you for teamwork? Are you willing and able to:*
- manage yourself well?
- build your competence and focus your energies to the greatest effect?
- commit to the team and organization's vision?
- take responsibility for delivering to the team?
- give and receive feedback?
- be self-confident and courageous?

*How effective is your team?*
- Are team goals and objectives clear, understood and shared by all?
- Is the team committed to goals and objectives?
- Are priorities established, realistic and relevant?
- Do priorities change in a timely and appropriate manner?
- Does the team regularly develop plans, set goals, establish future directions and steps to get there?
- Are tasks highly interdependent?
- Are members clear about what is expected of them? Are they prepared for their levels of responsibility and authority?
- Is the team well-structured? Are tasks organized effectively?
- Do all team members put energy and determination into achieving team tasks?
- Is the team open and honest in communicating between themselves?
- Does the team communicate appropriately with others beyond the team?
- Does the team operate informally? Are meetings useful and stimulating?
- Do high trust and confidence exist between team members? Do others trust the team?

- Is morale high? Is there a spirit of comradeship?
- Are decisions made jointly through group participation, with plenty of opportunity for input?
- Does the team make effective decisions with creative and appropriate solutions? Are people committed to the solutions?
- Does the team pull together in the same direction?
- Do team members co-operate with each other and co-ordinate their efforts?
- Does the team have appropriate direction? Is leadership shared?
- Do members give each other honest and constructive feedback?
- Are team members aware of each other's distinctive strengths and contributions? Are these highlighted and fully used by the team?
- Is performance evaluated on a regular basis?
- Are team members rewarded in a timely manner?
- Does the team have appropriate controls over performance?
- Does the team celebrate success?

Effective teamwork can certainly help an organization to achieve its goals. Another key ingredient to organizational success is effective leadership. Arguably this is more important in today's changing organizations than in the relatively stable times of the first part of the twentieth century.

## Why leadership?

For most of the twentieth century, organizations of any size have tended to structure themselves into a number of hierarchical levels, modelled on the military. Even the terms used to describe occupants of the different levels reflect this: the boss, or super-ordinate is in charge; the direct report or subordinate follows orders. This model of organization has worked well in producing standardized efficiency, such as is demonstrated in conveyer-belt production processes.

Hierarchical organizations work on the basis that decision-making is restricted to certain management levels. Information is passed up the hierarchy and decisions are passed down to be implemented. In such structures, especially in times of relative stability, the model of leadership is usually more akin to management. Managers manage the implementation of established processes. This usually involves telling people what to do and how, and supervising their performance. A popular image to describe the role of the manager is that of 'conductor' who is responsible for orchestrating the operation. According to Sir Christopher Hogg (Gretton, 1995), formerly of Courtaulds, now chairman of Reuters, management is about:

> ... an effective performance within an institutional framework, which secures the obedience of a lot of people.

In rapidly changing times, lean organizations, often with little middle management, require a different model of interaction. With the increasing power and availability of IT systems, employees often have the information they need to do their jobs, and the authority to use it. Decision-making often takes place at the customer interface. Information needs to pass down as well as up through the hierarchy. Teams are increasingly required to carry out some of the functions previously carried out by managers. They are 'empowered'. As Stephen Cronin (MacLachlan, 1995), director of Human Resources at Rank Xerox (UK), put it: 'We need to move from checkers checking checkers to leaders leading leaders.'

In lean organizations, the importance of the individual contributor becomes more apparent. More and more organizations pay lip service at least to 'our people are our greatest asset'. Getting the best out of people, especially when they are adapting to greater autonomy, involves more than putting in place a mass of management controls. Organizations want people to be 'firing on all cylinders', highly skilled and motivated to do the job. People need less to be managed than given the context and the support to exercise their skills to the benefit of the organization. Taking the human factor into account, leadership becomes a critical parameter. Leadership is essentially related to realizing the future of the organization. The leader as enabler is becoming the new model. The British Excellence Model, promoted by the British Quality Foundation and used widely throughout Europe, shows leadership to be a key enabler of good organizational results. The theory goes that a happy and contented workforce leads to good customer service, generating higher sales and out-performing the competition. With the right teamwork and the right leadership empowerment is the result, with more being achieved from less. Sir John Harvey Jones (Gretton, 1995) agrees:

> Today's leaders understand that you have to give up control to get results. That's what all the talk of empowerment is about.

The Business Excellence Model (Figure 4.1) and others seek to provide a practical way for organizations to see the links between business outputs (results) and organizational inputs, such as leadership. They provide a means for measuring the impact of employee-related issues on business performance.

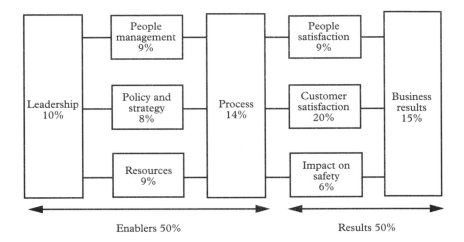

**Figure 4.1** *The business excellence model (printed with permission of the British Quality Foundation)*

In many organizations it is starting to be realized that employees tend to provide the same sort of service to customers as they feel they receive from others in the organization. Poor management and low morale tend to get passed on to customers, who can choose not to continue to deal with the company. In the UK, government-backed initiatives such as Investors in People (IIP) were introduced to encourage and reward organizations who develop and value their staff. Among the main reasons that cause organizations to fail to achieve IIP status are poor communication and inappropriate leadership.

## What is leadership?

So if leadership is so important, what is it? In this section we will look at some of the approaches to leadership identified by a range of theorists. According to Stuart Levine and Michael Crom (1994), leadership is about listening to people, supporting and encouraging them and involving them in the decision-making and problem-solving processes. It is about building teams and developing their ability to make skilful decisions.

Defining leadership is not always easy since the subject has been surrounded by debate for most of this century: are leaders born, not made? can you be a leader if you lack charisma? is it a question of McGregor's Theory X versus Theory Y? Transactional versus Transformational leadership? The shifts in organizations over the past two decades make some of the debate redundant: there is perhaps no absolute which will work in every situation; leadership may need to be contextual to be effective.

At its simplest:

> Leadership is that part of the organization that concerns itself with people. (Clemmer and McNeil, 1990).

Clemmer and McNeil suggest that leadership is not a role or position, but the ability to initiate action and move others to a shared goal. For them leadership is the foundation stone upon which other vital components of organizational high performance – management systems and technology – rest. All three of these elements need to be in balance in order to produce peak achievement and to avoid an excess of any, producing for example 'management madness'.

Warren Bennis, in his books *Leaders* (Bennis and Nanus, 1985) and *On Becoming a Leader* (Bennis, 1989), suggests that managers control contracts relating to jobs, security and money. They produce compliance at best. On the other hand, leaders empower people and ideas and create organizational cultures in which people are challenged and gain a sense of meaning and satisfaction from their work. Bennis coined the phrase, 'Managers do things right; leaders do the right thing.' However, Bennis is wary about over-emphasizing the role of leaders, and Peter Drucker, in his book *The New Realities* (1989), suggests that the principles of management and leadership need to be integrated, blending both innovation and stability, standardized systems and flexibility.

John Kotter (1995), professor of organizational behaviour at Harvard Business School suggests that leadership and management are complementary yet distinctive types of action and approach. Management is about handling complexity; leadership is about coping with change. The debate continues about whether both are required in the same person, although it could be argued that a good leader should ideally possess enough management skills to ensure that vision and goals, once formulated, are effectively achieved.

Whether we are talking about management or leadership, research suggests that both are lacking in the UK compared with other European countries. A survey carried out by International Survey Research of London in eight European countries found that workers in the UK were the most dissatisfied in Europe. Fewer than half believed that they were well managed or had the chance to develop their careers, compared with over 70 per cent of Swiss, Dutch, German and Belgian workers expressing high levels of satisfaction. The survey team found that companies did not put adequate resources into training and developing staff.

At Roffey Park, research into Career Development in Flatter Structures has produced a clear correlation between employee dissatisfaction and poor leadership. Employees seem to feel less loyal and more dissatisfied with their career prospects if they feel their organization is poorly led, especially through major organizational change. Conversely, where good leadership is having the desired effect on business results, teamwork thrives and career development is less of an issue.

## The qualities of leadership

If changing organization structures increases the need for leadership, what are the qualities of leaders and are they culturally specific? Few writers, academics or business chiefs seem to agree on what the ideal model of leadership might be. Indeed, it is probably more helpful if an organization has different types of leaders whom it can call on for different roles at different times.

For a European perspective, Philippe de Woot (1992) uses a Shell definition to describe leadership as 'a natural unforced ability to inspire people.' He suggests that leaders are leaders because they have natural authority and that the source of their natural authority is their acceptance by subordinates. For de Woot, there are two main ingredients to leadership:

- the capacity to articulate a vision – of the best future for their workers
- the ability to communicate (in many languages).

Indrei Ratiu (1983), a researcher and commentator on international leadership based in Paris, France, suggests that the 'multi-cultural' skills of effective leaders in multinational contexts are essentially the same as those working in any cultural context. These include being:

- adaptable to specific people in specific situations
- able to observe and listen
- willing to experiment and take risks
- actively involved with others
- able to learn intuitively, empirically from the immediate situation.

Perhaps a key distinguishing feature is their ability to create 'stability zones' into which they can withdraw when suffering stress, in their case from 'culture shock'. Do these leaders have particular strategies for dealing with change that may enable them to help their teams survive and thrive in the changing organization? Another key feature is their ability to make sense of what is going on in an unfamiliar environment, rather than being overly concerned with early explanation and rapid conclusions. As a way of experiencing and understanding a new experience, this approach is essentially forward-looking.

From Pacific-Asia, David Band (quoted in Yarwood, 1993), director of the Advanced Business Programme at New Zealand's University of Otago, suggests that smart leaders have three main strengths:

- the ability to identify the needs of current and prospective customers
- a capacity to communicate those needs to staff and colleagues
- the foresight to regard his or her prime task as the development of colleagues to add value for the company's owners.

For Max Depree, chair and former CEO of Herman Miller, and author of *Leadership Jazz: the art of conducting business through leadership, followership, teamwork, voice, touch* (1993), some of the attributes of leadership have an almost spiritual tone. They include:

- integrity – the core of leadership
- vulnerability – trusting the abilities of others
- discernment
- awareness of the human spirit
- sense of humour

- curiosity
- predictability
- ease with ambiguity
- presence.

For Depree, management is being recast as a leadership role and effective leadership is judged by the action of the 'followers'.

From the US, James Kouzes and Barry Posner (1993) take a similar view. For them leadership is not a spectator sport and you cannot be a leader unless people are willing to follow you. It is essentially a relationship in which followers or 'constituents' are motivated to confer authority onto the leader, not the other way round. For Kouzes and Posner, the key to effective leadership is credibility, hard won and easily lost. Their research among constituents found that certain attributes make up a common perception of credibility. These include:

- honest
- competent (in leadership)
- forward-looking
- inspiring
- driven by values and willing to make a stand on matters of importance.

Kouzes and Posner point out that the real battle of leadership is overcoming yourself, your fears and limitations. This calls for the leader to have a degree of self-knowledge and courage.

## The functions of leadership

Perhaps the core activity of leaders is to transform their organizations. How they do this is open to question, but many theorists agree that certain functions and the way they are carried out are particularly important. Thus providing inspirational motivation, idealized influence and intellectual stimulation are important. Let us look at some of these functions in a little more detail, especially those which seem particularly relevant, or are at least noticeable by their absence, in organizations with flatter structures in Europe.

*Providing direction*

Research carried out by Roffey Park in 1994 suggests that without a strong strategic purpose behind the delayering, surviving employees display relatively much less commitment to the organization than when a vision is known and believed. The vision should provide not only the reason but the inspiration for the changed organization. In many organizations, especially public bodies whose vision may be set for them by government or other elected sources, lack of an inspiring vision to which employees can commit can cause low morale.

In the past twenty years there has been a good deal of controversy over the process of developing strategy. On the one hand there is the conventional business school-type approach to strategic management, where you decide where you want to be (Figure 4.2), where you are now and how you are going to close the gap to get there. This works on the basis that the world is predictable and stable, that the external environment is to a large extent controllable and that you can expect to achieve what you set out to do. Strategy is essentially a top-down activity with logic and planning as key tools, supported by conventional management activity to help achieve your targets.

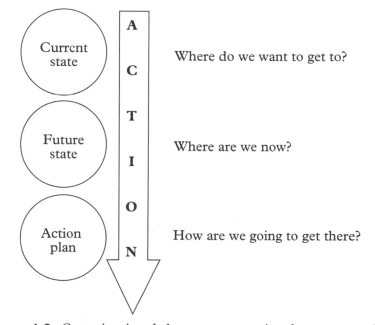

**Figure 4.2** *Organizational change – conventional strategy model*

A different school of thought has arisen over the past twenty years which takes a slightly more radical approach to strategic management. This 'emergent' strategy approach has its source in chaos theory. It assumes that major changes are essentially unforeseeable and unplannable. Some of the many changes in the world's political geography since the early 1980s would seem to reinforce this view. According to this approach, conventional strategic planning rarely produces the intended result in practice and business planning is merely a cosmetic annual data-gathering exercise rather than a real rudder for the business.

The emergent school would suggest that strategy happens on an ongoing basis if the organization is able to capture the information from key stakeholders such as employees and customers. Typically, an organization with such an approach will have flexible structures, supportive management and large numbers of projects exploring business opportunities or solving problems (Figure 4.3).

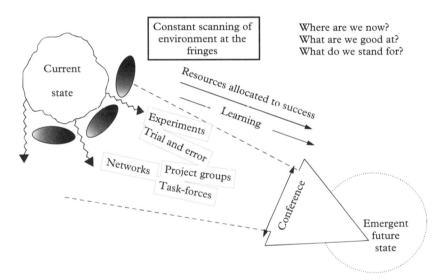

**Figure 4.3** *Organizational change – radical model* (from R. D. Stacey. *Dynamic Strategic Management for the 1990's: Balancing Opportunism and Business Planning.* Kogan Page)

The task of leaders in such an organization is to provide some coherence to what is going on, so that a sense of purpose and rationale for the organization becomes apparent. Though the emergent approach may be in evidence in many organizations, many employees still expect their leaders to provide a clear and explicit direction and become disillusioned when this does not happen. Often, this coherence only becomes clear when looking back, as is the case for many people when they look at their career development to date. It is rather like Winston Churchill's famous statement on becoming prime minister at the age of sixty-six: 'All the rest of my life was a preparation for this moment.' Effective leaders are perhaps those who define a vision of what they are trying to achieve and involve others in developing and realizing the vision, recognizing that the goalposts will shift as they move forward.

## Having the courage of your convictions

This implies that when the leader has a degree of self-knowledge and strong personal values, which ideally should be aligned to those of the organization, team members will align themselves to the leader. The leader should be prepared to make a stand as necessary. Effective leaders are clear about what is not negotiable for them, but offer some flexibility within that space. The power of senior managers to support or undermine the change effort by their behaviour should not be underestimated.

Increasingly, organizations that are experiencing continuous change try to provide coherence in the form of guidelines for behaviour. These are usually aspirational statements of purpose or values such as: 'We put our customers first.' If these remain as words rather than actions, they have little positive effect. In a major US financial services organization, the published statement of values was regarded with some cynicism by staff who perceived senior managers failing to 'walk the talk'. Lack of consistency was seen as a major barrier to empowerment at lower levels so leadership training was introduced as an expensive necessity.

The training takes the form of 360 degree feedback to the individual manager on how well he or she is implementing the values, followed by practical skills development based on the feedback. Workshop sessions result in development plans for participants which they share with their direct reports after the programme. So important is appropriate leadership behaviour considered to be that the feedback is no longer considered confidential but is now taken into account in determining a manager's pay. Needless to say, leadership is taken seriously by the managers in that organization.

## Leading the drive for change

The assumption is that leaders need to be scanning the competitive environment and encouraging innovation. They therefore need to welcome change, be willing to take risks themselves as well as encouraging others to do the same. There is plenty of evidence that change produces chronic insecurity and uncertainty amongst employees, which may make them unwilling to stick their necks out. Leaders are not immune from insecurity and pressure themselves. Research suggests, however, that many managers are risk-averse and dominated by short-term bottom-line demands. Even when an individual leader may be willing to take a longer-term speculative decision, for example to research a potential new product, pressures from owners or investors for short-term financial returns can make apparently 'risky' investments seriously career-threatening.

Another key area in which change may be needed is in the manager's own preferred style. In particular, many managers are unwilling to abandon or challenge the command and control style of management, especially if it has served them well to date. This may have the unwelcome consequence that, rather than encouraging people to try new things and learn from mistakes, managers punish them instead. A 'blame culture' is unlikely to produce innovation.

A confident prediction can be made that change is likely to be an ongoing feature of organizational life. It is perfectly possible that the pendulum will start to swing as ever to undo some of the shifts of recent years. The signs of growth are there and, according to some commentators, the trend towards devolution may be reversed in due course because of economies of scale. Other major international trends are not easily reversed. Organizations which have delayered during the recession are unlikely to revert to richer staffing levels even as national and international economies pick up. Similarly employees who have become multi-skilled and largely self-managing are unlikely to take kindly to being disempowered by stronger management cultures. Leaders will be required not only to cope with a wide range of changes but also positively to embrace change. Their role in guiding organizations through significant change, as well as releasing the energy and potential of employees, will continue to be essential.

### Bringing people with you

This function works on the assumption that managers as leaders will not be able to rely on the power of their position to get things done. Flatter structures usually bring managers' roles much closer to the 'action'. In many cases, managers will find themselves leading teams whose technical expertise is superior to their own. The challenge then is to influence others throughout the organization, encourage teamwork, be able to help people to motivate themselves. It also involves a key set of asset enhancement skills, namely coaching and developing others.

Coaching is the activity that focuses on the ongoing development of skills and confidence of an individual. It is in itself a skilled activity, requiring judgement and excellent communication skills. When carried out effectively, coaching, which includes being able to delegate appropriately, should release potential within the organization. Like the ability to manage, coaching should ideally be part of every leader-manager's toolkit.

In practice, action research into the subject found that coaching is not as extensive, particularly in Europe, as might be supposed. In some cases, the organization's culture, prizing output above development, may limit people's willingness to coach or be coached. Financial institutions in the City of London, for example, where time is money, expect employees to 'hit the ground running' and to keep abreast of new developments as they do their jobs. In some organizations there is an implicit policy of recruiting the skills needed rather than developing them. In other cases, the national culture may set a dominant example of management style. In countries with a highly structured approach to management interactions, as in Germany, or with a paternalistic approach to management, as in Central America, the concept of 'empowerment' at junior levels may seem alien.

There are a number of international organizations with bases in Britain that seem to be setting the standard on people development. In companies like Texas Instruments, DHL, 3M and Nokia, employees are on first-name terms, office doors are open and management and workers eat in the same canteen. The difficulty for the leader in these circumstances is to achieve a balance between approachability and distance. At least one general manager who took part in the Roffey Park research is experiencing difficulties with this issue.

A number of organizations are trying to provide managers with the skills and confidence to coach effectively. British–American Tobacco has introduced a worldwide training programme called the 'Line Manager as Developer' to equip managers for this role. Others are encouraging line managers to act as mentors or to provide ongoing training to their teams. In some cases, line managers are expected to share in the delivery of training programmes that are part of a larger culture change programme.

Coaching can lead to greater motivation. The question of whether a line manager can motivate someone else or whether the individual motivates him- or herself is open to debate. At the very least, the task of the leader is to provide the team with the positive environment in which they can find their own motivation. Given the negative effects of major change on employees' motivation, such as the consequences of flatter structures for people's career aspirations, this can be a very difficult task. However, there is evidence that some managers are able to do this. Why is it that in one organization employees are willing to make a lateral or even downward move in order to work with a particular leader? Perhaps it is because:

> ... outstanding leaders can probably be best measured by the degree to which those under them are empowered.
> Jacinta Calverley, Human Resources manager, FCL (Yarwood, 1993)

This will be explored in other chapters in this book. The trend towards encouraging line managers to develop others appears to be patchy in Europe. There seems to be an increasing emphasis on this aspect of managers' roles, even in organizations where management was previously regarded as a purely intellectual function, such as the British civil service, where government policy advisors are being encouraged to embrace this responsibility. How well equipped managers are for this role, or how willing they are to do it, remains to be seen.

## What do leaders actually do?

Some research carried out by Roffey Park in the UK set out to explore what leaders consider to be their main responsibilities, and how these might change as the new millennium approaches. We wanted to find out what the practising line managers, as opposed to the theorists, considered their role to be in the changing organization. In the main, the interviewees were owners, managing directors or chief executives of organizations ranging in size from fifty employees to five thousand. One was a board member of a multinational company with over fifty thousand employees worldwide. Most of the organizations had delayered or were planning to do so.

A key responsibility for many of these leaders is making decisions, typically for issues involving policy development, expenditure against functional or business unit targets, continuous improvement of service provision, resourcing and development of staff. Another major area of responsibility involves the creation of vision and strategy to underpin the business plan, as well as taking on a public relations role with clients. In smaller organizations the leader can find him/herself taking responsibility for all major decisions as well as the day-to-day operation, including being personally accountable for health and safety issues.

## What makes them effective?

In carrying out their roles, leaders consistently highlighted certain abilities and activities as being critical to their success. These are discussed below.

### Scanning the environment for opportunities and threats

One CEO described the process as being a 'hunter-gatherer of ideas'. Another talked of the need to be able to 'spot the rocks under the surface of the white water.' In addition, leaders agreed that the ability to understand the changing business scene, in order to identify new business and resources, is a basic requirement of leaders. Some do this by consciously networking within their industry and beyond. All are skilled at identifying trends, patterns and pattern-breakers, often looking beyond the national and European marketplace to the Pacific rim and global movements generally.

### Reconciling different interests

A concern shared by many of the leaders interviewed was the need to be able to reconcile the often conflicting interests of different stakeholders in the organization. The ability to manage conflict is only one part of the equation. Another key ingredient is excellent people skills, the ability to influence the internal political process without having to be heavy-handed. One senior Human Resource executive in a decentralized multinational spoke of the difficulties of obtaining critical business data when business units are virtually independent of the central operation. The ability to understand and influence the nature of corporate synergy in a devolved world is essential.

*Teamwork*

Leaders spoke often of the need for teamwork. The reason most often given was the effect of downsizing, with the entire operation having to work more cohesively to maximize individual output. Total Quality was another feature, calling for multidisciplinary teams. So often difficulties within the top teams have been seen to have an adverse effect on their organizations. One major multinational had introduced formal meeting procedures via training for the executive team in order to refocus attention on the core tasks of the group. Delayering in particular has highlighted the need to be able to manage without hierarchical control systems – to manage information, not people.

# Problems experienced by leaders

Three broad difficulties faced almost all of the leaders interviewed.

*Time management*

The broad-ranging responsibilities, including providing business direction and control, keeping abreast of market developments and human resource management, cause real difficulties for many leaders. The challenge is knowing what to prioritize, managing in the here and now without getting bogged down in detail while at the same time remaining forward thinking.

One leader, Julian Metcalfe of Pret à Manger, the UK sandwich shop chain, gets round this issue by not keeping a diary and having a three-hour meeting with his senior management team as the only fixed event each week. The meeting involves a brief discussion on the group's trading but mainly focuses on the major issues challenging the business. Of the remaining hours in the week, Metcalfe says he spends 95 per cent of his time listening to customers and employees. This unstructured approach allows Metcalfe to respond immediately to ideas and events (Bagnall, 1996).

In some cases leaders were open about preferring to manage in a 'hands on' way, often doing the kind of work normally carried out at a level or two below the leader's actual position. In a few cases this was because leaders did not fully identify with their senior management role, seeing their expertise to be in their former functional or technical responsibilities rather than in leadership of the business. This tendency was more pronounced among leaders whose career path had been mainly in the technical/functional route rather than a generalist route. In one case the leadership responsibilities of getting results from people were firmly delegated down the line.

In other cases, where the leader's role is changing from being primarily policy-making to more specifically managerial (as in the UK government departments) the need to acquire new roles and responsibilities as well as retaining the old is causing overload. Failure to delegate exacerbates the problem since subordinates hesitate to make decisions without the leader's involvement. One leader admitted that he knew this tendency was a major constraint on the organization.

### Interpersonal flexibility

Some leaders reported having difficulty developing the interpersonal flexibility they feel is needed in the role. One board member of a major international engineering organization felt that his relatively relaxed management style was now preventing him from being taken as seriously as he would like in implementing a company-wide change programme. Another leader found that his preference for a strongly controlling style of leadership was leading to 'palace revolts' which put his position in doubt.

### Managing self and others

Some found the hardest challenge was developing really effective management skills. Often these skills had been developed through practice, and several leaders felt the need to go beyond their current skill levels. Some were actively looking for external mentors and considering doing short- and long-term training programmes at international business schools.

## What will be required of leaders in the new millennium?

There was broad consensus on what will be required of leaders in the next few years.

*Being able to learn*

The ability to learn consciously and effectively was considered the key to long-term success as a leader. The paradigms of normality around which organizations have planned their future need to be continuously reviewed since they are constantly shifting. Who in the West, fifteen years ago, would have confidently predicted that the former Eastern bloc would become a major growth area for capitalist expansion? How many organizations have missed the opportunity to exploit a new product or service because they waited until they had all the relevant data to help them make the decision to go ahead?

Unless learning outstrips the pace of change, organizations will have all the data they need about missed opportunities. Often the pace of change is so great that the tendency is to move on to the next crisis before reflecting on what has been learned from the current problems. Ironically, it is almost as if learning is the one thing which is expendable if it takes time, yet without learning, an endless round of fire-fighting seems the consequence.

A positive step is required in order to break the vicious circle and consciously initiate learning. Leaders who placed a high value on learning had initiated a number of feedback mechanisms about their leadership style in order to increase their flexibility and effectiveness. Being able to learn and trust to intuition, that famous 'gut feeling', is likely to be an increasingly important asset in leaders. As one leader put it: 'We need to value learning as much as last quarter's figures.'

*Guiding organizations through change*

The ability to provide direction, inspiration and co-ordination to a work group, business unit or entire organization is likely to continue to be the core role of leaders. Although few people believe that organizations grow or die solely due to the impact of the leader, the style of the leader is part of a complex web of elements which have an effect on morale, productivity and organizational performance. The more the leader can provide the tools and the communication needed by employees to accomplish their tasks, the higher the productivity and satisfaction of the group. Again, the importance of knowing what is important and acting on it comes through. This implies that leaders need to have a clear sense of their own values as well as the personal resilience to adapt to changing times.

*Appropriate leadership*

The research highlights the need for leaders to recognize when other people can more effectively lead certain processes than they can themselves. Currently, where 'shared leadership' is happening, there is a discernibly high level of trust between leaders and their peers or subordinates. These leaders seem to be relatively more open to feedback than leaders who view their working situation as potentially hostile.

Perhaps this is where the practitioners agree with the theorists. According to Charles Handy, a leader must be a teacher, a consultant and a trouble shooter. His definition of the 'post heroic' leader is the manager who desires that every problem be solved in a way that develops other people's capacity to handle it.

## Conclusion

Teamworking and leadership are not new skills but in lean organizations they are increasingly important. The range of applications of both and the way in which they are increasingly expected of people at all levels in the hierarchy are, however, new. Managers need to be team members as well as team leaders. Likewise, team members need to be able to share leadership as appropriate. When teams and leaders are working together to forge the new organization, the results are likely to be robust and to stand the test of time.

# 5

*Introducing structure change –*
   *a strategic approach*

*Achieving what the organization needs to achieve through the way it brings about change*

Most organizations do not have the luxury of taking a strategic approach to implementing organizational change. By 'strategic approach' I mean a deliberate, planned approach to delayering which helps an organization to achieve its broad strategic goals. In this chapter we will explore some of the ways in which organizations become leaner and look at some different perspectives about what really works when introducing major change.

## Theory versus practice

*Conventional theory*

In theory, a strategic approach involves deciding **what** you (the organization) want to do and **why**. The next question is **how** will this be achieved and **who** will do it. Questions of structure, systems, processes and people should follow from the vision, being part of the strategy for achieving that vision.

So an organization wishing to become the most successful supplier of product A to the world market may believe that it is essential to provide superb customer service in order to secure repeat business (the **what** and **why**). It may then have to re-engineer its processes and design the organization around these aims. It may find that flatter structures make sense if the processes are horizontal, from customer to customer. It may need people to be able to work in process teams, understand customer requirements and be motivated to deliver to a high level. This may require a change in working practices, systems and people. Some may have the appropriate skills and attitude for the job, others may need time to adjust. Training may be required. Others may not have the appropriate mix of required skills and may have to leave (the **how** and the **who**).

### The practice

Even in relatively stable times organizations rarely follow the theoretical approach. There is sometimes too much at stake in maintaining the status quo for key individuals to allow the structure to be challenged. Especially in bureaucratic organizations or large, politicized multinationals, the **who** often determines **how** people work and therefore **what** can be achieved. Attempts to introduce quality initiatives in such organizations often achieve little because mapping horizontal processes across a vertically organized structure produces many issues that fail to be resolved.

In the relatively turbulent economic times of the past few years, radical solutions are often called for. The worldwide recession has been the backdrop to major shifts in employment. The trend towards major restructurings which refocus an organization's efforts onto its core activities, while the rest are outsourced, has contributed to destabilizing the workplace. When faced with the challenge to be ever more competitive, many organizations look on their workforce as a major cost and therefore a potential source of cost-saving.

The evidence of our research suggests that the majority of the UK organizations that have delayered in recent years have done so because they had no choice. In the mid-1990s, a survey carried out by Roffey Park Management Institute found that 79 per cent of employees in 200 organizations from all sectors in the UK considered cost-cutting to be the main reason for delayering. A survey carried out in Germany at the same time found a similar picture. Organizational survival was at stake. Other reasons included the need for greater efficiency because of worldwide competition. Some organizations were clearly following a trend set by other organizations. As one interviewee put it: 'The rationale is that everyone else did it in the 1980s and now we should do it.'

The picture which emerged from these organizations was one of confusion and uncertainty amongst employees, with the new structures apparently achieving the opposite of what they are intended to do. Typical of the comments made were these:

> 'I'm expected to work effectively in areas I'm not trained for or experienced in.'
> 'Negative effects on quality and project control.'
> 'Confusion in trying to deliver service in the field.'
> 'Decreased level of authority and responsibility leads to disempowerment.'

In each case, the decision had been taken to cut out a layer of management, in order to save costs or to remove certain individuals. Having done this, senior managers expected people working within the new structure to carry out the same amount of work as in the older, fatter structure, but more cost-effectively. The impact on employees – their needs, increased workloads, changing working practices and damaged motivation – was apparently not high on the agenda.

## Developing a team-based organization in a software company

An unusual approach to structure change was used at Company X, a software house providing services within the financial services industry and to government bodies. In the early 1980s, after a period of steady growth, the company floated and the money raised was used for reinvestment. By the late 1980s, Company X had established itself as a major provider in a niche market. In 1988, a major setback for the business led to a change of chief executive and growth began again. In 1989, a client service and quality initiative was introduced. However, massive change and increased competition in the software sector meant that profits once again began to stagnate.

By 1990, low margins and productivity levels led to major challenges for the organization. These were compounded by internal politics amongst the 600 staff, poor client service levels and bureaucratic inertia. Innovation was in short supply. Management decided that action was needed. Restructuring was considered in order to keep viable and a number of reorganizations took place. First there was a redistribution of staff into industry groups: by sector, such as financial services, government bodies; by functions, such as sales, client services and software development; by matrix, with vertical lines of business supported by horizontal generic services. None of these structures seemed to provide the improvements the business needed.

What quickly became apparent was that the perfect structure exists only at a certain point in time. The frequency of structure change required to keep pace with the changes in the industry was increasing. The small number of people, mainly senior managers and human resource staff, involved in shaping the organization could not assimilate enough information to make appropriate decisions. The frequent reorganizations were upsetting customers and suppliers since there was no prolonged point of contact with any one individual. It was felt that something more radical must be done to address the issues.

The key question was: What should be done? Which approach to change was most appropriate? The debate centred on revolution (let the pressure build until you reach a crunch point and then rebuild) versus evolution (lots of small-scale changes). The CEO opted for dramatic change, supported by the business imperative.

The next question was: which were the key targets for change? Certain major problem areas were targeted. Amongst these were leadership issues. It was felt that the dominant management style of command and control was contributing to the inertia. The hierarchical structure with defined job descriptions, rules and controls was to be replaced by teamworking which, it appeared, would result in high-impact delivery and maximum efficiency. The existing processes needed new technology and methods. Most of all, motivation levels of staff were low, despite pay levels matching or exceeding the average for the industry. It was felt that when motivation levels are higher, people will work well even if the structure is inappropriate. A key challenge was to find ways of increasing motivation levels.

## Approach taken

In June 1990 the CEO called for volunteers to join two design teams whose remit was to answer the question:

*How do we need to organize the company to resolve all our issues?*

Initially only a few people came forward to join these teams but, with encouragement from the CEO, who promised to implement their recommendations, the teams finally consisted of ten people each, mainly supervisor level or below. They were allowed to call in others from the organization for advice and information. Each group was supported by an external consultant and met off-site for a week. The families of team members were invited to join them at the hotel where the meetings were taking place and enjoyed a pleasant weekend as the company's guests.

The design teams presented their recommendations to directors of the PLC in a 'neutral' context. Following the presentations, the directors were invited to identify all the reasons why the proposals would not work. The issues raised fell into seven broad categories. The Chief Executive then presented the directors with the challenge cum ultimatum:

> These are the issues which we have to resolve **before** we implement the proposals!

Following the presentation to directors, seven task forces were set up to address the issues raised. Each taskforce consisted of ten people; three of the original design team, two directors and five 'volunteers' from the rest of the organization as chosen by other team members. Training in team processes was provided to enable the task forces to function effectively. The old-style directors took no part in the process but three directors, including the HR director, were attached to the task forces to provide specialist inputs on structure, design and the implications for training. The HR director put together recommendations based on the output of the taskforces. Checklists and handbooks to support implementation were prepared.

By the end of 1990, the task forces had done their work and were disbanded. Their presentation to the CEO recommended the creation of multi-skilled teams without leaders. These teams were to consist of thirty people, with a blend of all the skills needed to provide service to customers. This implied different roles, rather than different people. The teams were to have the following characteristics:

- client-focused – they must have external customers
- autonomous – they must be able to 'stand alone'
- self-led and self-managed – there was to be no appointed leader and there must be a 'constitution'
- commercially aware – they must have a three-year business plan and a one-year profit and loss
- co-ordinated – teams in similar markets must work together.

## Implementation

As promised, the CEO agreed to implement the recommendations, but at this point he disbanded the task groups and resumed a more directive approach to implementing the new system. He insisted that each team should have a mandate to exist, which could be withdrawn. To get the mandate, the teams had to obtain a certificate signed by the CEO.

A training programme explained the rules of the new organization to all staff. Teams were allowed to form themselves. Unallocated people found positions. A few senior managers, including functional specialists such as HR and Finance, were retained as a core business team. The other directors organized themselves into a team. The number of directors started to decline sharply, reducing from forty to eight within a matter of months. Those who remained continued to be paid the same as before but were now required to take on responsibilities that were much more front-line.

The introduction of multi-functional workgroups had a major impact on the organization's culture. The teams broke down the hierarchy and challenged all the previous 'givens' and power structures. The HR director, faced with endless queries about issues such as how invoices would be raised and expenses paid, decided that a framework of written rules would be necessary to replace the former 'natural law'.

Some of the policy guidelines were as follows:

- no one has the delegated right to tell others what to do
- there will be only two management layers
- there will be no appointed team leaders or managers (although in practice, teams did appoint individual leaders, or two or three individuals to act as a 'leadership forum')
- bonuses are available to everybody
- salesmen are not paid on commission
- budgeting is to take place from the bottom up
- there are no 'dead men's shoes'.

Employees were expected to be flexible in moving from activity to activity and from one location to another. The more senior employees had been in the previous hierarchy, the more they perceived themselves to be losing power in the new structure, with a few notable exceptions. Those directors who had been most closely involved with the process were the people least fearful of losing power and most disposed to make the new structure work.

The HR policy set out the different responsibilities of the organization and of employees. Individuals were told that they were primarily responsible for managing their own career. However, the company accepted responsibility for supporting individual development, in particular for career development within the organization. The company was also responsible for the benefits package and discipline. The teams also had to accept their responsibilities for achieving business goals and developing team members.

The self-managed element of the new teams proved fairly easy to implement. In some cases, team members shared the leadership role according to the specific issue they were working on at the time. Once established, the teams became unwilling to change, having established some internal continuity. When they were first set up, the teams underwent intensive training in team processes. Thereafter, individuals had to win support from the rest of the team if they wanted to spend money on specific training.

## Difficulties posed by the new structure

These mainly fell into the categories of career development and pay.

### Career structure

The lack of an obvious career structure caused problems both for existing staff, who did not know where they now 'fitted', and in recruiting new staff. The 'people' taskforce regrouped to address the issue. They proposed six levels which fell into two categories as follows:

*Skills level*

*Business level*

6　Expert
5　Intermediate
4　Beginner

3　Expert
2　Intermediate
1　Beginner

A career route was not necessarily through these levels. The ability to do the job was defined by experience, skills and aptitude. People either had these, or they did not. The difficult task of assigning levels and jobs to existing staff was carried out by a review board consisting of a director who brought awareness of the business overall, an HR specialist and people already in their new role. If the review board felt that a person had the relevant aptitude, they were assigned a role.

The new team structures and multi-skilling made the previous conventional job descriptions irrelevant. The review board decided to disconnect the concept of career route and current jobs. Broad banding was considered the answer. Role definitions were developed which outlined broad areas of responsibility, not specific tasks. The concept of 'jobs' was eliminated. Within the organization job titles were eliminated and employees were allowed to invent their own title for business cards. The prevailing idea was: 'You are what you do, not what you are called.'

In order for the new system to work, each role had to be closely analysed to understand what the skill area at each level would look like. What, for instance, would be expected of a secretary at 'beginner' skill level? For some roles, such as receptionist, there was no obvious progression to level two because the role itself was too small. The number of descriptions diminished as you went up the levels, until there was only one description of each role at level six. All new recruits were automatically put at the first career level.

Each employee could apply for their role level to be reviewed twice a year. If they moved from beginner to intermediate level, they were guaranteed at least the minimum salary at the next level, so moves were worthwhile. The self-managing element was that individuals who wanted 'promotion' were expected to speak to people at intermediate or expert levels and obtain any help they needed such as mentoring or coaching. They would then present their case to the review board, who assessed whether the individual had achieved the required level, in which case they were by definition 'promoted'.

However, the drawback was that if the team's goals did not require them to have an individual, such as a programmer, at the new level, the promoted individual was expected to carry on at their previous level and request transfers to teams where their new level was needed. Candidates for promotion also had to recognize the need for the previous activity they were carrying out and could not refuse to do what the team required.

The team and organizational responsibility for career growth was reflected in the process for moving around the company. People were expected to discuss their aspirations with HR and with their team, as well as with someone already carrying out the kind of role they were looking for. A 'Career Structure' book, containing all the role descriptions, was available to staff. People were expected to make opportunities for themselves, using this transparent process.

There were many difficulties with the new scheme, not least because people were not used to receiving feedback. Different forms of assessment were used, including assessment centres. In particular, people whose career levels were assessed lower than they thought was warranted, felt aggrieved and initially underperformed in the new teams. Higher up the levels there were fewer opportunities to change, with level six alone being by invitation only. In the second year of operating the new structure, people at levels four and five who were not performing up to the level required for some reason were assigned a mentor from level six. On average, one-third of employees were promoted.

### Performance appraisal

Performance appraisal was the team's responsibility. Each team had to identify two team appraisers, who must be at least at beginners' level in the business stream. They received intensive training for the task. Individual team members were able to choose who would appraise them and a variety of data-gathering methods were used. In addition to self-assessment, team members were required to collect 360 degree feedback on their team performance, including contribution to the team's objectives.

Each element of performance received a score out of 600 based on a 1–6 scale as follows:

- contribution in core role                                      60 per cent
- contribution to the team                                       30 per cent
- contribution to the company as a whole          10 per cent

The appraiser would then hold a team discussion about the individual and consensus, including the appraiser's own view, had to be achieved. More controversially, 'snitch' forms were used to allow team members to report on poor performance as well as the positives. These forms were not anonymous, but they were used. Objective setting was part of this process.

Individuals had the right of appeal, but generally appraisal decisions were accepted. This is where the credibility of the appraisers was critical since they had to appear well-motivated in order to avoid defensive reactions from appraisees. The system worked reasonably well and assisted in the development of the new culture. In assessing individual contributions to the company as a whole, for example, people were asked to volunteer new initiatives and suggest other ways of getting involved beyond their teams. The system effectively penalized people who simply wanted to get on with the 'job'.

*Salaries*

The most difficult area involved salary review. This is an ongoing problem which has still not been fully resolved. The review process is not a team issue, but is the responsibility of HR. While the team can decide the overall number of roles required in the team, the HR director decides on pay levels for individuals. To support the HR director, a salary review group was set up and HR 'agents', i. e. team members, and the Finance director were involved in the process. HR and Finance set the overall level of increase by calculating what the company could afford and by taking into account the marketplace salary levels of job types, such as programmer roles. Some of the overall 'pot' was kept back every year for promotions, ad hoc issues such as appeals and for special cases throughout the year.

The complexities of mapping across market rates onto the new structure proved enormous. It was decided that there should be a few general principles to guide decision-making. First, an across-the-board increase was awarded, then salaries were calculated using market levels. The company would pay at least the minimum of market levels, with no maximum level set. New joiners, though at the lowest level of the career scheme, were paid the maximum of market rates.

Perhaps the most controversial aspect of the new scheme was the use of the HR 'agents' to establish individual salaries within the points system used in performance appraisal. Agents were each given the brief to look at the pay levels of ten individuals. For each of these ten, agents examined details of the previous year's salary, bonuses throughout the year, the mid-points of the band the individuals were in and the performance appraisal scores of the individuals concerned.

Actual cases were then discussed to see if the pay decision proposed would be an anomaly. Factors such as performance and the likelihood of poaching by the competition were taken into account. In 20 per cent of cases it was felt that the pay level was out of step, with the individual being paid too much or too little. The recommendations of the 'agents' and the operational directors, aligned across the employee base, determined the pay level of each employee. Very few employees appealed against the decision.

On agreement with the board, pay rises were decided as follows:

| | | |
|---|---|---|
| below 300 | – | no pay rise (why are they here?) |
| below 400 | – | set objectives for half-year rise |
| 400–450 | – | 4 per cent |
| 450–500 | – | 6 per cent (excellent) |
| 500+ | – | 10 per cent  (why are they here?) |

Every employee became eligible for a bonus. Thirty per cent of salary was targeted, though in reality this never exceeded 10 per cent. A yearly customer satisfaction 'health check' was carried out. The team received 6 per cent of the revenue they generated. This was calculated on booked and cash revenue. In addition cash collection above set targets and profit above set margin levels were taken into account. The top team received on average £2500 a quarter. Sales commission was abolished and a sales-related scheme introduced on order achievement targets. Additional benefits were at or above industry average levels. These included pensions, cars and health scheme, and flexibility was introduced to some degree.

*Discipline*

Discipline was now the responsibility of the team since manager posts no longer existed. Peer pressure grew on individuals who, in the previous structure, might have been tempted to be lax. It was no longer considered appropriate, for example, for senior salespeople to celebrate a major deal by taking extended lunches for a week after the sale. Whatever the form of 'leadership' of the team, representatives received coaching in team discipline from the HR director once a month and were provided with a Personnel Handbook. If the team's efforts failed, the HR director issued formal warnings to the offending person. Discipline, such as time-keeping, proved particularly difficult for the teams to deal with, and co-ordinating standards across teams was a challenge for the HR team.

## Conclusion

The triggers for change in this organization were a strong business imperative and the mandate given to staff by a CEO who believed in the power of involving employees in the decisions which affected them and the business. The approach taken was both carrot (incentives) and stick (punitive). Within the change there was potential both for loss and for gain. The gains for the business were the improved profitability year on year from 1991, with clear benefits in terms of containing costs. Customers benefited from improved quality, with the company achieving ISO 9000 by the end of 1992. The more open culture meant that individual performance was much more visible to others. As one employee put it: 'You can't get away with anything these days – there's nowhere to hide.' For individuals there was much greater autonomy and a demand for recognition of achievement.

On the downside, senior managers found the changes hard since they were faced with the dilemma of authority versus authority. It was sometimes a question of having faith in employees and being prepared to let go. Respect had to be earned; it was not given with rank. Many of the 'givens' disappeared and leadership became more difficult since people demanded the rationale for what they were being asked to do. Other difficulties in the initial phase included co-ordinating transfers between teams, which produced some inter-team animosity. There was certainly increased stress on everyone.

Some necessary changes at the very top of the organization were not carried through, which limited the success of the initiative to a certain extent. Inducting new staff, especially at senior levels, also proved difficult because a relatively egalitarian culture was unattractive to many potential recruits. Those who did join were influenced particularly by senior directors who did not buy into the change and tried to undermine it. This is an example of one of the lessons drawn by John Kotter in his studies of why change efforts often fail. Obstacles to the change, whether they are in the systems, structures or the people, need to be removed if the momentum for change is to be maintained.

# 6 The Operations Development Project at Thresher

There may be no such thing as an ideal way to restructure an organization. So often, approaches which are tried and tested in one organization do not work so well in another. An approach which combines both emergent practices and conventional planning has been used by Thresher, the UK-based drinks retailer which is part of Whitbread Plc. In this chapter we will explore the introduction of the Operations Development Project (ODP) at Thresher, and examine some of the learning which the company has acquired through the process of implementing the change programme.

## The context

At the beginning of the 1990s Thresher was in a period of slow but steady growth. There were five established shop brands: Thresher Wine Shop, Drinks Cabin, Bottoms Up, Wine Rack and Huttons. In 1991 Thresher acquired Peter Dominic wine merchants, expanding the number of employees in its operations team. The 9500 employees who worked in these teams, as well as the managers to whom they report, were based in 1600 branches.

Unlike many other organizations, Thresher was not driven to introduce a major change programme by immediate financial pressures – the operating figures were more than adequate. They were looking instead to develop strategic and long-term solutions to strengthening the business. Competition within the drinks retailing industry is intense, with competitors to be found from a range of sources, including supermarkets and cross-Channel imports as well as other drinks retailers. Thresher was interested in finding ways of becoming more responsive to customers as a key to business success in this increasingly competitive market.

The ODP was introduced in response to this intention. The project originators were Brian Wisdom, Operations Director, Chris Johnson, Human Resources Controller, and Dick Smerdon, then Sales Director, who provided sponsorship of the project at board level.

## Operations Development Project objectives

The primary aim of the ODP was to bring about improved business performance. This aim was supported by a number of key objectives, the first of which was increasing employees' focus on the customer, since Thresher believes that customer service and satisfaction are critical to their future success. Secondly, the acquisition of a number of brands meant that ODP objectives included bringing the company's marketing strategy to life everywhere in the business. The third objective was to bring about significant business improvement by increasing both sales and profit.

The change team recognized that business objectives are fine in theory, but that they have to be delivered by a highly motivated and skilled workforce. The project team believed firmly that employees were key to improved business performance. They perceived a huge reservoir of untapped potential. It was unclear at the beginning of the project, however, whether that potential was of the calibre needed for the future. The business objectives were therefore supported by organizational objectives.

Recognizing that change programmes can have negative as well as positive effects on employees, Wisdom and Johnson made developing and energizing people a deliberate objective of the ODP. Chris Johnson stresses 'energizing' rather than 'empowering' – he feels that energizing is a more appropriate concept since he believes that people are responsible for their own motivation. The organization's responsibility is to provide them with appropriate opportunities to activate their own potential and motivation.

The project team recognized that employee morale and people's desire to give outstanding customer service are intimately inter-linked. For a number of years, annual 'Quality of Worklife' surveys had been used to measure job satisfaction and employee attitudes. There was some evidence that employee satisfaction at the time of the launch of ODP was beginning to tail off. The ODP was therefore intended to take into account the needs of employees. Developing and energizing people were not 'nice to haves' since it would be essential to have the enthusiastic support of employees if the ODP was to work. Taking into account the needs of employees would be the means of converting potentially low morale into getting the best out of current employees.

There were some cultural goals too. Recognizing that change was likely to be not only a feature of the ODP but a continuing need within the business in the future, the project team wanted to develop a climate where change would be welcomed and embraced. This would almost certainly require a more responsive organization structure to enable them to move faster in a changing world. The structure change would therefore be part of a more comprehensive set of activities aimed at equipping the organization for ongoing and future success. Flattening structures would not be an end in itself, as in so many delayerings driven by the need to cut costs. The ODP, in Dick Smerdon's words, was 'a careful look at the future without taking our eye off the ball'.

## Characteristics of the ODP

An important characteristic of the ODP was that it was envisaged as a three-year programme, unlike so many change initiatives which are dominated by short-term bottom-line considerations. The ODP was therefore underpinned by an investment perspective. Money saved through the ODP would not simply be shown as profit but would be reinvested in the project to provide longer-term benefits. As such, supporting the project would require an act of faith since results could not be guaranteed in the short term.

A danger with any long-term change programme is that it can drift over time, and therefore people lose interest in driving the change forward. Wisdom and Johnson therefore planned that they would share responsibility for driving change forward initially and that they would provide a framework for the evolutionary change process so that everybody involved would be able to understand what progress was being made.

Wisdom and Johnson developed the project architecture with five clear phases, beginning in Summer 1993. These were:

- information gathering
- blueprint
- design and trial
- road map
- implementation and reinforcement.

From the outset the ODP was to be underpinned by a few key principles:

- recognition of the need for change by all involved
- maximum involvement
- developmental, energizing of people
- innovative and experimental
- common values and beliefs
- not crisis-driven
- challenging sacred cows
- all aspects of the ODP should be measurable.

### Measures

These principles were put into practice from the outset. In particular, Wisdom and Johnson recognized the importance of measures. Conventionally, change processes are measured only on their bottom-line impact. Obviously it was important to be able to track progress on the business objectives, and 'hard' measures were set as follows:

- ongoing costs
- ongoing savings
- brand standards
- working practices such as drive time, wasteful administration, etc.

Given the nature of the ODP objectives, the change team took literally the accountant's cliché, 'If you can't measure it, you can't manage it'. The usual corollary is that 'you only manage the things you measure'. It was therefore important to make the cultural goals concrete. They decided to set measures on the 'soft' cultural goals, as well as on the 'hard' financial goals. These measures included, for instance:

- communications – upwards and downwards
- people development
- teamwork and coaching
- the implementation of operational values
- use of IT – both confidence levels and numbers trained
- functional interface
- survey results pre- and post-implementation.

By setting these measures from the outset, the project team would be well placed to make any connections between employee morale and business performance.

*Launch of the ODP*

A formal presentation was made to the operations team in May 1993. The operations team then consisted of three operations directors, twelve regional sales managers (RSMs) and ninety area sales managers (ASMs). It seems that getting buy-in to major change when the business is doing well is much harder to achieve than when there is clearly a problem. The audience was not expecting the message that change was necessary, working on the basis that 'if it ain't broke, why fix it?' However, the vision of a more customer-focused organization in an increasingly competitive market was compelling. The project proposal had to be costed and treated with the same kind of financial justification as building a new shop. Dick Smerdon in particular was aware that there was some pressure for change building from below. With Dick's backing, the board approved the project, giving the ODP team a much needed mandate for change.

**Phase 1 – Buy-in and information gathering**

The information-gathering phase began in the summer of 1993. The review was carried out over six months by the area management population, which had the effect of achieving their buy-in to the project. The emphasis was on identifying which operations could be effectively streamlined, and when, so that customers' needs were genuinely at the top of the agenda. Three task groups of various sales managers were established, with about eight people in each group. Each of the groups looked at different areas; one group looked at key operational roles, another looked at retail skills and the third group took a critical look at working practices, including the information and communication requirements of the operation's team. The groups met together for approximately six or seven days over six months. This represented an investment of approximately 150 person days in total.

The group reviewing key operational roles looked at what people were doing and considered what they were likely to do in the future and whether they had the skills and competencies required. Job analysis involved detailing the jobs as the job-holders themselves saw them. The roles examined included those of operations director, regional sales manager, area sales manager and branch manager. This was the first time that the nature and scope of the area sales manager role had been formally reviewed by operational personnel.

In order to collect views and data they designed a survey which was completed by 2000 employees, held focus groups and conducted fifty one-to-one interviews. They were helped in this task by Chris Johnson and an outside consultant. Chris acted as a bridge between the business and the consultant by being able to translate consultancy jargon into operations language. He was therefore able to bring in the benefits of some external creativity in a way that made sense to the employees.

The working practices group took a critical look at working practices such as the number of meetings and the amount of teamworking that was actually taking place. They also looked at the information requirements of the company's operations team, and examined the organization structure to identify which roles actually added value to the operation. The retail skills group set out to identify the critical skills needed within the business in the future.

The process of consulting staff and involving them in gathering information linked to a strategic review already produced a degree of interest from those involved.

The groups were charged with drawing the research to some firm conclusions and a working group, which included some of the members of the three task groups, was established to review the findings of the information-gathering phase. The findings and recommendations were then presented to the Thresher board in November 1993.

*Findings*

The group looking at operational roles found that there was significant overlap between the different levels. There were plenty of examples of 'checkers checking checkers'. Three roles were considered pivotal in the future; these were:

- operations manager
- business development manager
- branch manager.

New roles and responsibilities were developed and new competencies identified to give people a clear sense of what they would need to do to contribute to Thresher's success.

The group who were looking at working practices analysed how area sales managers (ASMs) spent their time. They found that too much time was being spent on basic administration and on routine matters rather than on asking fundamental questions about more flexible ways of working. Authority levels and budgets were examined and it was clear that there were many bureaucratic requirements which meant that ASMs were spending too much time doing unnecessary chores. The group decided to challenge themselves to 'scrap things that were not necessary to the operation'. They also aimed to develop more efficient meeting processes and to find hidden potential in people. Fundamentally this was about a shift of focus from administration to the customer.

The group looking at information requirements found similar evidence of unnecessary bureaucracy. The communications system as a whole was seen to be archaic and laborious. Collating for the first time information about all the paper-hitting operations, they found that each ASM received on average eight and a half pounds weight of paperwork per week. ASMs were therefore in a 'postman' role rather than being able to use their retail skills. They decided to ask the operations team what they really needed and to explore what was available from technology and how it could be exploited.

## Phase 2 – The organization blueprint

Following this first phase of gathering information, the project entered the blueprint stage, which used the findings to create organizational designs. Some members of area management who had been involved in the first stage carried on with the project to ensure continuity and ownership. Wisdom, Johnson and the working groups involved the senior management group in developing a set of organizational criteria for designing and testing options. The criteria included the following:

- the structure was to be designed with people in mind
- there should be realistic spans of control
- the organization structure should be flexible; the overlap between ASM and RSM roles should be reduced
- delayer if possible
- decentralize authority and responsibility
- introduce self-managing teams.

These were in addition to the criteria developed in the first phase of the ODP:

- brand emphasis
- customer satisfaction
- 'more than just implementers'
- better profits, overheads and sales than in 1993
- functional resources
- exploit IT and systems
- better communications and meetings
- bigger roles.

External benchmarks were established for the new organization design. The design group wanted to take some of the work from Phase 1 (the research) and make sure it addressed the key elements of business needs.

The decision was taken to organize branches into 'clusters', since it was believed that this would be fundamental to the future. In addition it was decided to remove regional offices and move towards flexible working. It was also decided that overlap between levels of responsibility should be removed so that decisions could be taken at the appropriate level. This led to a decision to delayer the operations team, but rather than taking the usual route of taking out middle management, Thresher made cuts at the top. In one case an operations director was redeployed and a number of regional sales manager posts were made redundant.

An important criterion established at this stage was that costs saved through delayering would be reinvested in the organization rather than recycled as profit, which has the temporary appeal of appearing to improve one year's figures. Thus the money saved was to be spent, for instance, on training and developing people lower down the organization, especially the area managers who have such a major influence over the branches they oversee. Similarly, in order to equip ASMs for their real role, they decided to move to a laptop environment and develop a management information system suited to the 1990s. This was a significant move from data to real information.

## Phase 3 – Design and trial

It was agreed that the blueprint organization would be tried out within one brand, Huttons, which consisted of 120 shops, and part of Thresher Wine Shop, the largest brand. The measures which had been established were to be audited; the hard business performance measures were to be audited by finance and the soft measures relating to organizational culture would be audited through surveys, focus groups and one-to-one interviews. The hard measures were to include significant profit before fixed growth (PBF) in the trial region over six months. It was expected that the new design would result in business savings, and targets were set for the six-month period. Shop refits, for instance, normally carried out by groups of specialists, would be carried out by the teams instead. Targets were also set for both business-to-business and for the worst performing branches. The trials were to be carefully monitored and evaluated.

The trials allowed experimentation to take place on a number of fronts. There were trials of alternative organizations, new roles and responsibilities and new processes. One team, for instance, developed a labour model which was subsequently adopted and rolled out to all parts of the business. Another trial involved introducing self-managing teams at the middle level. The area managers received support and coaching to enable them to manage team dynamics. The amount of training was increased and personal development was encouraged through peer group feedback and personal development plans.

Another trial involved investing in laptops and the development of a meaningful management information system to cut out unnecessary paperwork. As a result, operations personnel were provided with live relevant data for their part of the business. The use of laptops also enabled people to be more mobile and better able to carry out a sales role. The concept of clustering was introduced and teams were clustered around six shops. The new structure was to be put in place three years ahead of its projected implementation in 1996 so that it could be assessed over a reasonable time-frame. Assuming that it was successful, the new labour model developed by the Huttons team was to be rolled out across all shops.

The trials affected every employee in Huttons and two-way communication was vital to the success of the ODP. Johnson and Wisdom turned the established sales managers' conferences into ODP roadshows. Initially these involved conventional presentations where the senior managers talked about the purpose of the trials and invited employees to support the project. Johnson and Wisdom soon realized that the roadshow needed to reflect more closely the philosophy of the project and scrapped the hierarchical format of the events. They are now organized by the ASM teams and are used to gather new ideas and add impetus to the project. Their format is different and innovative every time. The roadshows had the effect of raising interest in the trials, gaining employee support for the project and developing the impetus for change. They also formed the key opportunity to recognize and reinforce operations' values.

## Phase 4 – Roadmap and implementation

The trial outcomes were evaluated and represented the reality of the business case for the ODP. Both hard and soft measures confirmed that the project had more than achieved its targets. The measures were externally validated in 1995 and included attitude surveys carried out in 1993 and 1994. It was clear that a significant shift in attitudes had taken place. Employees in the trial groups were enjoying much greater freedom of action than before and consequently were experiencing greater job satisfaction.

Area sales managers were able to concentrate on their primary responsibilities. Instead of acting like a 'policeman', the ASM was becoming more of a business manager. Employees reported being better appreciated and stated that they felt they could make progress within the company. In many cases this was already true, with employees whose previous roles had been relatively confined, taking on roles which carried much greater responsibility and more scope, albeit at the same level. People were encouraged to experiment and take action to put things right where necessary. This was a shift from the previous permission-seeking culture of 'you can do anything you like, but don't give me any surprises.' There was a sense that this was an environment of change where individuals could make a difference. As one employee stated: 'I had given up having ideas.' Another said, 'We get to solve our own problems.' The customer was firmly at the top of the trial groups' agendas.

On conclusion of the trial period, a cost–benefit analysis has proved that the investment of £2 million in systems, training and coaching people and bringing in the best calibre people for new jobs has already produced a major payback, both in terms of head count and greater operations efficiency. The ODP has resulted in much greater loyalty from the ASM groups, and Thresher estimates that it has saved at least £75000 in recruitment costs alone. In terms of customer focus and employee morale the evidence of the hard and soft measures is that the ODP has had major beneficial effects. The new working practices offer an excellent model for that particular business.

As Thresher seeks to extend the benefits of the ODP, there is a clear balance to be struck between imposing a model which has been developed successfully in one part of the business and maintaining high levels of employee involvement which ensures commitment and 'fit' in other parts of the business. To support implementation elsewhere in the organization the team has developed a Generic Implementation Guide (GIG) which has captured the learning from each stage and should serve as a change template. It is not intended that this should be prescriptive since the ODP team recognizes how vital to the success of ODP was direct involvement and the shaping of the change programme by the people involved. It is intended rather as a means of helping people avoid unnecessary time and expense in re-inventing the wheel.

ODP was extended into other brands during 1996 on a brand-by-brand basis, using the change sequence as follows:

*1   Plan*

- check business priorities
- confirm leadership
- establish key business processes
- construct teams
- marshal support resources
- establish operations ownership
- develop operations manpower plan.

*2   Launch*

- secure buy-in
- launch workshop

- set up brand sub-groups
- handle departures
- implement organization changes
- set up branch assessment centres.

## 3  Implement

- set up area workshops
- set up branch clusters
- commence priority training modules
- operate to new systems with laptops
- coach in all new roles
- monitor roles
- monitor evaluation of all new processes.

## 4  Commission

- review operation of roles, processes and people
- implement revised remuneration practices
- review operating performance against measures
- make modifications as necessary
- start longer-term training activity.

## Phase 5 – Commissioning and reinforcement

Wisdom and Johnson advise other parts of the organization to avoid the temptation to 'cherrypick' parts of the change programme without having in place some of the fundamentals to its success such as the cultural measures. This is typically where change efforts in many organizations backfire, as is the way in which the change process loses momentum.

In order to avoid these dangers, the change framework includes a commissioning phase. This is where the auditing of all the implementation takes place and the performance paybacks are seen to be a reality, especially the significant PBF growth. The latest part of the business to become eligible for commissioning is the Wine Shop brand.

Commissioning is the process that effectively ensures that the changes implemented are reinforced and built on in the future. It involves two board members evaluating the state of readiness for new working practices following a review of the implementation phase using twelve success criteria. The commissioners then produce a report which contains recommendations on the installation of the implementation and reinforcement phase, which have to be acted on in the six months following commissioning. In the Wine Shop brand, for instance, the commissioners required that the appraisal process be revised since the existing system was no longer appropriate to the way the business operated. The implementing group have to produce evidence after six months that the commissioners' recommendations have been acted upon. The process is exacting, which adds to its credibility. Commissioning is not seen as the end of the change process, rather as the starting point for the future. It is only when the commissioners are satisfied that measures established at the outset are being met that the changes are implemented and become the new way of operating.

## Benefits

In terms of PBF, performance in the trial brand has exceeded forecasts in the Thresher business plan. Brand standards have also improved. Communication has improved, both in terms of speed and quality of implementation. The effective use of systems has provided better and more relevant information. The training focus within the ODP, including personal coaching and skills development, has resulted in overall improved personal development for operations personnel.

The new roles have resulted in RSMs becoming operations managers, less involved in paperwork and policy implementation and more involved with business building and being team leader and coach. Increased clarity about roles has allowed people to build personal goals. This has reinforced one of the key Thresher principles of change: that the 'duty' of managers is to develop and energize people. As such, their role has become much more strategic. The shift of management style from command and control to enabling has been consistent with the overall vision and allowed managers to walk the talk.

Some of the biggest successes are to be found in the creation of a more flexible and change-oriented culture. By setting 'soft' as well as 'hard' measures for the project, Johnson and Wisdom have been able to keep track of shifts in employee morale. There have been improvements on all the values measured through attitude surveys. From the point of view of employees, the company is now more open, honest, informal, flexible, participative, caring, innovative and trusting than before. Innovation is now welcome, as opposed to threatening.

Much of the credit for getting the change effort under way initially must go to Wisdom and Johnson, but the effective implementation and maintenance of that initiative have demanded the active participation of a larger group. The creation of a guiding coalition has ensured that the vision has become institutionalized, part of 'the way we do things around here'. Involving employees in the changes which affect them has produced enthusiastic owner-ship of the initiative by employees at all levels.

The way in which Chris Johnson and Brian Wisdom have worked together is a good example of strategic activity carried out as a partnership between line and Human Resources personnel. They have each appreciated and complemented the other's approach and provided a key driving force for the project. It is often loss of faith or short-term pressures coming from the top which cause change processes to be abandoned. Dick Smerdon's championing of the project with the board and shielding the change agents so that they could get on with their job was a vital contribution to the success of the project.

## Reinforcing change and career development

Roffey Park research suggests that perceived career development has a potentially strong effect on employee morale. With respect to career paths, at the outset of the ODP, Thresher had few exciting options for the majority of staff. Few Thresher employees moved to other parts of the Group as a whole since the company was not known as a leader in innovative practices.

In the past, turnover at ASM level was roughly 10 per cent per year. At the beginning of the project, a number of employees who were keen to see change hoped that the change process would be quite dramatic and result in major changes overnight. Despite the important initiatives early on in the ODP, not all the people who were eager for change were prepared to wait for the effects of change to work through. Some employees left the organization voluntarily.

Johnson and Wisdom saw this as a strategic opportunity in line with the objective of creating an organizational climate attuned to change. They wanted to introduce people into the organization with a crucial role, that of being 'an architect of the future'. These would be area managers with specific attributes who would be likely to prevent the change effort from sinking back into complacency once early success was achieved. A key characteristic which Johnson and Wisdom are looking for in potential recruits is a future orientation and a history of successfully implementing change programmes in other organizations.

Normally the recruitment process for an ASM role would involve candidates seeing a member of the HR team and then having an interview with their future boss. So vital is the role of 'architect of the future' that Johnson and Wisdom took charge of the recruitment and induction process themselves. This results in consistency in terms of recruitment and 'fit' with what they are trying to achieve. When recruited, the new employee can request time out with either Wisdom or Johnson, who recognize that they may be under pressure from peers to conform with the old ways of doing things. This mentoring role is considered vital in maintaining the employee's momentum for change.

These new recruits are involved in all the task groups. The common features are that they all have to be able to deliver high-level operations performance, which gives them credibility and a 'licence to operate'. They also have to have high energy commitments and usually work on average ten to fifteen hours above the standard working week. They have to find ways of coping with the extra load, handling the status quo as well as being innovative and taking risks. They must be prepared to take knockbacks, mainly from their peer groups, and to tolerate a degree of 'background noise'.

Gradually, although they have been seeded into the organization at all levels, the impact of these new recruits is being felt most keenly at the ASM level. Examining the culture within Thresher, a working group found that the starting point was a demand for high performance and accountability. The fact that the environment was demanding and non-participative became particularly evident when things went wrong. ASMs were perceived by most people reporting to them as 'helpful disciplinarians who think they are above a lot of other people'. As the role has become more that of coach and team leader, new ideas and role models are helping bring about a more appropriate style of management in the middle ranks.

Of the fifteen area managers recruited since 1994, fourteen are still with the organization today. Most of these are performing bigger, more developmental roles, such as managing major projects or taking on leadership or coaching roles. Such is the perceived value of such employees that Whitbread are now actively recruiting within Thresher. The developing reputation of Thresher as a 'can do' type of organization is making its employees more employable. Ironically, perhaps the biggest challenge then is the retention of such highly-prized employees, though the signs are that people who are motivated by opportunities to grow are more likely to stay in an organization which enables growth – at least for the time being.

The intuition of Johnson and Wisdom that there was unrealized potential within the organization has been confirmed through the renaissance of the 'old guard'. Johnson has maintained a tight control on succession planning as he develops the pool of area managers to be team leaders. These are high-calibre people whose readiness for taking on significant roles is assessed regularly. An important consideration in assessing potential is whether or not people are really buying into the change and beginning to demonstrate new ways of working. He is particularly keen to identify catalyst types, especially among established managers, who can bring other people with them. Typically such individuals are highly people-focused.

## Learning

As the early successes started to become known, other parts of the business started to copy some of the processes used, but without some of the same context issues or principles. Thresher has learnt that taking ideas without trialling them usually results in failure. The challenge now is to extend the benefits of the learning without at the same time shortcutting employee involvement, which has been such a key part of this trial process.

Indeed, creating an agenda for change under a project title enabled the change team to create a protected environment. Within this environment, experimentation was not only accepted but encouraged. The 'Trojan Horse' approach to organization change has created a group of skilled internal change agents who can now spread the benefits of change to other parts of the business, very much in line with the original objectives. As a result of the trials, Thresher has produced some key principles for change within the organization. They are:

- We have a duty to **develop our people** to their maximum potential.
- We must use **technology** to make things **simpler, faster** and **better**.
- We must **value** and recognize an individual's **contribution** but particularly when it benefits **the team**.
- We must embrace change and **become players** not spectators.
- We must **welcome the surprises** that innovation brings but guard against shocks due to negligence.

The lessons learned by ODP team members themselves are as follows:

- You need to take every opportunity to reinforce the change; the use of sales conferences organized by the trial groups themselves has gone a long way to maintain the impetus.
- Change takes time; you need to win small battles in order to make larger gains.
- You need to see the whole picture and plan within it; having a vision of what you are trying to achieve is vital.
- The leadership body must 'walk the talk'.
- You can measure the bottom line.
- During times of change you need a balance of 'architects of the future' and 'maintenance engineers'; too many of either would cause problems.
- You need to create the right environment for change.
- It is important to challenge routines, history, politics. As Brian Wisdom says: 'When you're looking at the sun, you don't see the shadows.'

## Delayering an organization – a change agent's checklist

What lessons can be drawn from these case studies about the strategic implementation of structure change?

- Know why you feel change is necessary and develop the vision you want to realize.
- Support the vision with values, so that the vision can be realized in the 'right' way.

- Mobilize commitment to change through the joint analysis of problems and opportunities. Involve as many people who will be affected by the change as possible. At the very least, develop a core group of drivers of the change effort.
- Ensure that you have strong commitment to change from the top. Without this, change is difficult to sustain.
- Understand the culture of your organization – what is going to help or hinder your change effort. Identify the levers for change with the maximum chance of success in your organization.
- Build a working climate which is responsive to change. Encourage learning from mistakes as well as success.
- Establish the need for change through hard data. Set measures for tracking progress.
- Build the internal capacity to manage the change before implementing it.
- Break the change programme down into actionable parts and make individuals accountable.
- Delayer to the minimum number of layers that can be made individually accountable.
- Promote acceptance of the change by making sure that people understand the strategic reason for the change and how it will affect them.
- Restructure the remaining layers into multi-skilled self-managed work teams.
- Communicate goals relating to the vision and frequently report on progress made towards the goals.
- Ensure that employees' behaviour is in line with the organizational values, especially that of the senior management group.
- Reinforce and celebrate the first successes, then tackle the bigger changes.
- Set up effective systems that support the organization vision, values and structure. These include communication, appraisal, reward and recognition, recruitment and promotion. Ensure that these systems are in line with what you are trying to achieve. Modify systems or start again from scratch if they are inconsistent with the vision.
- Monitor the implementation of change and people's reaction to it. Make tough decisions, if necessary, if people are unwilling or unable to support the change.

Above all, remember that the implementation of change is difficult. There will be delays and set-backs. For the change agent, an optimistic and persistent disposition will be an asset. Safeguarding the most important parts of your plan by having a few practical contingencies up your sleeve will help. Even the best laid plans have to be adjusted, and strategic restructuring should not involve sticking to the plan no matter what. Unless you are able to adapt your plans you may miss the vital opportunities which you could not have foreseen before you started. As Mintzberg (Post, 1989) suggests: 'Effective strategies develop through experimentation, through design and through a combination of the two.'

# Introducing lean organizations: cross-cultural experiences

In this chapter we will be exploring how various cultures deal with introducing lean organizations, often with flatter structures. As the world becomes a truly global community for trading purposes, and approaches to management and organization are exported internationally, lean organization structures are being applied in multinationals worldwide. We will be looking at how transferrable is the model of the lean organization or whether the model is so culturally specific that it is essentially non-exportable. My co-author in this chapter is Michel Syrett, Visiting Fellow of Roffey Park Management Institute, who has prepared the case study of General Electric in Hungary.

## Organizational change in Asia-Pacific

Introducing lean organizations in Europe and the US usually involves simply cutting staff. In Japan, where the tradition of life-time employment remains deeply engrained, the inexorable global trend towards flatter corporate hierarchies is posing an awkward challenge. So far, the restructuring of Japan's business sector has focused mainly on cutting production lines and paring manufacturing costs. In recent times, attention has switched to the difficult issue of how to reduce the many layers of white-collar workers.

The methods chosen by the Japanese have necessarily been different from those employed by their western counterparts. Some of Japan's blue-chip companies have been forced to announce sackings and early-retirement plans. However, the public outcry has been so great that others are now trying to find new ways to increase the efficiency of their existing white-collar staff without getting rid of them. Some companies have tried to deal with the problem by shifting unwanted employees to subsidiaries or to smaller client companies.

Others are trying to introduce more 'Japanese' solutions through comprehensive reorganization schemes. Some companies are placing stricter quality requirements on their managers. Ultimately, business leaders will need to set new ground rules for employees as the traditional social contract breaks down. In the past, companies guaranteed workers a path up the corporate hierarchy in return for their loyalty and service. One major company now places a strict time limit on managerial posts. If a manager fails to be promoted within twelve years, he or she will be forced into a non-managerial post without subordinate staff. The loss of 'face' implicit in such situations can be more than demotivating. Research suggests that there may be links between such organizational actions and the increasing incidence of suicides amongst white-collar workers. In situations where division managers lose their titles and become ordinary staff, companies need to map out a new direction for them.

While structures may or may not drive behaviour, behaviour may be an enormous barrier to structural change. Two North American multinationals decided to re-engineer some of their business processes, one in Singapore, one in Thailand. One of the requirements of re-engineering is that employees become innovative, creative and show initiative. This proved extremely difficult in Singapore, where it was found that the average Singaporean employee finds it difficult to perform without knowing exactly what they are supposed to be doing. Structure, system and order are very important to most Singaporeans. Similarly, the idea of broadening the nature of work in Thailand was considered not only impossible but dangerous, with the result that Thais cannot easily relate to a western dimension of job enrichment.

Another result of re-engineering which sits uneasily in both Thai and Singaporean organizations is the concept of 'empowerment'. In broad stereotypical terms, the role of management in Singapore is paternalistic and in Thailand the duty of the boss is to control. To 'empower' employees would therefore lead to chaos at best and business collapse at worst. Flattening organizations is therefore out of kilter with the force of societal hierarchy, which overrides that of the organization, particularly in Thailand. Flat structures are not necessary for speedy decision-making because only those at the top could possibly make decisions; that is their obligation, to act as 'fathers'.

Consequently, the challenge for international organizations that are looking to ensure a common standard of service delivery worldwide is to query how much their organization structures need to be consistent everywhere. The 'glocal' ('think global, act local') message may mean that lean organizations are not the best way to produce the outputs the organization needs. Similarly, the links between organizations, individuals and society as a whole are much more closely drawn in cultures different from those in which lean organizations prosper. Societies which consider businesses to be a cornerstone of the community, supplying employment, status, well-being and continuity, are perhaps not going to accept so easily models of employment which view people as dispensable.

## General Electric in Hungary

General Electric is one of the few truly global corporations, with a significant presence in sixty-five countries, many of them with emerging economies. The turnaround of the company in North America in the 1980s was achieved by the combination of a dramatic disinvestment of unprofitable subsidiaries and a corporate restructure which laid heavy emphasis on breaking down internal barriers and creating what its CEO, Jack Welch, terms a 'boundaryless' organization, shifting resources and expertise to wherever they are most needed. 'People seem compelled to build walls between themselves and others', Welch wrote in a recent annual report. 'These walls cramp people, inhibit creativity, restrict vision, smother dreams and, above all, slow things down. We must break them down if we want to release the flood of ideas that are so important to the future.'

On the back of this philosophy Welch transformed a company with a declining market share in every sector in which it competed into a US$60 billion operation which, by 1991, ranked number one in the Forbes 500. Having used this formula successfully in the US, Welch has seen little reason why he cannot apply the same methods in establishing a hold in the many emerging markets in which the company has a presence. 'Change has not constituency', he said in a well-publicized quote in 1993.

However, Welch's definition of what this change means differed radically from the expectations of the workforce that his company inherited from the many companies that GE acquired or set up in its expansion overseas. In terms of the impact on the company's career management the best illustration is GE Lighting's acquisition and turnaround of Tungsram, an ailing state-owned Hungarian lightbulb manufacturer in a former command economy.

When GE Lighting acquired a half share in Tungsram in 1989, the Hungarian company had nearly 20 per cent of the market in eastern Europe. However, this had been built up largely from the then Comecon countries of central and eastern Europe, which accounted for around 30 per cent of Tungsram's sales, and when their economies collapsed in the year following GE's initial investment, revenue from this source fell to near zero.

As a result, the company lost a record US$1–5 million in 1993 – 'the biggest blot of red ink in the history of Hungary', according to Lazlo Mohr, the former deputy general manager at the Hungarian Credit Bank, then Tungsram's largest minority shareholder. GE's more leisurely investment plans for the company had to be abandoned in favour of a radical restructure which, coupled with GE's planned job cuts, resulted in half of Tungsram's workforce, slightly less than 9000 people, being laid off.

It was in this climate that Welch's philosophy of a boundaryless organization was put into place. Under the supervision of production director Don McKenna, time between order and delivery was slashed from ninety days to thirty-two in less than two years (McKenna, 1995). Over the same period, manufacturing cycle time was reduced by half and breakages on the production lines were cut from a staggering one in two lamps in pre-GE days to its current level of near-world standards.

All of this was achieved using western-style teamwork and project management, backed by systematic skills training of a kind unheard of in a company with a previous culture founded on rigid demarcation. 'Our world totally changed', said one project manager, who saw Tungsram's layers of management cut from eleven to three in less than a year. Tamas Palotai, senior leadership technology director at the time, agrees. 'People who were used to a hierarchical structure where the boss gave the orders had to adjust in a very short time to the idea that decisions were now taken by teams, not individuals.'

In economic terms the strategy, supported by an internal investment by GE of nearly US$600 million, paid GE back in full. After two years of heavy losses in 1991 and 1992, GE Lighting Europe was back in profit by 1993, having doubled in net sales in less than five years. The transition was not without its problems, however, and in the context of this chapter, two issues are worth stressing:

* Getting the new message across: in the Communist era that immediately preceded GE's acquisition of Tungsram, exhortations to greater productivity and efficiency were seen as political slogans to be ignored and bypassed. The result was that, while GE executives regarded concepts like empowerment and promoting 'a culture of winning' as articles of faith, to workers on the factory floor and their supervisors they initially bore a confusing similarity to the slogans of the old order. GE had to invest considerable time and effort to transform their thinking.

* Breaking down the old mentality towards pay: workers at Tungsram had been used to wage settlements negotiated annually across the board, largely based on job title and seniority. In line with modern TAM strategies, GE held that companies should only reward measurable improvements in quality and teamwork. Tungsram's unions also expected productivity deals to be negotiated year by year. GE's policy is that increases in quality and productivity should be continuous and not linked to specific wage deals.

The twin philosophies of empowerment and continuous improvement, taken for granted in most North American and European companies, were initially regarded with great suspicion by many Tungsram workers, who saw them simply as devices for increasing responsibilities without providing greater reward. 'Our approach to pay and performance was entirely new to Hungary at the time we introduced it', GE's director of technology commented in 1994. 'It has not been easy to implement it in this part of the world.'

Charles Pieper, GE Lighting's CEO at that time, stresses that the problem was largely overcome by a systematic approach to training and development which provided supervisors and middle managers with the teamworking and project management skills they needed to provide local credibility to GE's corporate commitment to continuous improvement.

In the key period immediately after the total acquisition of Tungsram, 800 of the company's staff received intensive training in English, 650 took part in TQM courses and 650 were placed on general management programmes. The influx of new skills that resulted was accompanied by a systematic effort to break down the barriers between departments. As Steve Marbut, Vice President and Director for European Logistics, pointed out at the time: 'The real key is communication. Every Monday we conducted telephone conversations with our different locations and held video conferences and business strategy consultations. Direct communications between managers has always been a priority at GE. Our information architecture is designed to support learning and sharing but it is used essentially as an enabler not a driver. Jack Welch has always preferred face to face communications, and our CEO Chuck Pieper and his team travelled to every location.'

Pieper saw the newly trained Hungarian management team being used to convert local staff to the new way of thinking throughout the company's expanding operations in central and eastern Europe. 'The Hungarian team will support our other eastern European operations in the way our UK and US managers initially supported changes at Tungsram – by transferring know-how', he commented in a 1994 interview (1).

In this sense he was also putting into practice Jack Welch's philosophy of boundaryless business, in which resources and expertise are shifted to wherever they are most needed. The money GE has poured into GE Lighting Europe – including building a plant at Nagykanizsa at a cost of US$300 million – has done much to allay scepticism about the company's intentions among most of Tungsram's key supervisory and management staff, but the job cuts that were necessary in the early stages of the turnaround have left a lingering resentment among the local trade unions that could still bubble over into industrial action.

# 8 *Motivating and retaining people – the roles of the line manager and the Human Resource professional*

Changing business drivers are producing different sorts of organization. Increasingly network-based operations are becoming a reality, with strategic alliances and partnering arrangements between erstwhile suppliers and customers becoming commonplace. There are frequent mergers and acquisitions and the days of the so-called 'virtual' organization seem to be upon us. Typically organizations are opting to move away from structuring themselves along functional lines to more multidisciplinary and team-based approaches.

No matter where the impetus for change comes from, the main implementers of change are line managers and Human Resource professionals. Inevitably, many of the changes in the ways organizations structure themselves to do business are having a direct effect on the role of managers. Such arrangements call for managers to be able to communicate effectively across organizational interfaces. They often find themselves co-ordinating the work of a new mix of workers, some full-time employees, others who are on a range of flexible work arrangements. To managers falls the responsibility of reorienting and motivating their teams. The resulting mix of responsibilities and tasks represents for many managers a substantial shift from a previously clear-cut role.

Similarly, in changing organizations, the goals of the business are unlikely to be achieved if the workforce as a whole lacks the skills, resources and motivation to carry out the goals. Often organizational processes work against the business goals because they are out of step with what the organization is trying to achieve. Human Resource processes such as recruitment, development, appraisal and pay need to be aligned to the business strategy.

Unless they are, employees can unwittingly sabotage organizational goals through inappropriate behaviours and working practices. This is where the role of the Human Resource professional becomes critical in ensuring that the organization is 'fit' for its tasks, both in the short and medium term.

## Are managers an endangered species?

Recent research suggests that both HR professionals and junior line managers, but middle managers in particular, are an endangered species. Middle mangers in particular are vulnerable to redundancy (Holbeche, 1997). In our Roffey Park survey alone, we found that 15 per cent of junior–middle line manager positions had disappeared in less than two years. In many cases this is because many of the 'management' processes and functions have been redistributed or re-engineered out of the system. It seems that there is a general trend in Europe towards removing middle management positions through restructuring. Yet it could be argued that line managers have a potentially critical role to play. It is often line managers who are in the front line of the battle to motivate and retain key employees, let alone gain even higher levels of output from teams whose morale may be negatively affected by change. They are perhaps best placed to be aware of the issues confronting staff and affecting their motivation. Some organizations are recognizing this and are reintroducing manager positions that had been phased out, though typically the mix of responsibilities is different from before.

Like that of everyone else, the workload of managers has expanded through increased spans of control and devolved responsibilities for finance and human resources, as well as being expected to maintain their previous output. Similarly, previous 'support' roles have often disappeared so that managers are having to do work which was previously carried out by personal assistants and secretaries. Technology is helping, and indeed information technology literacy is becoming an essential requirement of executives, according to head-hunters. Perhaps not surprisingly, many line managers seem to be experiencing stress and overwork.

There is a small trend towards managers choosing to go self-employed rather than continue in unsatisfying jobs. Similarly, there is a slight indication that more managers, particularly women, are developing job-share arrangements or going part-time. One former senior manager decided to leave her financial services company because her employer was unwilling to accommodate her need for more flexible working arrangements. Having become freelance, she found herself re-contracted to her former employer on much more favourable financial terms than before, as well as with a shorter working week. As we have already seen, the trend towards so-called 'downshifting' is more marked in the US.

Increasingly, executive search agencies are aware of increasing demands from both employers and employees for a good 'fit' at the values level. Job fit involves a good match for competencies, interests and aspirations as well as what an employee can commit to. Research carried out in the UK (Ashridge Management Index, 1996) suggests that career progress for senior people will increasingly depend on business or management qualifications, together with a broader business knowledge. It is thought that Master of Business Administration degrees will continue to be in demand.

For many managers in multinational organizations, job opportunities involve international assignments. There is, however, a noticeable trend towards treating such assignments as 'local', with expatriate pay and conditions becoming a rarity. Similarly, such assignments fail to include provision for family arrangements and managers are increasingly having to 'commute' on a regular basis from their assignment rather than disrupt family arrangements. Executive search agencies in the UK are finding that many major international job opportunities are being refused by potential recruits because their partner's career is as important as their own.

# The big challenges: retaining and motivating people

Before we look at how line managers respond to the challenges of getting the best out of people, let us look at some of the issues that form part of the background against which managers are operating. Why, for instance, is it harder to motivate people in a changing organization? What are the issues relating to retention, especially with respect to employee loyalty? How can managers retain and motivate people in this context?

## Retention

Retaining key staff is a big challenge in times of major change. Even in relatively 'stable' times, some turnover is to be expected and can be healthy for the organization, since new people can bring with them new ideas. Typically, turnover amongst graduates is relatively high in the early stages of their career, since graduates are often ambitious for rapid career progress and financial success. It has been customary for many young people to enhance their CVs with experience in a good range of blue chip or Fortune 500 companies before pursuing a particular career route. It would seem that the 'pull' factors connected with the next job tend to be the incentive for moving jobs.

Conversely, many employees in their late twenties or thirties, especially if they are happy with their employer by and large, often move to go to other jobs because they become unhappy with some aspect of their current position. Roffey Park research suggests that some of the biggest 'push' factors include frustration with lack of career development and dissatisfaction with leadership. Some of the main attractions of other positions are the challenge of the new role, greater autonomy and a stimulating work environment. Increased salaries are important for some people, but are not the primary motivation in most cases.

## Loyalty

One of the main reasons that organizations retain good employees is that the employees feel loyal to the organization. There is plenty of evidence that organizations should no longer rely on this as a means of retaining people. A noticeable characteristic of delayered organizations is the decrease in loyalty towards the organization on the part of employees. One of the most common measures of employee loyalty is staff turnover, on the basis that satisfied employees tend to be the people who stay longer. My research suggests that this may not be a reliable guide to assessing loyalty. Staff turnover can seem artificially low when the job market is relatively static or appears to be shrinking. The real test is when growth returns and people choose to be more mobile.

When, in 1996, I interviewed managers in 200 organizations who had helped with my initial research in 1994, I found, not surprisingly, that 35 per cent were untraceable –usually because their job had disappeared. The most vulnerable groups were junior or middle line managers and junior personnel specialists. The remaining group broke into three: 21 per cent had been promoted, 34 per cent were in the same job at the same level and 45 per cent were at the same level but their jobs had grown.

The most dissatisfied group were the people whose jobs had not grown. They were all actively looking for jobs, even though many of them stated that they were still loyal to their employer. They recognized, however, that they had a higher loyalty to themselves. They could no longer be loyal to an organization at the expense of their own interests. The people whose jobs had grown, albeit at the same level, were the most satisfied and least likely to be looking for a job. The promoted group contained a high proportion of people who were actively looking for jobs, suggesting that promotion alone does not increase employee loyalty to the organization.

The importance of the job mix and the reputation of the employer are not to be underestimated. In the highly paid world of investment banking, I have come across a number of examples of attempts to lure specific individuals to leave one firm and join another. Investment banks are knowledge-dependent to a very large extent. This knowledge is embodied by the individuals who work in the sector, making them a valuable commodity. In at least two cases, people were given the 'blank cheque' option, and could no doubt have demanded any salary they wanted. In almost every case the employees chose to stay where they were. Granted they were already well paid, but the main reasons for staying were the degree of autonomy and variety currently enjoyed; adverse factors such as the relative size or lack of reputation weighed against the prospective employer.

Organizations cannot afford to take employee loyalty for granted. In cases where people felt most loyal to their organizations, it was because the individuals in question felt valued and respected by their employer, and in particular by their line manager. As Richard Heard, Chief Editor of *International Forum* magazine (1996) put it:

> If loyalty is synonymous with emotional attachment to a company, if it is bound up with a belief that the firm will always stick by me, then let's bury it, the sooner the better. If, on the other hand, it can be interpreted as a community of purpose where individuals identify with their team leaders and the projects for which they are responsible, then it is definitely a quality which should be nurtured.

Where commitment to the organization remains reasonably high, loyalty is becoming less institutional and more personalized. Relationships within the team and especially with the manager are likely to grow in importance as organizations continue to evolve.

*Motivation*

As we have already seen, Abraham Maslow's well-known hierarchy of needs suggests that progressing to higher levels of need, such as 'self-actualization' or self-fulfilment, tends to occur as other more fundamental levels of need, such as the need for security, are being satisfied. There is certainly a good deal of research evidence to support this. Organizational change of any kind can carry implicit threats of potential job loss. In such circumstances, holding on to the job they have becomes a prime consideration for many people, rather than thoughts of career progression. Not surprisingly, when people feel insecure they are less likely to take risks. Consequently, the opportunity to satisfy some of the higher levels of need and gain job satisfaction becomes elusive.

Similarly, according to expectancy theories such as the motivation calculus, the amount of energy and effort people are willing to expend on a task is directly related to the relevance of the activity to a goal which is important to them and the reward they believe they will gain from it. If organizational change, such as delayering, upsets the likely achievement of a goal, such as being promoted, it is less likely that people will want to make the effort to raise their game unless they have other goals which can be fulfilled through the change. If an individual is given some say in deciding desired results, the person will at least be able to complete a calculation. However, if an individual is rewarded according to performance against those same results, the individual will normally set lower goals than if rewards are not tied to performance against standards. Ironically, management by objectives can actually lower performance.

# How can line managers retain and motivate people?

It is arguable that motivation is very much the responsibility of the individual, rather than their manager. Equally, it might be argued that the manager is responsible for enabling people as much as possible to find what motivates them or at least eliminate sources of demotivation. Often, just asking people what motivates them can be a useful starting point for understanding the range of issues involved. One group of senior managers in a public body considered what demotivated them. Their list was lengthy and included:

- working for idiots
- lack of interest from above
- lack of promotion prospects
- internal politics
- people not pulling their weight
- overload
- lack of recognition
- conflicts with the rest of one's life
- bureaucratic obstacles
- lack of prioritization from above
- low morale
- lack of control
- routine
- boring tasks
- lack of clear responsibilities
- belittling of contribution
- failures (team or individual)
- lack of ownership
- poor surroundings
- criticism from above
- manager changing mind
- personal objections to policies.

The group were challenged to think how much any of these might apply to people reporting to them, and how much they were able to control some of these factors so as to reduce the number of demotivating factors. Their other strategy was to look at the areas which motivated them and see how these might be strengthened for themselves and other people. Their motivators included:

- challenge
- pride in job
- being respected for what you have done
- having fun/enjoyment
- competition
- winning
- doing something worthwhile
- career advancement
- peer recognition
- interest in work
- deadlines
- variety

- seeing results
- reward – not only monetary, but other kinds
- status – being valued by the system
- human contact
- delivering for the team
- appreciation from others
- successful outcomes
- taking decisions
- educating others.

While every individual and group may be motivated by different things, nevertheless there appear to be some general ways in which a line manager can make a difference to other people's motivation, especially if they are consciously working on eliminating some of the sources of demotivation outlined above or on strengthening potential sources of motivation. Some means of satisfying employees' intrinsic forms of motivation, such as the chance to learn new things, or to have greater job variety and autonomy, may well be within the gift of line managers.

*Through contact*

In fact, contact with the line manager seems to be a fairly consistent motivator to employees, even if they do not like the manager. This poses a particular problem for managers whose span of control or geographical location makes regular contact difficult. In some organizations, especially when they are operating internationally, the flat structure operates as a matrix, with different reporting lines for functional and operational activity. For career development purposes these structures can pose problems unless individuals maintain active networks with their bosses and others.

In many project-based structures such as consultancies, there is a designated responsibility for 'staff management'. Typically this is seen as a temporary and essential piece of experience for people who aspire to more senior positions. Perhaps not surprisingly, it seems that practising staff managers (who also maintain a high client case load) spend more time on development issues for staff who are typically highly self-motivated than managers in more 'conventional' organizations.

## Through empowering people

Line managers have a crucial part to play in developing new customer-focused processes, in stabilizing systems and in motivating their teams to deliver high outputs. With decentralized and flatter organization structures the old management paradigm of decision-making is no longer appropriate. It makes no sense for decision-making to be focused exclusively on a small group of very overworked executives. The notion of empowerment, by which employees at all levels are trained to take on appropriate levels of decision-making, with improved customer service as the consequence, should enable even lean workforces to achieve higher levels of performance than under the old system.

## Through helping people develop

The challenge for managers is to mobilize people whose morale and motivation may be adversely affected by change. In flat organizations, spans of control typically expand. In one financial services organization, the average number of direct reports per manager expanded from six to twenty when the organization partially delayered in 1990. The system proved unworkable and team leader positions were introduced to ensure that the increased need for manager–employee interface could be met. The challenge is far greater in an existing organization with a strong corporate culture and entrenched working practices than in a 'greenfield site' situation. The line manager is at the cutting edge of the development of the new culture, using vital tools such as coaching, dealing with people on individual solutions and the recognition of desired performance.

## Through providing clarity and direction

Managers have a key responsibility in helping employees develop a sense of purpose and new working practices more appropriate to what the organization is trying to achieve. This may involve being fairly ruthless in prioritizing what the team needs to achieve and in clarifying roles. In many cases, the conventional practice of setting objectives implies that the targets are to be achieved in particular ways. Some organizations are moving to the framing of what is to be achieved as 'Key Results Areas' (KRAs), or areas in which results are to be achieved. This implies a much greater involvement and ownership by the postholder in deciding the 'what' and the 'how' of performance.

Setting objectives is an important factor in raising performance, but performance will tend to improve in proportion to the quality and quantity of feedback, especially from the line manager. Absence of feedback can lead team members to become hostile or to lack confidence, whereas high feedback, even if some of it is negative, can lead to higher confidence.

### Through developing trust

A key element of mobilizing people, and the foundation stone of empowerment, is trust between manager and team. This affects the degree to which managers are willing to delegate responsibilities and thus grow the team and the extent to which the manager is able to relinquish control of decision-making. I have come across numerous examples of line managers interfering with decision-making when tasks have been delegated, with predictable consequences for staff morale.

### Through helping people to thrive on change

Another element of mobilizing people is helping them to adjust to change and find opportunities to grow. The line manager is closest to employees and by rights should be best placed to spot potential. The challenge then is releasing that potential. Roffey Park research suggests that a supportive, enabling culture, such as that at Sun Microsystems, and good manager–employee relations are key ingredients to achieving this. The difficulty is that at the one-to-one level factors which can inhibit growth are numerous – personality clashes, unwillingness of the manager to release an individual for another assignment, incompetence, to name but a few. This is where an essential ingredient in managing is the ability to relate to people and to listen.

## Managing those who stay

For many line managers, the toughest challenges are not so much retaining key performers as motivating people who have no intention of leaving. Many people hang on to their jobs despite their dissatisfaction. This is probably no different from trends of years gone by, except that as a consequence of flattening of structures, more people are likely to find their career progression stops at an earlier age. These 'plateaued performers' pose particular challenges for line managers.

Jacobson and Kaye (1993) distinguish between two types of plateau – the structural plateau, where the employee no longer makes vertical career progression, and the content plateau, which can be reached at any level in the hierarchy when the job no longer stimulates the job holder and slowly, often imperceptibly, their performance loses its edge. Content-plateaued employees may have achieved a happy balance between work and home life. Often employees do not wish to advance in their jobs and are reluctant to go beyond its demands. Line managers often have the twin pressures of being unable to promote people in line with their aspirations as well as the day-to-day responsibility for motivating people to produce high levels of performance. For a more detailed look at ways of helping people to develop, see Chapter 14 on Mobilizing Development.

## The role of the Human Resource professional

Another group apparently under threat in changing organizations is the Personnel or Human Resource profession. Despite a lot of company rhetoric about 'people being our greatest asset', the reality is often very different. The key measures which matter often appear to be the 'hard' indicators of organizational performance such as return on investment. This applies both to management attitudes towards employees, their development and expendability, and towards the personnel professionals whose contribution is often considered as a necessary cost for the business.

In the UK in the 1980s the investment community effectively rewarded companies that cut costs. This resulted in many of the mergers, downsizing and other structural changes that were introduced. Short-termism dominated strategic decision-making, and few companies which cut down spending on research and development were penalized. There was a perception that companies which embraced employee-friendly approaches such as those encouraged under Investors in People were 'soft'.

In many cases, the quest for improved efficiency has pushed concerns for employee motivation and welfare well down the list of management priorities. A survey of business leaders in thirty-one countries carried out by Research International (1996) reported that in English-speaking countries, concern for employee satisfaction and security ranked lower than in countries in Asia. In 74 per cent of cases, concern for customers was the key corporate consideration, with only 38 per cent ranking employee satisfaction as their top priority.

## The evolution of Personnel

To some extent this is reflected in the relatively small numbers of Human Resource professionals on the boards of companies. This can be perhaps be explained by the evolution of the Human Resource profession over much of the twentieth century (Figure 8.1).

1900s **Operational role**
- data storage
- respond to requests for information
- tea and sympathy
- wages clerk.

1960s **Managerial role**
- employee relations
- administration of procedures
- corporate policies
- service provision.

1980s **Strategic role**
- developing partnership roles with line management
- creating HR strategies to support business strategies
- providing tailored response to line needs
- consultancy roles
- change agency
- organization development.

**Figure 8.1** *The evolution of strategic Human Resources management*

In terms of development, the Personnel function started primarily as a welfare and administration role in medium to large organizations. Typically carried out by women, the role often consisted of being a pay clerk and the stereotypical dispenser of 'tea and sympathy'. Gradually the role broadened in larger organizations to embrace the management of a number of internal systems and started to attract an increasing number of graduates. Their preoccupations were predominantly operational.

A more managerial role began with the era of industrial relations in the 1970s. This saw the rise of specialists in dealing with the unions and taking part in collective bargaining on behalf of management. The organizational changes of the 1980s called upon personnel specialists to become experts in de-hiring and outplacement. For a brief period, they were also seen to be experts in the skills associated with managing change. During this period, some personnel heads effectively operated as power brokers and often took on a more integrated role in the business by managing quality initiatives, communications and organizational development. Meanwhile, in many organizations, the same core functions related to maintaining personnel processes such as appraisals, pay systems and responsibility for training were being maintained.

The current stage of evolution of the role of Personnel has been influenced by the recognition in some organizations of the importance of having and retaining employees. The term 'Human Resource' is an acknowledgement of people being an asset, though there seem to be few companies that have investment strategies relating to employees. Very few HR managers are asked how the assets of the workforce can be leveraged with respect to information technology. The Rover Group is amongst the highest spenders on employee development in the UK, spending over 5 per cent of its salary bill on learning, compared with the average spend of 10 per cent by Japanese companies.

'Strategic' Human Resource management involves understanding in depth the needs of the business and being able to align all aspects of the company's decisions about people to the needs of the business. Typically this will involve:

- gaining top level commitment to people development processes
- benchmarking best practice on people development processes
- designing and managing the change process
- modelling the new behaviours required in the organization
- designing the new organization
- thinking through the consequences of new policies to ensure that they are consistent with what the organization and its employees need
- monitoring the effects of change.

The challenge for HR professionals is that expectations – management's and their own – may be caught at different stages of this evolution, making it difficult for them to break out of the role expected of them to one which more clearly adds value to the business. In some organizations, for instance, there has been a conscious move to devolve responsibility for some personnel processes, such as recruitment, to line managers. There is often an attempt to produce standardized procedures so that the task becomes less daunting for line managers. One consequence of this is that junior operational personnel roles are fast disappearing. Roffey Park research found that there has been a clear polarization in personnel jobs, with many middle-ranking personnel specialists taking on more senior and potentially strategic roles. This shift towards a more strategic Human Resource role should be underpinned by ensuring that Human Resource strategies are completely aligned to those of the business.

## Aligning business and HR strategies

Human Resource professionals are uniquely placed to influence the development of employee-related policies and strategies which will serve the interests of both employer and employee. All aspects of the Human Resource cycle have a bearing on motivation, including selection, appraisal, development, training, reward strategies and outplacement. These must be completely aligned with business strategies.

There are many frameworks and models that suggest how business and Human Resource strategies can be aligned. At its most basic, alignment involves finding satisfactory answers to questions such as those that follow.

*Planning and organization design*

*Business*

• What is our vision? How will we carry out the vision? (planning, resource assessment, investment contingencies, communication, etc.)

*Human Resource*

- What will we need to carry out the vision in terms of skills etc.?
- What is the time plan for achieving the vision? Can we create a plan which defines and measures a high-quality organization?
- How will work best be organized to achieve business goals? With respect to what we want to achieve, have we the right structure, with the appropriate types of roles and numbers in those roles? Are any roles superfluous? How will these be eliminated or remodelled?
- Do we have the human resources to achieve the business plan? Do we have current information on all our employees? How is it assessed? What systems do we use/need? Who do we have with the skills we need? What are we lacking?
- How will we handle processes such as redundancy, redistributing responsibilities, training people in their new responsibilities? What are the business costs and benefits of alternative organization designs? Who decides?
- What are the implications for the workforce? How will morale be affected and what can we do to address issues of morale? How, for instance, will this affect career prospects, roles, information requirements, working practices, support requirements?

*Recruitment*

- What do we need to bring into the organization in terms of skills and experience, and why? Is it just one skills/person template that we need or are we looking for greater variety? What will be the most appropriate way of identifying and recruiting the best people? How will new people best be integrated into the workforce? What induction, mentoring or other forms of support can help them to be productive quickly?

*Identifying potential*

- What does potential look like in the changing organization? How will we assess it? Who will be involved in assessments? How will they be trained? How will we ensure that our assessments are up to date? How will we nurture and develop the potential we have identified?

*Development*

- Are we prepared to invest in developing our staff? What do we need longer term, e.g. how will people be working – with more/less technology, etc.? How will we want senior managers and others to act, e.g. will we need people to be more flexible and customer-focused? How will development opportunities be made possible and for whom? Who is ready for a development move and what might this be?
- How can line managers help people to develop? Will helping people to develop be a core part of every manager's role? In which case, will we make this a key result area for performance? Do we want all managers to do this or only people with appropriate skills? If we want line managers to coach staff, what is a reasonable span of control? Will we recognize and reward managers who do this well?
- What is our attitude towards accreditation? Will we support employees who wish to take higher qualifications? If so, what and whom? What form will our support take? Will we expect an immediate pay-back to the organization?

*Succession planning*

- Who do we define as 'key'? Is this a small group of potential executives or a broader group? How can we convey the message that people are valued without raising unrealistic expectations?
- Do we have contingency succession planning for specific jobs, and more general planning in place to support internal development? What will be our attitude towards employees who leave? Will we welcome back former employees in the future?

*Career development*

- What are the implications of change on people's careers? How will this affect morale? Do we need to do anything about it? How can we help people adjust their career expectations? Can we create a range of development opportunities that move away from the notion of vertical career progression? Who else will be involved and how will they be integrated into the process?
- What development opportunities will we consider beyond the organization? If development moves include overseas assignments, what are the issues for employees, such as dual-career

families, and how can we support them? Will we make career counselling available to employees?

## Working practices

- What will be the impact of change on working practices? How will technology affect roles and what is the implication of the IT strategy for training? How will roles be clarified? Will competencies be helpful? If so, how can these be developed so that people will actually use them?

## Training

- What do we want to achieve through training and what are the priorities? How will line management be involved in training? Will this include line managers identifying needs, choosing appropriate training, following up the training and evaluating the effectiveness of the training? Do we also want line managers to deliver training? If so, why, and how will we prepare them for this role? What cost–benefit assessment has been done? What are we measuring?

## Assessing performance

- What do we mean by performance? Will we assess performance in terms of bottom-line delivery, behaviours such as team-working and leadership, skills including competency development, etc.? Do we want everybody to produce similar kinds of performance? What are appropriate standards of performance and are they understood? How will we set targets for performance? Who will assess performance? Will it be HR, line managers, peers, customers, the individuals in question? What mechanisms will we use? Will training be required and for whom? Who will keep appraisal data? Will we encourage discussions about development to take place during discussions about appraisal of past performance? Will the processes be separate? Who will own development discussion data?

*Rewarding performance*

- What will we reward and how? Will we reward performance or contribution/value? Who are our competitors for staff and how do our packages compare? How does our current system block other things we are trying to achieve, such as encouraging people to make lateral moves? How can we remove the blockages? How can we develop an imaginative compensation strategy? What will have to change in the way we currently reward people  so that we are rewarding what the organization really values? How will we communicate this to employees so that they understand what and why?
- How much are we developing intrinsic rewards such as job satisfaction? What do our total compensation packages consist of, i.e. the value of benefits, salary and 'psychological income'? Are employees aware of this? How flexible is our compensation strategy? How much scope is there for meeting individual needs?


*Organizational culture*

- What kind of organization do we want to become? Do we want an empowerment culture and what will this mean in practice? What are the current values operating in the organization? Do we have organizational values which support the organization's longer-term vision? How will we develop the culture as we change the way we work? What cultural issues may block positive change? What actions should be taken on these and by whom? How will we develop effective two-way communication systems? How will we manage the implications of any acquisitions? How will we balance local with corporate culture? What recognition schemes can we put in place to reinforce desired behaviours? How will we encourage teambuilding? How will we deal with regulatory issues? How will we deal with moral dilemmas? How will we support managers as they manage change? How will we monitor what is happening to employee morale? What will we consider an 'acceptable' level of employee morale?

**The Balanced Business Scorecard**

Numerous management frameworks, such as the Balanced Business Scorecard approach, attempt to make the point that measuring business performance using only financial measures provides a purely retrospective look, with no attention paid to the drivers of future business success. The BBS approach is a means of measuring performance in a way that balances current and future needs. The four BBS perspectives are Finance, Customer, Internal Processes and Learning and Growth. Organizations are encouraged to find appropriate ways of achieving balance between the dominance of Finance and other Scorecard perspectives. The BBS works on the principle that measuring business purely in financial terms provides only a backward-looking perspective. The three other measures – Customer, Internal Processes and Learning and Growth – relate more to sources of future success. The idea is that measures in all four areas will be required to ensure that a balanced approach to running the organization can be achieved. The BBS approach does not imply that any of the four areas is more or less important than the others. It suggests that balance can be achieved in a number of ways according to the needs of the organization. In some organizations employees are encouraged to develop a Personal Scorecard reflecting balance between required outputs and inputs such as behaviours, knowledge and skills. The Scorecard notion is useful in helping people realize the need for balance and the dangers of imbalance when outputs seriously outweigh inputs.

Many organizations now acknowledge that demanding more outputs from employees without providing appropriate inputs is a no-win strategy in the long term. Increasingly organizations are adopting the principles of the BBS to ensure that their improved outputs are sustainable.

The difficulty lies in helping employees understand how their performance contributes to the business results. Employees may well perceive that the balance is in favour of outputs for the business as opposed to support and growth for them. To achieve a better balance and to help employees measure their own development, business scorecards may need to include job-specific competencies. At the individual level, a balanced scorecard in terms of performance may consist of improved outputs balanced by improved skills, knowledge and experience. The BBS approach will be discussed in more detail in Chapter 11.

**Helping employees achieve balance**

Another aspect of balance that falls within the Human Resource arena is whether the current high workloads of many employees are sustainable in the long term. It has become fashionable to talk about the need for 'balance' between work and other aspects of life. Many organizations consider that maintaining balance is the employee's responsibility, and this is perhaps realistic. However, organizations can accept that current pressures have the potential to damage morale, motivation and overall employee effectiveness.

There are various actions that can be taken to encourage employees to achieve balance between their work lives and personal lives. This is one of the key areas in which Human Resource policies can work in both the long- and short-term interest of employees and employers. Suggestions include:

*   clarify roles so that people know when they can say 'no'
*   support flexible work patterns
*   get senior managers to act as role models with regard to leaving on time
*   extend occasional 'leave on time' days to become the norm
*   reduce the number of conferences and business meetings that require employees to work or travel at weekends
*   encourage the development of peer mentoring and other informal support systems
*   ensure that staff take their annual leave
*   offer an employee-counselling service and stress programmes
*   include child care and dependent care in benefits packages
*   include employees' families in decisions relating to relocation, promotions, etc.
*   do not penalize employees who do manage to maintain a balance
*   include 'the ability to achieve and maintain a balance' to the list of core competencies which employees are encouraged to develop and for which they are rewarded.

# The 'new' Human Resource professional

Of course many HR departments and personnel professionals find themselves in 'no-win' situations, with many conflicting demands on their time and efforts. In the most successful examples we have found of HR contribution, HR professionals are working in partnership with line management. The process of gaining credibility with the line to make this possible varies widely, but there are certain common approaches and characteristics which these individuals share.

### They see their role as that of change agent

First of all, these professionals understand the organization's vision and are able to translate the operational objectives into organizational implications. Some of the most influential HR professionals think of themselves as business people first and HR professionals second. This affects the way they perceive issues and communicate with line colleagues. As one person put it: 'I need to be able to talk to line colleagues about issues and concerns affecting their business. I make sure that I read what they read, including trade press, so that I can initiate conversations with them and be taken seriously as an ally.'

In every case they have challenged the status quo and had the courage of their convictions. This may give them the reputation of being renegades, but their proven track record in the field gives them a degree of freedom to challenge. They have sophisticated influencing skills and often have one or two top-level supporters who win backing for their ideas amongst the supporters' peer group. The most effective contributors are those who focus the change effort and see projects through to fruition.

### They have earned credibility with line management

This is often achieved when the HR professional's role is considered less as a policing or power-base role and more as a consultancy role. Tailored delivery of solutions as opposed to mass policy imposition seems to help HR win support from the line. So does being willing and able to co-ordinate the outputs of line initiatives. In some organizations, middle managers have taken the initiative to develop competencies appropriate to their part of the business. Where several operating units are producing different sets of competencies, potential benefits to the business, such as job rotation schemes, can be difficult to introduce because the information is not transferable. In this sort of case, the HR team can add value by integrating the different sets of competencies into a common framework, while retaining local ownership of the competencies.

This in turn calls on HR professionals to see the value of such a role, which may be a radical departure from the conventional central systems approach. Ironically, the consultancy-type role can produce opposition from the line if line managers feel that they are losing a service with which they are familiar. This sort of role also depends on clear prioritizing on the part of the HR consultant. Often with much smaller teams than a few years ago, HR managers frequently have to juggle demands for advice on industrial tribunals, for example, with major change programmes and projects for important internal clients.

Often HR groups have the same difficulty adjusting to flatter structures and their career implications as everyone else. Some departments are taking the lead in setting up placements in and out of the department for themselves and line managers. It is useful if their practices embody the culture change they are meant to be leading. Teamwork is often a very visible element of culture change. HR specialists need to be accepted members of project groups and client teams. Some very successful HR teams have led the change process by restructuring their own team. In the Employee Development group at London Transport the team has developed its own vision in which titles are unimportant. They are consciously modelling the benefits of the flatter structure.

### They become experts in change processes

Many organizations pay attention to people management processes only when the new structure does not seem to be working well. Although this may be incremental strategy in action, the consequence can be a sort of 'domino effect' in which one part of the system, such as appraisals, receives attention at a time and does not appear to fit within an overall strategy. Many recent interventions have successfully encouraged people to think seriously about managing their own careers. This type of initiative can have only limited success unless some help is given to people to make lateral and other moves, and typically this help is not forthcoming. This can result in frustration within the organization and the impression that HR is merely reacting to events by this piecemeal approach.

While taking each stage in turn may be a pragmatic approach, the more successful HR departments are adept at showing how the HR strategy as it evolves is clearly linked to changing business needs. They are good at putting the pieces of the jigsaw together.

This involves thinking through the knock-on effects of new policies, testing with end-users, monitoring policies when they are implemented and advising senior management of any changes needed. Moreover, they do not simply monitor issues such as employee morale through attitude surveys and focus groups. They act on the information and target improvements.

In some organizations, the importance of employee welfare is treated as a business issue. The semiconductor industry is fiercely competitive in attracting skilled new recruits. In that industry there is open acknowledgement that people are the organization's main asset. One organization is actively planning to enhance its future profitability by attracting the very best employees it can find worldwide. In this company, business decisions generally take employee considerations into account. The sign-off of the siting of a new factory, for instance, and its furbishment are very much the responsibility of HR, since employee morale and working conditions are seen to be their prime concern. In such a company, the senior HR specialist is an active member of the board, initiating and influencing business decisions as well as simply implementing them.

## The role of HR in career management

This is perhaps the area where the HR professional has the greatest contribution to make, as it lies at the heart of many employee morale issues. On the whole, research suggests that employees are very dissatisfied with the career possibilities open to them in flatter structures. Some of the biggest problems lie in the apparent imbalance between the organization's needs and those of employees. According to Rosabeth Moss Kanter (1994), organizations need to change incentives from status, careers and promotion to teamwork, personal reputation and challenging assignments. Making work challenging and satisfying will, she believes, translate into what she calls 'employability security'.

How will this work in practice? There are certain potential solutions to the challenge of attracting, motivating and retaining key staff. They involve a partnership approach on the part of HR, line managers and employees in general to dealing with these difficult issues. Suggested strategies include the following.

- Work with line managers to ensure that jobs have an element of challenge built into them.
- Develop the ethos that learning is critical to organizational and individual success.
- Ensure that employees genuinely have the chance to enhance their skills.
- Provide systematic training in 'new' skills and working practices.
- Design processes to enable employees to contribute their own ideas and to participate in the decision-making process.
- Encourage innovative recognition approaches, both corporate awards and individual schemes – people need to feel valued.
- Develop reward systems that offer a sense of progression and reinforce what you want to see.
- Scan the organization for signs of overload or burn out; help people work in ways appropriate to the new organization.
- Ensure that the dominant management style is appropriate to empowerment.
- Encourage shared leadership at all levels.
- Build cross-functional teamwork.
- Manage career expectations and help people develop an appropriate concept of career.
- Pay attention to the induction process.
- Consider introducing a 'revolving door' policy for employees who leave.
- Build commitment by recognizing individual values and developing shared values.
- Disengage performance review from development discussions.
- Decentralize performance appraisals, giving employees and line managers more responsibility.
- Make lateral moves possible and reward those who make the moves.
- Remove barriers to change, whether these are systemic or particular individuals.
- Learn from exit interviews what needs to change – and be prepared to change it.

## Conclusion

The range of people issues facing most organizations is fairly daunting. Retention and motivation are critical business issues since without the right people, the business cannot deliver. Finding the solutions to some of these issues is beyond the scope of any one individual or team. The best chance of finding the most appropriate solutions to the challenges of the short and medium term is to pool expertise and bring goodwill to bear in a shared way. Few groups are better placed to ensure a strategic approach to planning for, managing and developing employees than line managers and Human Resource professionals working in partnership.

# 9    *Changing roles*

Are roles really changing? If so, what lies behind the changes and what might the future hold for careers? These are some of the questions we will explore in this chapter.

## Are roles really changing?

There are without doubt some subtle and not so subtle shifts going on. When we revisited our original research population after a gap of two years, we found some surprising changes. Junior line managers as a group had almost disappeared, which is not unexpected given that the flattening of organization levels typically takes out people in junior to middle management roles. Other groups of workers had also disappeared. Junior personnel employees had found their jobs phased out over a two-year period. Looking back to the original research, these people were feeling very dissatisfied and uncertain about their future in the changing organizations, and they proved to be right.

On the other hand, some things appear to be much the same as they always were. Flatter organization structures do not seem to have put an end to vertical promotion in quite the way many people expected. In our research we found that a fifth of our sample population had achieved promotion in the two-year period. These tended to be people who were already reasonably senior. They included senior personnel managers who had in some cases reached the board of their organization. This probably reflects the increasing trend that specialist jobs become consultancy-type roles.

*Changing employment relationships*

Some of these shifts reflect broader changes in the working environment. The ongoing evolution of organizations can sometimes be genuinely chaotic, with every restructuring followed rapidly by yet more change initiatives. Understandably, people can get weary of change. Very few organizations offer continuous employment these days. One exception to this is the Rover Group in the UK, who see affirmed employment as a foundation stone of the trust which they feel is an essential prerequisite of employee commitment.

*The growth of the flexible workforce*

Another big shift is the range of types of contract that people are working to. It is predicted that by the year 2001 up to 41 per cent of the UK workforce will be working on some form of flexible working arrangement. These include part-time working, fixed-term contract working and teleworking, to name but a few. Such forms of working can offer both the employer and the employee some flexibility, in theory. Often the changes have come about because of increased use of technology.

Not all forms of flexible contract benefit the 'employee'. In the UK there is an increase in fixed-term contracts in all sectors, including the British civil service. In many cases, restructurings provide organizations with the opportunity to review staffing levels and benefits arrangements, and the workforce is often placed in a 'take it or leave it' situation. Despite this, very few employees seem to be making provision for their pension arrangements.

There is an increasing trend in Europe towards part-time employment, especially for women, mainly in clerical or 'front-line' roles. Some sectors of the economy, such as retailing and the leisure industry, have a higher proportion of part-time workers than others. In the retail sector in particular, the increase of shop opening hours is likely to promote this trend. Part-time working offers many advantages to employers – increased flexibility and lower expenditure on benefits and training. The challenges for the organization include managing and aligning people on part-time contracts to what the organization is trying to achieve.

For employees, being part-time often means exclusion from the communication processes and a lack of opportunity to develop or participate in teamwork. Often the term 'part-time' is reflected in the pay packet only, since research suggests that part-time workers are frequently called on to exceed their contracted hours. Nevertheless there is a small but significant trend for professional women in particular and some men to opt for part-time or job-share arrangements that allow them to balance other needs. Often when the employee takes the initiative to ask for job-share arrangements, the organization finds difficulty in responding flexibly to meet employee needs. People then have to leave and recontract their services on a different basis or be approached by prospective employers who are more willing to consider flexible arrangements.

It seems that the idea of long-term employment with a single employer is long past. In times gone by it was customary for lowly paid workers to supplement their income with one or more part-time jobs. This tendency seems to be spreading to other groups of workers, including professionals. There is already evidence, for instance, that young doctors are opting for locum positions with a number of practices rather than a full-time engagement with one.

### Core versus periphery

Increasingly, organizations use their full-time staff to concentrate on their core activities, outsourcing those parts of their operation which are seen to be peripheral, such as facilities management. The roles of people in the core workforce are therefore likely to change. People will probably be required to have broader business awareness and multi-skilled approaches to delivering their contribution, whereas specialist services will increasingly be bought into the organization on contract. Part of the rationale for outsourcing non-core or value-adding activities is that this is a way of saving money on employees' salaries. In reality, of course, contract work often commands higher sums for the contractor, though as these sums do not appear on the salary bill, the organization appears to be trimming its employee costs.

The tendency to concentrate on core activities has meant that many 'peripheral' activities are outsourced. This can be bad news for the employee, such as the security guard employed by a financial services company who found her job outsourced to a security company on very different (and worse) terms. To the former employee, this move represented a betrayal by her original employer since they continued to require the service. In other cases, contract workers whose roles have been outsourced from previous employers often find themselves at the mercy of the employer in areas of high unemployment such as the north-east of England and parts of Scotland.

The situation is most difficult for contract workers whose skill level is not particularly high, or who lack a specialism, or where there is acute competition for contracts. The safeguard in this case is to develop very marketable and high skill levels in areas which are of great interest to potential hirers. The 'catch 22' for many contractors is that they are afraid of turning away work in order to train or become better qualified. The contract market does seem to require that people are ready to 'hit the ground running'.

Contract employment can also be good news for the employee, especially where contract working is well established, such as in the IT industry. It can offer high payments, greater freedom and less requirement for them to become embroiled in the internal workings of any one organization. To be successful, contractors find that they really do need to see themselves as a business. They usually have to be independent but well connected and highly customer-focused. When work is plentiful they have to be able to prioritize and focus in on things that are important to them. If the increasing tendency in organizations is to suggest that employees should be responsible for their own career development, there are perhaps some tips which employees in full-time employment can pick up from contractors.

*Purchaser–provider split*

In the UK public sector, another interesting shift is the increased division between so-called 'purchaser' and 'provider' activities. This is particularly marked in local government and the National Health Service where provider services are often set in competition with each other to meet market conditions. Though this was originally intended to produce higher-quality and more cost-effective services, the effect in many cases was a severe culture shift within the organization. Purchaser units took on a clear management role, with many provider units being effectively outsourced. Ironically, although such moves initially appeared to put all the power in the relationship in the hands of the purchasing bodies, highly skilled specialists, whether they were trainers or clinicians, were soon able to thrive in the new environment. As a result they are now able to be more selective about the kind of work they choose to do, putting the boot on the other foot.

**Managerial roles**

How do these broad changes affect individual roles? Will roles as we know them continue to exist? Consider manager roles, for instance. When flatter structures were first introduced in many organizations, middle manager positions were often the first to go. There has already been a significant swing back to reintroducing managerial positions, but with some differences. The first is that many managerial positions have a much clearer developmental role built into them since the experience of many companies is that flatter structures call for managerial clarity and support. In some cases this has meant separating out 'technical' management from people management responsibilities. This is commonplace in matrix and project structures but is increasingly adopted in consultancy-based structures.

*The line manager as developer*

Managers are also increasingly required to act as coaches and mentors to their teams, a task which is very difficult when in flatter structures spans of control can typically number as many as twenty direct reports. Such large spans of control make performance management very difficult, especially if the line manager is expected to help individuals in the team to develop. Just finding time for twenty development discussions can overwhelm a manager's workload if, at the same time, they are required to be technical manager as well.

In parts of Glaxo Wellcome the two types of managerial responsibility have been separated out to some extent – within a sales division the role of 'team coach' has been devised to support teams that will gradually become self-managed. Sherrie Charlton is an example of such a team coach. Her role is to provide support for the team as it learns the processes of managing meetings, managing performance, hiring and other team processes which replace to some extent what the manager would previously have done. At the same time she provides individual coaching to ensure that each member of the team is able to deliver their peak performance. Of course, not all teams will find it possible to be self-directed, even with lots of help, and likewise many managers find themselves ill-equipped to take on the role of coach and developer of other people.

*The manager as cog in the wheel*

The role of managers has increasingly become that of being the cog in the middle of a bigger operation. In many cases they are managing big projects which employ large numbers of subcontractors. They have to provide the coordination and linkages between different parts of the project, ensuring that quality and other standards are met, even though they are not directly managing the individuals concerned. Given the essential sensitivity of the human resource asset this is likely to prove an increasingly complex task, especially when it comes to team building.

The challenges of managing are likely to become more rather than less complex. Increasingly, managing 'knowledge workers' means that the majority of people being managed are more expert in their particular fields than the manager. If those individuals have highly marketable skills, providing them with the sort of environment in which they are highly motivated and committed will be the manager's responsibility. Understanding how to coach and 'shield' such individuals from the organization's negative effects may involve the use of sophisticated skills by the manager.

Some managers already have the challenge of coordinating so-called virtual teams, people who never meet face to face but have to communicate via technology. In such situations, the manager needs to have cross-cultural skills as well as understanding the art of teambuilding at a distance. Often this is not helped by conflicting organizational objectives. In an international software business, for instance, the business operated as a global group of separate selling operations coordinated by the headquarters in the US. As the business grew, and providing good follow-up service was recognized as essential to further growth, the company decided to restructure its services so that sales would be carried out by groups from the UK and US, leaving customer service to be supplied at the local level elsewhere. The manager trying to motivate all the former sales staff, who were now half-heartedly supplying customer service to what they saw as colleagues' customers, found the task impossible. Senior management initially saw this as the manager's inability to manage a virtual team. The manager's challenge was to manage the situation with senior management, acting as the organizational interface so that the team's problems could be addressed. He was able to arrange for targets to be revised so that teams would achieve joint bonuses based on the combined effect of both sales and service. Managing the interface between team members became relatively straightforward after the core issue had been resolved.

## Generalist or specialist?

There is an increasing tendency for organizations to imply that they want all employees, especially those whom they consider key to the future, to have multiple skills rather than to specialize in one area only. This has the effect of reversing old professional status hierarchies. In some team-based companies in the construction industry, for instance, architects are feeling effectively downgraded because their specialist contribution is valued and rewarded perhaps less than that of the multi-skilled project manager.

On the other hand the increasing polarization between deeper specialization and multi-skilling can favour the specialists. Where knowledge workers are able to acquire consultancy skills so that they can not only enhance their professional knowledge but also sell their expertise internally or externally, they are able to increase their employability. If at the same time they think and act as business people first, subject specialists second, they are likely to increase their influence within the organization. Given that there appears to be a lessening of loyalty towards employers, it could be argued that employees are increasingly likely to find their long-term employability best secured through developing their professional skills and increasing their external networks, especially with customers.

### Teamworking

Flatter structures often favour teamworking, whether in cross-disciplinary or functional project groups. There are undoubtedly many advantages to teamworking where this is appropriate. There is also some debate about whether teamwork is appropriate in all circumstances.

In some circumstances teamworking may be required, but not everybody is able or willing to be a team player. Managers are then faced with the dilemma of deciding what to do about excellent sole contributors who do not see themselves as team players, but who nevertheless contribute well in other ways. Developing teams relies on the will and skill of all involved. Training can help to some extent but there are plenty of examples where 'self-directed' teams are exposed as a myth. The commonest problem is where managers retain a 'command and control' management style which tends to undercut any attempt by the people reporting to them to make their own decisions. Other problems arise when teams become complacent or subject to the 'rut of group think' as Denis Waitley (1995) puts it. This can lead to reduced performance rather than the benefits of a group of people working synergistically.

### The end of jobs?

Many pundits predict that jobs as we know them will cease to exist. William Bridges, for instance, argues that technological and economic shifts are already making the notion of a fixed 'job' obsolete. Fixed jobs are becoming flexible roles. Even the notions of part-time and full-time are anachronisms. In some organizations, people work according to the demands of the project, rather than to any preassigned schedule.

William Bridges (1995) suggests that this trend is already under way and that many people are currently working within organizations under arrangements too fluid and specific to be called jobs. In many types of organization, especially in the software industry, people work in project teams in which they are not accountable to management but to other members of the project team. In such a context individual performance is very visible. An individual's prospects are dependent on the credibility established in every project. Traditional marks of status count for little. In such teams, a leader's authority lasts only for that project and today's manager may be tomorrow's team member.

## Adjusting to changing roles

When we first started researching the effects of flatter structures on people's careers we found that in organizations which had recently delayered there were enormous problems caused by the introduction of the new structures. Typically there was lack of clarity, confusion about roles, job overlap and in particular job/work overload. Statements were made such as:

- 'we're expected to do better with less; there's far more actual work with less support'
- 'less resources and people to deal with larger responsibilities'

- 'less support for those in staff roles'
- 'morale is lower, commitment is lower'
- 'responsibilities less clearly defined, therefore increased stress'
- 'expected to work effectively in areas not trained for, or experienced in.'

For some people their new role meant less, not more, responsibility. Senior people in particular reported decreased levels of authority and responsibility, which left them feeling disempowered. The confusion that surrounds the allocation of authority and responsibility seems to be a key factor in causing problems.

## The need for clarity

Lack of clarity seems to be one of the main sources of dissatisfaction in changing organizations; the consequences of not addressing this can be harmful to both employee morale and organizational goals. In the Roffey Park research we found that there is a close relationship between lack of clarity and people contemplating leaving the organization, loss of motivation and frustration. People were often expected to work in areas that they were not trained for or experienced in. This had a knock-on effect on quality and project control as well as on service in the field. We also found that when people did not know the limits of their decision-making authority they became hesitant and less efficient. Clarity therefore is useful, but what is it important to be clear about?

## Making clear the long-term goals of the organization

It seems to work best when people are clear what the organization is trying to achieve in the long term and understand where they can contribute to achieving the vision and strategy. Often, even where there is a clear organizational vision, it is not well communicated to employees, and they do not understand how all the disparate efforts to achieve the goals are connected. This lack of coherence can often then seem chaotic and add to the stresses on employees, especially when they retain all their old responsibilities and are expected to carry out new tasks. Ambiguity decreases the motivation to make an effort because it makes people believe that their effort has little chance of producing the desired results. By making organizational plans and individual opportunities clear, it is possible to help employees develop positive work attitudes. Understanding what needs to be done, and why, is important if employees are going to be able to understand how best they can add value.

### Providing clarity through competencies

Many organizations try to provide role clarity by identifying competencies which are then used to provide people with an understanding of what behaviours are appropriate for effective performance both now and in the future. Competencies can be very useful in forming a framework that leads to job profiling, skills profiling and eventually to the widening of the opportunities for people as they move across organizational boundaries which would previously have been closed to them. The competencies are usually only as good as the way in which they are devised. If the people who are likely to be most affected by the competencies are involved in developing them, the words used will reflect the actual situation and the employees can buy into the value of the competencies.

### Providing clarity through standardizing procedures, not roles

Some companies try to provide clarity through systematizing their processes and procedures, especially when they have quality initiatives under way. When procedures are standardized, documented and continuously improved it is easier for a mobile workforce to maintain high levels of output to identified quality standards. The downside is that there can be a huge amount of documentation generated which can suppress initiative rather than encourage it.

When recruiting for new positions or defining what roles will be needed in a new structure, it is important to define the elements of the roles in some detail. However, this should be a starting point rather than an end point. In fact, research suggests that, when it comes to roles, too much clarity is not a good idea – it is often when there is some ambiguity that people are able to sense the biggest opportunities for themselves. Of the people who helped in the Roffey Park research, those who were the most unhappy with their work were those whose jobs had remained the same, with tight boundaries, but with increased workload. Most of these people reported a lack of job satisfaction. Some jobs in particular need a degree of ambiguity so that people can use their initiative to grow the role. The challenge then is to get the right balance between confusion and clarity.

*Setting standards*

In particular, people need to understand what is expected of them and how they will be judged. This means clarifying levels of performance so that people are clear what represents an entrance level of performance and what represents truly excellent performance. Often what constitutes performance is poorly understood and people then find themselves trying to conform to stereotypes of effective behaviour rather than what truly makes the difference.

Once the standards and targets are set people need regular feedback on how they are doing. This means specific observation and encouragement based on a detailed awareness of the value being contributed by each individual. There seems to be a direct link between feedback and performance. The more an individual believes that they have clear objectives, the more feedback they receive on specific tasks and on the whole of their performance, the clearer their idea of the responsibilities they have to assume, then the better is their performance.

*Opportunities for personal growth*

Of course not everybody responds with despair to the confusion caused by organizational change. Some people in fact see organizational change as an opportunity for personal growth. Flatter structures often cause relatively junior people to be promoted to management positions without the intervening levels of supervisor and so on. The challenge is often managing people older than yourself without having gradually acquired people management skills on the way.

In other cases the gap between levels has widened significantly due to delayering. The effect of this can cause problems for junior people who are reporting directly, for example, to directors and who need to be able to communicate appropriately but often do not have the insight into the business which is needed for them to communicate the right information. Training can help. This is particularly where development in role may involve exposure to other parts of the business through project work.

# Are people managing their own careers?

Another key area of role change is in the field of career development. People nowadays are frequently told that they are
responsible for managing their careers, and to some extent it seems
that people are accepting this message. However, when we interviewed groups of high-flyers within organizations we found that
few, if any, considered making their career sidewards. Looking at
the research population as a whole, very few people have made
financial provision for themselves other than through their
company pension scheme. So how much the message 'manage
your career' includes mobility is questionable. Similarly, very few
people do seem to be contemplating a portfolio career rather than
continuous employment in a few organizations. In some cases this
is in spite of evidence from their own lives that this is how they have
managed their career to date.

# Conclusion

Changing roles call for people to be willing to adapt and develop
new skills and approaches. Career and employment patterns seem
to be undergoing major shifts, but what will emerge as the 'new'
pattern of employment and career development is not yet clear.
Increasingly people are demanding more from the work they do
than just pay. 'Career' in that sense carries with it the implication of
satisfying important individual values. It is quite possible that as
time goes on there will not be one career pattern but many, with a
wide range of life experiences contributing to a rich blend of work,
paid and unpaid, which provides meaningful employment. This
rather implies that a key characteristic of someone who is likely to
thrive in the new work environment is a positive approach to
learning and change. We will look at the characteristics of the 'new
employee' in more detail in Chapter 10.

Why is it that some people seem to be successful no matter what the circumstances whereas others fail to make the grade? Is it purely down to personality, looks, credentials or luck, or is there more to it than that? Everyone is entitled to their own opinion on this. I was interested to know if organizations are developing any consistent views about what successful employees will be like in these changing times. One of the initial objectives of my research into career development in flatter structures was to identify how organizations were managing to retain employees whom they considered to be very effective. As part of my research, I spoke with twenty-six chief executives or managing directors in a range of organizations and asked a rather strange question: 'Who, out of all your employees, would you be most keen not to lose?'

Some were reluctant at first, but they all eventually named one person whom I then met, as well as some of their peers. Of the twenty-six, fifteen were women, some of whom were very surprised to find themselves identified as a key player. Some were in positions of considerable influence, others occupied relatively lowly customer service-type positions. Only five had been or were on conventional 'fast-track' schemes. None was a paragon of virtue. I was interested to find out what, if anything, they had in common. Here are some of the distinguishing features.

## The vital characteristics

### Thriving on change

All twenty-six individuals accepted change as normal. They were willing to challenge the status quo to find better ways of doing things. This sometimes caused ruffled feathers at the next level in the hierarchy. Rather than worrying about the changes, they were constantly on the look-out for new opportunities for their departments or themselves. They enjoyed the challenge of the unknown. They were not concerned about potential job loss since they were confident of being employable elsewhere. They encouraged their own teams to develop a problem-solving approach to the challenges facing them.

### Self-starters

They had an entrepreneurial approach and accepted responsibility for making things happen – for themselves as well as for their organization. One woman had created an international professional network from which her organization was benefiting. She also got to travel and mix with people from different cultures, which increased her awareness of the value of diversity.

### Taking responsibility for themselves

This certainly applied to the way they described their career. They considered that this was their responsibility, but that by and large their employers were supportive and had encouraged them to take on responsibility. They were opportunistic in getting on to project groups in which they could learn new skills. Most were taking, or had taken, qualification programmes that had increased their skills and knowledge.

## Interpersonally effective

### Able to influence

Most were able to influence others since they had excellent interpersonal skills. They were confident about dealing with people at different levels in the hierarchy and in some cases were able to adapt their communication styles as appropriate. This was not just a case of good presentation skills but a more sophisticated ability to communicate with people in ways which they find most acceptable. One manager in particular was able to flex his message so that he delivered the right level of information to different audiences. This skill was also helpful to him in dealing with the needs of a potentially very difficult team. Some used this skill to influence political processes within their organizations.

### Networking

I wondered why it was that so many of these people were highly visible within their organizations, especially when some were in relatively junior roles. The answer may be partly to do with their networking ability. Many saw networking as an essential part of getting things done.

## Seeing the big picture

### A business perspective

These key people also thought beyond the boundaries of their job, acting as business people first and departmental specialists second. As a result they were able to see linkages between what was happening in the marketplace and the work of their own department. In a real sense they were able to think and act strategically as well as translate strategy into clear operational plans. Through their business acumen they were able to enhance the contribution of their department to the organization.

### Knowing what is important

The overriding characteristic that they had in common was their strong sense of what was important to them. Some had clear personal goals, others did not. However, they all had strong views on what they stood for. They were also keen learners, taking every opportunity to review and refocus as necessary.

## Retaining new employees

Ironically, of the twenty-six successful individuals interviewed in mid-1994, fifteen had left by the beginning of 1996, mostly to join other organizations or to go self-employed. In every case their departure was voluntary. The very skills which made these employees so desirable to their employers also increased their own options. The main reasons for leaving were frustration at the slow rate of change, especially with respect to management behaviour. Most of the leavers did not consider that their primary job loyalty was to their employer but rather to their profession, clients and most of all themselves.

One person commented that she had developed a different approach to changing jobs in recent years, largely as a result of the frequent changes and her own increased awareness of what she wanted and what she had to offer potential employers. She said: 'The next time I am ready for a job move I intend to use my networks to help me find a role which really suits me and allows me to grow. In gaining my current job I realize that I was interviewing my boss rather than the other way round – I suppose I'm getting choosy.'

In some cases, people opted for self-employment or for more flexible work arrangements so that they could achieve a better balance between work and other things which were important to them. This suggests that organizations are going to have to take more serious account of employee needs if they wish to retain key players. According to Tom Barry of Blessing/White, some of the main values which employees are finding important are having a sense of control, and getting the balance right between home and family. Increasingly people are expressing a sense of idealism and a need for a sense of purpose in work.

This links with other research which has found that high personal control, which relates to an individual's beliefs that they are able to bring about change in a desired direction, is positively linked with career success such as job satisfaction and higher pay. To what extent are aspects of personal control, such as self-efficacy or the belief in your own worth, developable? The effect of having a high belief in your own ability to deal effectively with any situation does seem to be something of a self-fulfilling prophecy.

To what extent is our career path set for us during our early work experiences? Edgar Schein (1996) developed the notion of 'career anchors', which are occupational self-concepts based on one's inherent needs and motives, one's values and one's known talents. Of the eight career anchors identified so far, perhaps the 'pure challenge' anchor is put to the test most in changing organizations. People with this self-concept measure career success by meeting difficult challenges and overcoming barriers. This may involve having to win over colleagues in order to achieve the objective.

**Retention checklist**

So how can organizations retain people who have valuable contributions to make but who are not prepared to tolerate ongoing frustration of what is important to them?

- Understand why this individual is so valuable to your organization. Are you using their skills and talents to the full? If not, how could you?
- Find out what is important to these individuals – what motivates them, how they like to be managed. As far as possible, give them the chance to satisfy what is important to them in their job. Be prepared to think creatively about what is possible.
- As far as possible, eliminate or minimize sources of major frustration. If that includes the way in which people are managed, see what help can be given to managers to develop more appropriate styles. Examine what they point out. These may be sources of frustration for many others too.
- Give the individuals the mandate to tackle some of the biggest sources of frustration as business issues.
- Give them the chance to exercise autonomy as much as possible, but having taken the precaution of providing adequate coaching and guidance about what is acceptable.
- Encourage and recognize behaviours which are in line with what the organization is trying to achieve.
- Give them the chance to use their initiative on things which the organization really values.
- If they have leadership potential, give them the chance to lead a project team addressing an important business issue.
- Encourage a real balance in workloads so that they have time to satisfy other important aspects of their life.
- Be prepared to lose them anyway. If they are conventionally ambitious, they may need to look for opportunities elsewhere. Be prepared to welcome them back in years to come, with their experience enhanced. After all, they were only managing their own career.

# New skills

This links in with other information emerging from the Roffey Park research about the abilities many organizations are now encouraging their employees to develop. As one senior manager put it: 'We no longer look at a job as a function or a certain type of work. Instead we see it as a set of skills and competencies.' So what are the skills that will help people to succeed in the future? Most people agree that job-specific skills alone are not enough, though they are critical. In the new, more fluid organizations of today and tomorrow, it will not be enough to have technical know-how. The importance of so-called 'transferable skills' is becoming more obvious. For some people these skills are far removed from their previous experience and they may underestimate their value.

*Political skills*

Effective employees will need to be able to get things done when they do not have direct authority over others. This calls for an awareness of the political processes or 'shadow' side to the organization. Political skills include 'managing up' the organization as well as down. This involves knowing how to communicate effectively and influence decision-making at different levels. Knowing how to influence these processes so as to achieve your objectives will be important, and a few UK organizations are now beginning to train employees to be more politically aware and effective. Effective political actors are able to build strong networks and see this as a means to get things done.

The importance of being able to influence political processes can be a matter of survival within an organization. More than one 'head-hunter' has discovered the increasing trend in Europe for 40–45-year-old managers to become casualties of targeted redundancy. The common feature of the circumstances surrounding their departure is a belief on the part of the job holder that their skills and excellent contribution to date gave them the security to stand apart from their senior colleagues. As one Belgian manager put it: 'I forgot to play power games and how decisions are taken within the company.'

Cross-cultural skills are also growing in importance as many organizations become global operators. These involve having higher awareness of one's own stereotypes, an appreciation of cultural difference and a sensitivity to people and situations. Many of the skills which make people effective as international leaders, such as their tolerance of ambiguity, can be useful in their 'home' organization if it is undergoing major change.

*Team skills*

These include both team membership and leadership skills. Increasingly people are called upon to work in various forms of team. These can be short-lived, ad hoc project teams, permanent departmental teams, cross-functional quality teams and many other variations on a theme. Some organizations are structured on a project basis and people are required to integrate quickly into new teams and be able immediately to add value to the team. In other cases, people can be members of several teams simultaneously. This can cause difficulty for the individual if the teams have objectives which conflict to some extent with those of the individual's own department or manager.

At a basic level, people find it useful to understand something of team processes, team dynamics and the stages of teambuilding. It is also helpful for people to have insights into different team roles and types so that they can understand and maximize the benefits of diversity. Facilitation skills are helpful. Another important element is the ability to handle conflict since this seems to be a common feature of much of contemporary organizational life.

More sophisticated skills are required of people working in certain sorts of teams. Many organizations, particularly in the manufacturing sector, are attempting to set up semi-autonomous teams. In such teams, some management responsibility is delegated to the teams so that arranging shifts, ordering resources, setting targets and monitoring performance are all areas managed by the teams themselves. In 'self-directed' teams, responsibility for the team's outputs and composition is largely decided by the teams. This can involve recruiting, disciplining and deciding on the level of reward for individual team members.

*Information technology skills*

Increasingly these are considered to be core skills, especially as more organizations are finally developing more effective use of IT. This usually involves people being able to use the company's Intranet and e-mail facilities, though as yet few organizations seem to be making extensive use of the Internet. Through technology, there is no need for anyone to be out of touch. International companies are encouraging travelling executives to communicate via their modems and laptops, or else to avoid the need for travelling though the use of video and Internet conferencing. In many cases, technology has been used to replace office jobs as well as to automate manufacturing processes. The days of the manager's secretary seem to be numbered, though often former secretaries are able to move into interesting, challenging and sometimes prestigious roles because they have skills which are much in demand.

People who remain unable to do even basic word processing are starting to be at a disadvantage. Several outsourcing firms are providing accelerated IT training for former executives who have been made redundant. A popular proposal by the UK's Labour Party at the end of 1996 was that members of the public should be given vouchers to encourage them to learn IT skills at their local colleges. This seems sensible given that the changing work patterns, including teleworking, have to a large extent been made possible through technology and the trend looks set to grow in years to come.

## Self-management skills

At an individual level, flatter structures generally result in much higher workloads. Self-management skills, including time management and prioritization, are becoming essential for survival. Similarly, given that the nature of many roles is changing, many people value project management skills which enable them to structure and manage complex activities.

Similarly, people need to take to heart the message that they are responsible for managing their careers and for thinking through the consequences of that. Depending on their age and situation, many people will wish to carry on working for their current employer. Will they hope to be doing the same job in five years' time? Often just beginning the thought process about what would be the next step stimulates a more proactive, opportunity-spotting attitude. People who become genuinely independent of any one employer, because they are employable and have made financial provision for their long-term security, are much more likely to be able to negotiate their career needs on an adult–adult basis with their employer.

## People management and leadership skills

Increasingly managers are required to develop more enabling and participative styles of management that may not be their personal preference. Yet research evidence suggests that managers' behaviour in leading and shaping the new organization has a profound effect on its success or otherwise. Some of the main causes of employee frustration in changing organizations revolve around managers expecting other people to change their way of doing things, but not being prepared to do so themselves. This failure to 'walk the talk' causes cynicism amongst employees. Another common cause of frustration is when managers are unwilling to empower others to make decisions, often blaming people when things go wrong.

Leadership training is often provided to help senior managers develop behaviours which are consistent with the aims of the organization. Such training usually includes the use of feedback instruments including 'upward' and 360 degree questionnaires as a means of making managers aware of what it might be useful to change. Typically, one of the key areas of difficulty lies at the heart of performance management, namely managers being ineffective at giving feedback and delegating.

Coaching and mentoring are increasingly seen as part of a manager's role since it is widely recognized that providing people with the help they need to peform their new roles is essential. The difficulty is that many managers have such wide spans of control that giving individuals the attention they need can prove very difficult. Managers are widely criticized for not recognizing improved performance in their team members. Training managers in coaching skills can help, but often the basic problem remains if the manager is overloaded. Increasingly, line managers are also required actively to supply training to their teams and many organizations are providing them with train-the-trainer courses to enable them to do this.

### Financial and business skills

Most employees in changing organizations need a clear under-standing of the business dynamics of their own organization. Without such an understanding, employees are less likely to make shrewd decisions and empowerment remains a myth. At a basic level, an understanding of how work is costed, and whether it is better to aim for market share, profitability or both, can help people in their day-to-day interactions with customers and suppliers.

In one truck distributorship, a small but apparently profitable sideline was repairing the local bus fleet. This became a very large part of the workshop's activities since they were the local specialists, and the workshop team, who were perfectionist by inclination, clearly enjoyed taking considerable care over the repair of the venerable engines. The only problem was that, because the chief engineer failed to cost the work accurately, much of the actual cost was being borne by the repair company, which was too busy to take on the repair of trucks, which would have been more profitable! Fortunately, a new managing director was able to sort out the problem in the nick of time.

It is also important for people at all levels to be able to think and act strategically. This means thinking beyond the boundaries of their own role and understanding how their organization operates. Having broader business acumen is especially important for people in staff roles, such as HR specialists who need to understand their (internal) customers' business so that they can provide a more credible service.

*Consultancy skills*

Many 'support' roles have changed in nature dramatically over the past few years. Gone are the days when IT and Human Resource managers had large teams providing a mainly operational service on demand to the rest of the organization. With the ever-growing emphasis on value-add and the tendency to outsource areas that are seen to add cost rather than value, many support teams have shrunk to small numbers. Those who remain are increasingly in internal consultancy roles, which involves working with line clients to address key strategic and operational requirements. For many internal specialists, repositioning themselves as consultants can be difficult. Consultancy involves not only developing and upgrading expertise, which many people can do, but also selling that expertise, which many people find more difficult. Training in diagnostic skills, intervention and problem-solving skills can be helpful.

## Up-skilling and re-skilling

It is now frequently predicted that school-leavers in Europe can look forward to a lifetime of employment if they are prepared continuously to improve their existing skills and learn others. The average 'credentials' required of young people entering the job market is rising year on year. For many jobs that previously required only high school qualifications at entry level, there is now a minimum requirement of a first or even higher degree. Add to that the frequent technological breakthroughs and their commercial applications, and retraining is likely to be a necessity in most jobs.

*Learning and knowledge skills – the 'meta' skills*

This of course requires a willingness on the part of employees to continue learning, whether through taking part in active learning processes at work or through the acquisition of professional qualifications. People who feel they left learning behind at school are likely to find themselves squeezed by the competition. In the UK there is relatively little uptake by employers of vocational qualifications, such as NVQs, whereas their equivalent in Germany is highly regarded by employers. Already there are some signs that employers are demanding that employees be better qualified, if only so that employers can protect themselves against possible litigation if things go wrong. In the insurance industry in the UK, increased regulation is making some form of professional qualification in all its staff a requirement for organizations to do business.

## An employee's checklist for career self-management

Managing your own career involves using all the skills described in this chapter and more besides. It depends on developing a degree of self-insight, a realistic awareness of strengths and weaknesses, an opportunistic approach to making things happen and a willingness to do this. It means that people need to understand what they are worth on the job market by doing their homework. They have to be prepared to ask for what they want, which may involve developing confidence and negotiation skills. The negotiation skills for new careers include:

- committing to yourself
- taking time to develop a personal strategic plan with a five- to ten-year time-frame
- taking this plan as seriously as you would advise others to take a corporate strategy plan – or more seriously!
- reminding yourself that you deserve this time and attention
- identifying the subject of your negotiation
- setting goals and targets and asking for what you want and need
- developing good networks and managing impressions and visibility
- enjoying the pursuit of your goals and the achievement of success.

# Conclusion

The sad irony is that many organizations are aware of the kinds of skills, attitudes and behaviours which will make a difference, yet they fail to make good use of those skills when they have the opportunity. Very often this is because the organization's culture is not really ready for new ways of doing things and is out of step with what the organization is trying to achieve. This is also often the result of sloppy thinking about what is needed to help the organization achieve its objectives. If innovation, for instance, really is considered essential, this will involve new ways of doing things. This may ruffle some feathers and may be a cost which the organization is not prepared to pay. Similarly, an organization which believes it has the template for success and recruits only entrepreneurs is likely to find itself in a state of anarchy before long.

The end result is that it is the very people the organization needs most who leave. 'New' employees are unlikely to be motivated to stay in an organization which talks 'new' but continues to act in hierarchical ways. Deciding what the organization needs, valuing people's contribution and enabling them to use their skills may result in the 'new' organization getting the best out of its 'new' employees.

# 11  *Should organizations care about career management?*

*Gaining senior management commitment to the retention of high-quality employees by demonstrating the bottom-line benefits of this strategy*

Is there a business case for addressing issues relating to career management? After all, most people recognize that they have responsibility for managing their own career; why should the organization care if people's aspirations have been frustrated? In this chapter we will look at some of the factors that are beginning to be recognized as having a bearing on the viability and success of the organization – factors such as attracting and retaining key employees, motivating core employees (the 'survivors' as well as 'plateaued' employees) to higher levels of performance, the link between morale and bottom-line performance, and the loss of valuable experience. All of these factors relate to employees and how they feel about their careers. Organizations ignore these issues at their peril.

## The return to growth?

For many companies over the past few years economic survival has been the key priority. In many ways, attempts to strip out wastage and improve processes have led organizations to produce short-term savings that have indeed ensured their survival. People issues have taken a back seat to business issues. Typically employees have endured ongoing job insecurity, heavier workloads, flatter structures with reduced promotion prospects and a demand for ever higher levels of performance. So great has been the turbulence of change in many cases that employers may perhaps be forgiven for taking tough business and organizational decisions while neglecting the effect of change on employees. After all, they at least have been the lucky ones who have retained their jobs. At least it is a plausible argument.

There have now been changes in the economic climate, and management gurus such as Stephen Roach (1996), Chief Economist at Morgan Grenfell and previously an advocate of downsizing, admit that their advice to downsize and continuously re-engineer has been carried too far. This perhaps reflects a sea-change in priorities. Downsizing as a strategy is essentially short-term since there are limits to the extent that profitability can appear to improve by cutting the salary bill. If 20 per cent of the workforce is slashed in any one year, the finite life of a company as a going concern is essentially limited.

Downsizing, linked with new working practices brought about by improved processes and flatter structures, can slow the attrition rate but, as a strategy for growth, it has its limitations. Only one-third of organizations taking part in a recent survey claim to have seen improved productivity in the short term as a result of down-sizing. Some job losses are bound to continue as a result of the impact of new technologies and increasingly global competition. However, treating employees as expendable costs is no long-term strategy for survival.

In fact some companies are recognizing the importance of retaining high-quality employees by developing specific retention strategies. Part of the battle to win high-level support for such strategies lies in convincing senior management that the business can suffer if certain people leave. Some senior managers are convinced of the need to address the issue of retention by the calculation of the cost of losing and replacing high-quality personnel. They may become sceptical when there are no imme-diate results from a retention strategy. Pilot schemes to gain the necessary facts and figures can win the support needed to give the strategy a chance to work.

A few companies, like the Rover Group in the UK, have recognized that ongoing uncertainty about jobs creates an atmos-phere which is counterproductive to the organization's strategic ambitions. Rover has understood the importance of committing to their workforce if they hope to see the levels of performance which will make the company successful in the longer term. They have committed to ensuring employment in return for loyalty and high performance from staff. This strategy is starting to pay off in business results and other key indicators. Ironically, there are early signs of several organizations following Rover's example in the UK, while countries elsewhere in the world, such as South Korea which is experiencing the revoking of guaranteed employment, are experiencing widespread strikes.

Where previously survival was often the key priority, now growth is returning. Where ingenuity was to be exercised in containing costs and lowering risk, now innovation and creativity are called for. Where short-term fire-fighting and tactical survival dominated thinking, longer-term strategic perspectives are needed in refocusing organizations on their next phase of development.

## The need for innovation

Different circumstances call for different ways of thinking. Where once strategic thinking was strictly the province of the executive, flatter structures offer both the possibility and the challenge of a wider group of employees contributing their insights and knowledge to the strategic debate. The problem is that few organizations have managed to create the kind of organizational culture that is supportive of innovation and responsibility being exercised at different organizational levels. Hierarchical thinking, which causes people to be limited by their role, is the antithesis of the empowerment culture that is supportive of innovation, creativity, responsibility and sensible risk.

Take the case of the borough treasurer of a local authority located in the leafy south of England. In his early fifties, the treasurer has controlled the purse strings of the authority for the best part of twenty years. His political acumen is such that he has managed to survive councils of different political hues as well as changes in chief executive. So great is his financial acumen that his position seems secure. He plays at espousing the team approach advocated by the new chief executive.

In reality his team knows (as does the entire council staff) that he exercises a vindictive and demanding regime. His large team are all overstretched, though he claims to operate a clean desk policy himself. His approach to managing is delegating or dumping unpleasant tasks, retaining those which maintain his sole access to power, and punishing those who dare to complain or get anything wrong. When the second-tier officers were offered the chance to carry out a strategic project as part of a management development programme he squashed the idea of people being involved in anything which exceeded their job level, even though some of the ideas emanating from the group were potentially very valuable. This was less a case of value add than value subtract.

The main problem is that the chief executive is insecure in his role and actually approves of the borough treasurer's approach. The chief executive also has an autocratic approach, though he is aware of which 'politically correct' notions it is appropriate to appear to espouse. Teamwork is one of these notions. Of course, officers throughout the authority are aware of the real situation and as a result few people dare to challenge the status quo. Many are cynical about prospects for real change.

Hierarchical thinking and behaviour can be difficult to break out of and can sometimes emanate from subordinates who are not used to taking responsibility for decision-making and who want to perpetuate a relationship of dependency on the boss. The challenge for managers wishing to develop more adult–adult relationships is to be able to phase delegation in such a way that employees see for themselves that they are capable of making appropriate decisions. The biggest test for the manager comes when the direct report makes a mistake while they are learning new skills or developing new responsibilities. How the manager reacts will usually have a significant effect beyond the incident itself. The damage caused by a blaming approach can undo any inclination of the direct report to experiment in the future.

## Corporate memory loss

During the process of becoming lean, many organizations have shed numbers of older employees through voluntary and compulsory retirement or redundancy. In some ways this may seem a sensible policy from the organization's point of view, since by removing older workers career bottlenecks lower down the organization may be removed, as well as making often considerable savings on the pay bill since more senior employees are often at the top end of their salary band.

While this may seem a sensible and even humane policy, since many workers are pleased to retire early, many organizations are now realizing that short-term benefits may be devalued by more serious longer-term loss. Several organizations are experiencing a loss, or even a haemorrhage, of experience. Of course, experience alone may not equip an organization for the future, as implied by the oft-quoted remark about a thirty-year career being 'one year's learning repeated thirty times'. However, several organizations are finding that at a time of rapid change, learning from what worked or failed in the past can be helpful in assessing strategies for current market conditions.

Arnold Kransdorff (1995) has found that in many UK organizations the percentage of managers with at least six years' company experience has dropped significantly in recent years. The effect of loss of experienced staff is felt particularly keenly in so-called 'veteran' businesses. Many organizations are therefore having to reinvent the wheel on areas of former expertise since that expertise is no longer available to the company. In fact several big name employers, including DIY chains such as B&Q and supermarkets such as Safeway, are deliberately employing older workers since they consider them to be more versatile, flexible and customer-focused than younger staff. Ironically, these are core skills and attitudes required by many organizations as they move forward.

### Skills outflow

Another effect of becoming lean is the net loss of key skills when employees are given the option of voluntary redundancy. One large company which had a policy of lifetime employment had to revoke this policy in recent years when trading conditions became difficult. Wishing to be as fair as possible to employees who were likely to be angry and disillusioned about the revoking of the policy, the company offered generous redundancy packages for those who opted for voluntary severance. The consequence of this policy was that many key personnel did leave and were promptly snapped up by the competition, in some cases without a single day's unemployment between jobs. The same company has learned the hard way that the core assets of the company are its people, and has spent time and money painfully rebuilding its expertise.

Conversely, enabling people to have rewarding and challenging careers is proving to be a key means of retaining able employees in the City of London. For City high-flyers, levels of pay are high, hours are long and the pace of life can be hectic. There are relatively high turnover levels among certain groups who change organizations and receive much more money, though it would seem that money *per se* may not be as motivating as it might appear, for some people at least. In several recent cases, executives have been offered major salary rises by other companies but they have refused to leave their current employer. In one example, an executive in a merchant bank was offered a 'blank cheque' salary if he was willing to join a new bank in its start-up phase. Although the move would have had many attractions, the executive preferred to stay since he saw that some of the development opportunities he was enjoying were related to the established nature of his employer. He was finding his job too stimulating and satisfying to risk giving it up for something potentially untested.

## Becoming the best employer

In the semiconductor industry there is a sharp recognition of the value of certain employees. More than in many industries, the link between profits and the skilled input of employees is very obvious. A key consideration, therefore, is to hang on to employees who in some cases hold the financial fortunes of their companies in their hands. In several companies, the needs and aspirations of employees are receiving board-level attention. Sun Microsystems in particular is addressing the career development needs of the majority of its employees through a career development process called 'Managing your career in Sun'. The effect of this programme has been to slow down turnover of key staff significantly in the period since the programme started. More details of this programme are given in Chapter 13.

Other organizations in the same sector are aiming to gain the reputation of being the best employer. One, for instance, takes a monthly sounding of all employees worldwide to assess levels of satisfaction with issues such as morale, career development and job satisfaction. The results are discussed at the top level and initiatives are put in place to address those issues that seem to be the biggest causes of concern. Career development is the area receiving the greatest amount of attention. Another organization is trying to change its relatively staid and dull image in this fast-moving sector by seeking to shape thinking in the marketplace. By setting up a form of learning resource centre which brings together leading academics, thinkers, opinion formers and executives from other sectors it hopes to develop an image of thought leadership, which should make it attractive to both investors and potential employees.

### Loyalty

Research carried out by Roffey Park has found that loss of staff loyalty is beginning to be a problem for organizations when it shows through in a lack of commitment by staff. The research found that many people remain loyal to their organizations despite the many changes, although most people felt less loyal to their organizations than before, particularly in the public sector which, in the UK, is undergoing major change under the public sector reforms.

On a small scale, loss of loyalty is starting to be felt in the way in which employees safeguard the interests of the company, or not. We found several examples of the effect of erosion of loyalty. One engineer, for example, whose work required him to travel frequently by plane, had changed his previous practice of arriving at the airport in time to be able to use the long-term car park. He had decided to put his own interests first and now regularly parked in the more expensive short-term car park. Another organization discovered that people were being less rigorous over expenses, often using the most expensive options within the policy. They increased controls and policing measures, which only served to aggravate the situation and reduce employee loyalty further.

A more sinister example involved a case of computer fraud perpetrated by contractors over a period of time. The company had outsourced the skills required to manage the project, so that it took some time before the extent of the fraud was detected. The contractors could not be expected to be loyal to the company, yet a former employee of the company who now worked for the contractors was the person who 'blew the whistle'. The value of employee loyalty should not be underestimated.

While the research found surprisingly high levels of loyalty, in view of the stress and dissatisfaction with their employer reported by employees, it is questionable how sustainable these will be in the long term. The same research found that half of those interviewed were planning to leave their organizations in the near future or were actively looking for jobs. The main source of dissatisfaction for almost all of these people was the lack of good career prospects. People were having to put loyalty to themselves ahead of loyalty to the organization. And this is surely to be expected. After all, how loyal to the organization can people be expected to be who take the career self-management message seriously?

## Motivating the survivors

While attracting and retaining effective staff are important reasons for paying attention to the needs of employees, one of the biggest issues is obtaining high levels of performance from the bulk of employees who remain after downsizing. In any time of change there can be casualties. It is not always recognized that many apparent 'survivors' can be damaged by the change process. Many suffer from a range of destructive feelings which can have a bearing on their performance. Feelings of guilt about retaining a job when others have lost theirs, stress caused by ongoing uncertainty and overwork, frustration at lack of opportunities, fear of sticking one's neck out and being the next to go, make up a depressing cocktail of emotions.

On the other hand, some people can become complacent and unwilling to put into their job the 110 per cent which most jobs seem to require. Others become expert at appearing to be effective even if there is little substantial achievement to show for it. With the proliferation of meetings people often lack the time to follow through on decisions taken. There is ample scope for activity to be valued over results.

Other issues which can affect performance are those sometimes described as the 'plateaued performer syndrome'. This is where employees' careers may have stagnated, or where they have no structural promotion to look forward to. In the case of 'structural' plateauing such as this, the challenge is to motivate these people to higher levels of performance when the manager does not have conventional bait such as promotion at his or her disposal. These issues will be looked at in more detail in Chapters 14 and 15.

Career plateauing can occur at any level when the person stops growing in the job and is less motivated to maintain high levels of performance. Some commentators claim that this can occur to anyone once they have been in a job for more than two years. In the case of 'content' plateauing, one damaging consequence for organizations can be that people become unwilling to embrace change or to develop new working practices. Solutions to plateauing are not easy to find, but if the general principle of 'carrot or stick' is applied, there may be ways of helping people to 'supercharge' their performance through appealing to their intrinsic or extrinsic motivation (the 'carrot'), or forcing people to attempt to change (the 'stick').

Some companies are attempting to shake up attitudes among existing employees by deliberately introducing large numbers of new recruits with specific attitudes and skills. This is a recognition of the effect on profits when the attitudes and performance of the bulk of staff remain set in old ways. Such a policy may, in the short term, be a way of forcing changed attitudes and behaviours amongst older workers who see the newcomers as a threat. If at the same time there are clear corporate messages about the behaviours that are now valued in the organization, there may be some success in bringing about relatively rapid change. However, the policy of recruiting externally in preference to developing needed skills internally may backfire in the longer term if people feel that there are few real opportunities to progress once they become an established staff member. If the only way to progress is by leaving the company, reduced loyalty to the organization is a likely result.

Similarly, some employees do a good job and their performance is not at fault. However, what is required in the job may change and they may be unable or unwilling to change as required. They can gradually become a bottleneck and prevent mobility within a team. Similarly, some people use their expertise or area of responsibility to exercise control over internal customers. When the 'expert' needs special coaxing to provide appropriate levels of internal customer service, more time ends up being spent on organizational issues than on dealing with customers and winning business.

## The challenge of the truly strategic perspective

More and more organizations appear to be acknowledging that there are limits to the extent to which re-engineering processes can produce better business results. The link between sustainable sources of competitive advantage, such as superb customer service and innovative products, and the source of these – people – is becoming apparent. There is an increased interest in appearing to take the needs of employees into account, especially in the area of career development. In the UK, as opposed to countries such as Germany or France where trades unions or workers' councils have a much greater say in issues relating to employee needs, the approach is essentially voluntary. Britain, after all, opted out of the Social Chapter.

A major problem in addressing the issue of 'Should organizations care about career management?' is that there seems to be a disconnection between the apparent recognition by senior management that employee needs should be taken into account and a real understanding of what that implies in terms of policies and priorities. While there is plenty of company rhetoric about the value of employees, the reality as perceived by employees may be very different.

These contradictions become apparent through corporate values statements such as 'Our people are our greatest asset.' However, very few organizations appear to take employee needs into account when making business decisions. There are exceptions, of course. One major company in the semiconductor industry insists on siting factories in areas which are most congenial for staff, since they wish to attract and retain the best people.

Unfortunately, in the majority of cases, people issues only receive attention when they start to cause problems to the business. This often results in hasty, ill-considered or expensive solutions being thrown at the problem. In several of the major oil companies, for instance, the needs of the business require employees to spend long periods overseas on 'difficult' postings. In the past, when such postings often led to promotion, people were willing to make short-term sacrifices in return for bigger gains and the problems relating to dual-career families received little attention. Now, with flatter structures and less promotion available, employees are increasingly refusing such postings. Companies are belatedly having to address the problems of employees since business is likely to suffer unless they do.

The contradictions between intention and reality are also reflected in the way professionals who are responsible for devising policy relating to staff are viewed by senior management. In many organizations 'Personnel' has given way to 'Human Resource management', which implies that the value of employees as resources is recognized. However, the emphasis is often on managing employees as a cost rather than an asset that can and should appreciate in value. Few organizations appear to have an 'investment' perspective with respect to employees and, when times get tough, people-related processes such as training and jobs are the first to be cut.

There is often an implicit hierarchy of importance in which 'front office' is valued more highly than 'back office', 'line' more highly than 'staff' roles. This is reflected in the degree to which decision-making is a joint process, as opposed to being the province of one group, while the other group has simply to implement the decisions made. On the whole, for instance, 'Human Resources' personnel are excluded from the process of making business strategy. It does not help when Human Resources professionals lack understanding of the business needs and face the dilemma of trying to meet short-term needs, when their area of responsibility is essentially long-term. Developing a human resource strategy which supports the business strategy can then appear piecemeal and reactive.

The contradictions also show through in senior management behaviour. Sometimes senior managers cynically exploit corporate messages for their own purposes and cheerfully ignore the needs of staff. Others are genuinely self-deluded and believe that they are team players, for example, when others see them differently. One financial controller, for example, frequently boasted of his participative style of management, while his team saw him as autocratic, temperamental and a bully. The management development professional who dared to point out to him the anomaly found his career to have been severely compromised. The person who has to give feedback to such an individual should be wary!

Of course many senior managers are well-meaning individuals who are genuinely concerned about the welfare and morale of employees. Many companies have introduced various forms of feedback, including 360 degree, as a means of enabling managers to lead more effectively. However, no matter how well-intentioned managers may be, they are actually accountable to a broader range of stakeholders than just customers and staff. Whether these stakeholders are owners, trustees, shareholders, boards, or the community as a whole, most organizations are governed by the means of financing their activities. In many cases, these are pension funds that are managed by people whose key accountability is to secure the best returns. Allegiance to, and support of, an organization's long-term business strategy is not likely to be a pension fund manager's priority, especially if investment strategies appear to reduce dividends.

To the extent that they are in business at all, most organizations are affected by the vicissitudes of the money markets. With the exception of some major multinationals, who are perhaps able to create financial trends rather than merely follow them, most organizations find themselves unable to take a long-term perspective or to plough back profits into creating some slack in the organization since the money market perspective is essentially short-term. And human resource development requires an essentially long-term perspective.

## Does caring about employees make a difference to the bottom line?

How can you tell when something makes a difference? A difference implies a change from one thing to another. In travel terms this can involve knowing where you are starting from, where you are aiming to go and what you will look for on the way to check that you are on the right route. In business strategy terms it involves aiming to achieve a particular business vision, understanding your starting point in terms of resources and constraints and planning a strategy to achieve the vision. The measures or metrics which are set at the outset are intended to guide progress toward the vision.

Given the financial perspective which dominates most decision-making in organizations, it is understandable that 'hard' measures such as the impact on the bottom-line are often taken into account much more than the 'soft' measures such as employee morale. Measures are often seen by employees as a management control rather than an enabling tool. So great has been the emphasis on measures in recent times that the phrase 'if you can't measure it, you can't manage it' will be familiar to most readers. The corollary of that is that perhaps managers only consciously manage the things they can measure and underestimate the things which may produce the real results the organization is looking for.

Very often 'soft' measures are not even set, so there is little evidence that people-related activities make a difference, even when they do. As such they are then easy to discount. Even where employee soundings are taken through opinion surveys and turnover statistics, little use is made of them in terms of setting targets relating to improving morale, for example. Measures focus the mind on what is seen to be important. The lack of measures on areas such as career development and job satisfaction may mean that the importance of these issues to morale, performance, productivity and ultimately profits is understood only intuitively. Without the data, there is no 'proof', and investment decisions are rarely taken from a 'hearts and minds' perspective, except by rather visionary leaders who have the courage of their convictions. In these areas above all, evidence is often easiest to collect retrospectively, when the damage has been done.

Where organizations have attempted to set 'soft' measures they are better able to assess the impact on the bottom-line of volatile and fragile employee morale. One organization that has established the link between employee morale, customer service and business results is London Underground (Holbeche, 1994). Six-monthly soundings are taken on a Key Performance Indicator on employee satisfaction. In business planning, a value is placed on a one point improvement or decrease in employee satisfaction according to the measure known as the 'Net Passenger Social Benefit'. This is a customer satisfaction measure established with customers. A one point variance is felt to be worth £5 million to the business.

## Conclusion

So is there a business case for attending to career management? Each employer must decide for themselves what they believe. If they need the figures, these are easy to calculate. Lack of career development is the biggest single source of dissatisfaction for many employees. Assuming that people who are dissatisfied with their careers will move on, they must calculate the cost of attracting and recruiting good replacements. They should factor in to the equation the fact that increasingly recruits are expecting development to be part of their package. They also need to take into account the 'opportunity costs' while the employee adjusts to the new organization and the cost of providing support in the form of mentors. They should also recognize that increasingly recruitment is back-firing as a more discriminating workforce is requiring that the place they work fits with their own values. If the organization does not match up to expectations, the new recruit often leaves.

The real case lies not so much in cost as in opportunity, for which figures are only available retrospectively. Good career management can produce the multi-skilled, valuable contributors that the organization needs in order to build for the future. It is part of the payback to loyal and committed employees who are the organization's best asset in an increasingly competitive world. Organizations who recognize this are already doing something about it and trying to become the 'best employer' in their field. The best employer looks after the interest of its employees.

*Developing commitment to the organization from high-quality employees and to employees from the organization*

In this chapter we will look at some of the effects of change on the career aspirations and expectations of employees. After tracing some of the broad trends in organizations we will explore the question: Whose responsibility is career development?

## Economic stability – 1950s to 1980s

In the period from the end of the Second World War until about the mid-1980s, Europe saw the return of relative prosperity together with the growth of major corporations and the prospect of long-term employment for the majority of people who wanted a job. Large organizations in particular have had mainly paternalistic policies of employment and career management, and to a large extent it is understandable that many employees entering the job market in the 1950s and 1960s could anticipate employment and career progression within a single company. While career development and job security were considered to relate largely to white-collar jobs, relative affluence and buoyant job markets meant that most people could anticipate a lifetime of employment.

Many people indeed took the view that the company would look after them. Few UK organizations went as far as was common in post-war Japan, where the company often became the hub of the local community, providing schooling, education and healthcare for employees and their families. Nevertheless, the clear policies and processes relating to progression, such as promotion boards in the civil service, encouraged people to believe that the organization was responsible for managing their career. All that employees had to do was to perform well and learn how to put themselves in the best position for promotion, and all would be well.

Nor were such practices confined to Europe – they seem to have been prevalent throughout the developed world. In the US the phenomenon of the 'company man' who was intensely loyal to the powerful organization, and who would receive status and money through promotion up the company hierarchy, was seen as the approved model of achieving, other than being a highly successful entrepreneur. So great was the stereotyping of behaviour of people climbing the corporate ladder that it was parodied in novels such as *Stepford Wives* (Levin, 1991).

## The old 'psychological contract' – job security and vertical promotion

The system seemed to work in the interests both of organizations and employees. The organization obtained what it saw as the best people for more senior roles while employees at best would see themselves as having been fairly treated even if they did not achieve promotion. At the very least, employment would be guaranteed as long as the employee continued to perform. The so-called 'psychological contract' on which these assumptions were based was an unspoken agreement between employer and employee based on mutual interest. From the employee's point of view, it went something like this:

> In return for my loyalty and hard work I expect long-term employment with this organization and to be considered for promotion up a vertical hierarchy as long as I am doing my job well.

Of course, in practice promotion was not available to every employee, but there was nevertheless an assumption of fairness and that doing a good job should be enough to ensure that rewards came along. As long as times were economically buoyant and there was business growth there was usually enough potential for promotion within a business to disguise the fact that not everybody would reach the top of the organization or anywhere near it. Job titles were usually indicative of status and understood outside the organization. Becoming a manager or director was 'something to tell the mother-in-law'. By the time employees neared middle age their career growth had usually stopped, but financial rewards linked to seniority cushioned disappointment about being passed over for promotions.

### Vertical structures

From the organization's point of view the contract worked well too. Typically they organized themselves along lines of maximum stability and order, enabling them in theory to plan for the future based on known resources. Loyalty amongst employees was therefore required and, with few exceptions, people choosing to leave an organization would be treated as deserters and judged unreliable. Most large organizations organized themselves on functional lines, often with large corporate headquarters wielding power over operations. Promotion tended to be up functional 'chimneys' or 'silos' in which unspoken promotion criteria involved pleasing the boss.

Such structures seemed appropriate in a seller's market in which the organization could rely on incremental growth year on year. Customers were often seen by such organizations as a regrettable necessity whose redeeming feature was their good sense in buying the product. When customers were keen to buy, it was tempting to adopt a mentality of providing goods rather than selling.

## Times of change – 1980s to the present

The drawbacks to such systems of organization became more apparent when economic turbulence started to challenge corporate strategies. At a time when flexibility, rapid response and the ability to make maximum use of market information were critical to survival, many organizations found themselves bogged down in bureaucratic procedures, interfunctional power games and wrangling, and lack of real customer information.

Coinciding with recessionary times, the increasing selectiveness of customers was shifting power in the marketplace from suppliers to customers. Customer loyalty could no longer be guaranteed and technical excellence alone was insufficient to maintain market lead. Increasingly customer service was becoming critical to economic survival and many organizations found that their structures had tended to focus employees' attention internally – on pleasing the boss – rather than on meeting customer needs.

Customers started to vote with their feet and many organizations found that their corporate complacency and arrogance made it difficult to see the need for change until it was too late.

Even corporate giants like IBM, which had prided itself on a lifetime employment policy, found that by the early 1990s market conditions were such that change was inevitable. They began a process of downsizing which many other organizations had embarked upon several years earlier. In the 1980s, a wave of management gurus produced recommendations for change in both business strategies and organizational development. Rather than diversify, many organizations started to concentrate on their core business and to outsource activities which were seen to be peripheral to this. Size was no longer seen to be a good thing, and managers in many organizations started to describe the effort of introducing change in terms reminiscent of trying to change the direction of a supertanker in a minefield.

## Quality

Approaches such as Benchmarking and Total Quality Management, together with Process Mapping and Business Process Re-engineering, aimed to identify best practice, streamline the flow of work and increase efficiency and effectiveness. Awards for Quality started to be seen as commercially desirable, and many organizations aspired to the Baldridge award, ISO 9000, as a means of enhancing their reputation. The monolithic organization divided along functional lines was increasingly inappropriate to the effort to achieve greater flexibility and efficiency. Experiments in organizational structures became commonplace, with matrix organization structures, reduced central headquarters, regionalization, centralization and other pendulum swings in organization.

## The customer service revolution

Quality approaches tended to raise organizational awareness of customer needs since the processes targeted for mapping or re-engineering usually start and finish with the customer. The increased attention to the needs of the customer led to an awareness of the internal customer concept. Henceforth departments or functions should no longer see themselves as being in competition but should operate quality processes on a customer–supplier basis. Various initiatives, such as customer service training, were widely introduced and were claimed to have produced appropriate attitudes. British Airways, for instance, put staff through 'Putting People First', a training programme which helped raise awareness of what was involved in good customer service, and many other organizations used similar approaches.

## Flatter structures

In tandem with quality processes and increased customer focus, it became apparent in many organizations that the dominance of a vertical hierarchy, with its concentration of decision-making at or near the top of the organization, was increasingly getting in the way of business success rather than supporting it. The tendency in vertical structures for the line of command to have clearly demarcated levels of decision-making and accountability that were known to all began to backfire.

This became apparent when front-line or customer-facing staff were unable to put their training to good use and use their initiative to service customer needs since they usually required authorization from higher up. The dominant belief on which these checking practices were based was lack of trust in those below to make sensible decisions. How could they, after all, since the information to which they had access was restricted to what was considered appropriate to their level? Many organizations found that 'management' had become a system of 'checkers checking checkers' with little value added by each level.

One of the commonest responses to this was the introduction of flatter structures in parts or throughout organizations, achieved by removing several layers of the hierarchy. Research carried out by Roffey Park in 1994 found that 95 per cent of organizations had undertaken delayering in the previous three years or were intending to do so. Whilst the trend was in practice patchy, with some organizations reintroducing layers, usually at the top, almost as soon as they had delayered, nevertheless many organizations claim to have flattened their structures and intend to keep them 'flat'. The 'flat' structure sometimes has as many as eight layers but represents fewer layers than before restructuring. The average number of layers from front-line staff to managing director is often four.

## The rhetoric of empowerment

Flatter structures make sound sense in theory since they should make cross-business teamwork easier. The logic of teamwork is that better results are produced by a team than by a range of individual contributors working independently of each other. Similarly, flatter structures should enable employees to make decisions at the level where the decisions are needed, often at the customer interface. 'Empowerment' of people at every level is the obvious implication of having fewer management layers. If decision-making of every sort continued to be concentrated in the hands of a decreased band of executives, organizational processes would grind to a halt, or so the logic goes.

Similarly, while flatter structures reduce the number of vertical promotion opportunities, this only reflects what was true for most people anyway. In theory, increased challenge and opportunities to broaden skills and experience should prove satisfying to most people. People can no longer expect a job for life. Promotion is a thing of the past. Job titles and other obvious forms of status symbol should become an irrelevance, or so it is argued.

Of course, the reality of flatter structures is somewhat different, as we saw in Chapter 2. Some of the biggest issues lie in the area of career development and the frustration caused by lack of promotion and the wide gaps between levels. This is made worse when poor management adds to the pressures experienced by employees. Job insecurity compounds the problems.

These issues hit deep at the British psyche. In the past, and still today, people have derived status and security from being employed, especially in an organization with a good reputation, and from having a job title which implied seniority. The stigma of being unemployed or being made redundant has largely evaporated because this experience is so widespread these days. Nevertheless, attempts to eliminate status inside an organization, such as by removing job titles, are often not understood by the outside world. Clients still want to deal with the 'top' person. Many organizations are addressing this issue by eliminating titles for internal purposes or by using ambiguous terms such as 'head of ...', while using conventional titles such as 'manager', 'director', etc. on business cards.

Even when employees are willing to adjust their career expectations to the flatter structures and consider sideways moves rather vertical promotion, their adjustment to the new career concept can be rudely arrested by mixed messages sent out by the organization.

## Mixed message 1: 'Manage your own career'?

During the last decade downsizing and a host of organizational restructurings have fundamentally challenged the old psychological contract. Few people these days believe that a job is for life. Flatter structures in particular have challenged the idea that career development is 'onwards and upwards'. The idea that the organization will look after career development seems fanciful. So what, if anything, has replaced these ideas?

Many organizations have discovered that conventional career planning has not worked well in the past few years. Career planning based on a stable state and employee loyalty seems inappropriate. In some cases, organizations have wished to be honest with their employees and encourage them to take more responsibility for managing their own careers by openly asserting that succession plans have failed. Others simply state that employees are responsible for managing their own careers and relieve themselves of any responsibility towards employees with respect to this. Of course, in a situation where the employer has plenty of skilled staff from whom to draw for a limited number of promotions, this message effectively absolves the organization from any responsibility for planning and places all the onus firmly on employees.

The trouble is that few employees seem to be taking this message to heart. Taking responsibility for managing your career can be extremely threatening to people who may be part way through what seemed an assured career path. Particularly for people who were attracted to occupations such as banking or the civil service because of the job security and career development implied in these once most stable of institutions, the prospect of contemplating a change of occupation, self-employment or a highly competitive 'dog eat dog' approach to promotions can seem threatening.

The careers playing-field may be very uneven indeed for those people who have perhaps spent twenty years or more with one employer, where they have built up considerable expertise, but whose appeal on the job market may be limited precisely because their experience is limited to one employer. Similarly, people who have built up pensionable service with one employer can incur severe financial penalties when changing pension schemes on changing jobs. Only those whose skills and desirability to prospective employers put them in a strong negotiating position are able to avoid losing out financially. Telling people that they are responsible for managing their career in such circumstances often appears to be an abandonment of loyalty towards staff, unless the employer is prepared to help employees see how they might best do this.

The career self-management message seems out of kilter with support systems in the broader infrastructure of society. For people to be able to manage a career which will increasingly include changing employers, periods of self-employment and various forms of flexible working such as contract work or tele-working, true independence and responsibility will come from having financial security and good health provision.

On the health front, recent changes in the management and funding of the National Health Service in the UK have encouraged people to be more, not less, dependent on private health insurance, which is usually provided by an employer. Job flexibility is still frowned upon by financial institutions when people apply for mortgages. People who opt for self-employment or who are on fixed-term contracts find getting a mortgage difficult. For many people the option of self-employment becomes too risky to be seriously contemplated because long-term security seems bound up with employment. This encourages a degree of dependency on the employer which the 'manage your own career' message does not take into account.

In the third stage of the Roffey Park research into Career Development in Flatter Structures (1997), we explored the extent to which employees in organizations that had delayered in the previous three years were beginning to take responsibility for developing their own careers. One of the areas that we probed was the extent to which people were making financial provision for themselves other than through their company pension scheme. We were working on the basis that since long-term employment with a single employer is increasingly unlikely, potential career mobility is likely to be limited unless people have made provision for their long-term financial security independently from their pension scheme.

We found that the vast majority of our respondents (85 per cent) had made no financial or healthcare provision for themselves or their families other than through company schemes. Only those who were most seriously dissatisfied with their jobs were considering making provision for themselves. This perhaps suggests that the implications of the message 'manage your own career' are not percolating through.

So if organizations are encouraging people to manage their career, what form of career and type of 'contract' might be emerging between employers and employees? What might each party expect to put into such a contract, and what benefits will each derive? Will the contract have benefits for both or continue to appear somewhat one-sided, as it does at the moment? In which case, as job mobility returns, how likely is it that employers who appear to have abandoned their employees will hang on to their best employees?

## The new psychological contract – employability and sideways development?

Whereas the old contract was based on job security, the emerging contract is based on the nearest alternative – employability. While some organizations take the view that they do not wish to train up employees so that they can leave and go to the opposition, more and more employees seem to be demanding opportunities to learn new skills and become better qualified. It would be short-sighted indeed for employers to insist on employees acquiring skills for use within the company, but not qualifications which might make them more employable elsewhere.

Organizational changes have profoundly reinforced the idea that employees must consider their employment options since nothing is guaranteed. More and more people are looking to enhance their curriculum vitae by acquiring qualifications. In some ways this can benefit the current employer. Sponsoring a key employee to do an MBA may retain that person in the organization for a year or two. Similarly, many management and professional training programmes now include a practical element which involves working on a work-based issue. Where this learning is captured and valued within the organization, the benefits can be extensive. The difficulty is that in many cases the learning acquired through the person doing the qualification is ignored or undervalued within the organization, adding to the frustration of the employee.

Though many employers are sceptical of the value of National Vocational Qualifications and Continuous Professional Development, the pressure for continuous upgrading of skills is starting to be felt from both the government and professional bodies. Similarly, in some sectors, such as the insurance industry, increased regulation has made qualifications an entry requirement to trade. As a result many employers find themselves, whether they like it or not, sponsoring employees as they try to upgrade their qualifications to the appropriate level.

Research among headhunters suggests that investing in people's development is not optional. Potential recruits are becoming much more demanding of development packages when they are considering job offers. Many job candidates are considering how each job might help them in their longer-term career development rather than committing to a new organization for ever.

For many people, employability lies in broadening their skills and experience and becoming generalists instead of functional specialists. This reflects the trend towards multi-skilling which many organizations have encouraged amongst their 'core' workforce. In the Roffey Park research we found that senior managers were more likely to consider a generalist cross-business route while more junior people were anticipating developing their functional or technical specialisms. The British Civil Service, which has for decades encouraged generalism by posting people to different departments, is now supporting people who want to develop specialist skills such as personnel responsibilities and qualifications. This is in recognition of the fact that, with public sector reforms, many people will have to contemplate becoming employable on the open job market.

### Lateral moves

So if employability replaces job security, what replaces vertical promotion? Promotion was often the external sign of progress, often bringing with it greater responsibility, visibility, status and financial rewards. Promotion ideally occurred just before the point when an employee had outgrown their job and while they were still learning and contributing. If vertical advancement routes are blocked, people are still going to want to find ways of moving forward. Logic suggests that sideways moves may be the obvious organizational routes to enable people to feel they are making progress.

Roffey Park research suggests that, for a time at least, people do find lateral moves or the expansion of their own role satisfying. When we re-surveyed a group of 200 people in 1996, two years after our original survey, we found that, of the people who still had a job (65 per cent), there was a group of people whose jobs had grown, although they were at the same organizational level as in 1994. In some cases they had moved laterally and in almost every case they had taken on greater responsibility. These were the people who considered themselves to be enjoying career development and who were least likely to be actively looking for other jobs outside the organization.

However, within the same survey findings were indications of possible limitations in considering lateral moves as the solution to lack of vertical promotion. First is the fact that vertical promotion is clearly still taking place. While many organizations claim to have flat structures, these are frequently on paper only. The structures are often operating in a multi-layered way made ambiguous by obscure job titles and broad banding. Our survey found that nearly a quarter of our respondents had been promoted in the course of the previous two years. Clearly people who accepted the message that lateral promotion was the only way to progress might feel cheated in the long term.

## Difficulties with lateral moves

There can be logistical and other difficulties in making lateral moves happen. Even people who are only too keen to make a sideways move find it difficult to do so for a host of reasons. Typically there is no formal mechanism for facilitating such moves. Consequently, arrangements have to be made through existing contacts or where one manager accepts a member of another team as a favour. Often managers are unwilling to release a good performer for a sideways move, especially if there is unlikely to be a replacement for that person.

Sometimes people would like to make a move but there is a real stigma attached to moving sideways. In vertical organization structures, sideways moves were often seen as either a sign of failure – a last chance to prove yourself – or were part of a clear career path for future general managers. Though structures are flatter, old attitudes may still remain. Some organizations are trying to address this by deliberately repositioning sideways moves as advancement. People who make these moves are given publicity in company newsletters, gain access to senior managers and in other ways are treated as heroes. Other companies are incentivizing lateral moves by making modest payments to counterbalance the inevitable loss of performance which takes place while the person is learning the new job. Other ways of helping people to develop laterally will be explored in later chapters.

Lateral moves may never prove acceptable to some employees for various reasons. Some people do not wish to move out of their area of specialism. The person who has become the company expert on something is often unwilling to abandon the status and, in some cases, power related to being the expert. Moving to another department or role would cause them to lose face and credibility in their own eyes. At the same time they can cause career bottlenecks to others over time or may become set in their ways.

It might be argued that rather than becoming more generalist, some people have greater contributions to make as specialists. They may find career development through enhancing their own reputation and that of their employer by an increasingly outward-facing role. Speaking at conferences or becoming visible within their professional body may offer a sense of advancement and at the same time ensure that the person remains in touch with the latest thinking. These and other forms of job enrichment may be highly motivating for individuals who are prepared to abandon conventional ideas about career development.

### Mixed message 2: 'Fast-track' schemes

Another issue is the reintroduction of 'fast-track' schemes for graduates or high-flyers. In the past few years many organizations cut down the numbers of graduates they recruited but have recently stepped up the numbers in preparation for growth. In one major retailer in the UK, people who entered the company on the last graduate entry scheme are in their late twenties. They now find themselves on the same organizational level as the new recruits who are being assigned mentors and other opportunities for rapid development. Some of the older graduates feel that the company has exploited them by encouraging them to accept development at the same level and will pass them over in favour of younger people.

When organizations are recruiting people for such schemes, there is an understandable tendency to imply that rapid progression is possible. Some companies are actually marketing themselves to undergraduates on the basis that they have well-established career planning and can offer an exciting career with vertical promotion. In the rare cases where this is the case companies are able to meet the expectations of the people who join them. Where, as is more commonly the case, rapid advancement is not possible, graduates are left feeling disillusioned and more often than not leave at the earliest opportunity. At the very least, managing expectations is a challenge in such circumstances.

*Avoiding raised expectations*

Some companies are refusing to promise things which they may not be able to deliver, even though they may miss out on some of the best qualified recruits, who may be attracted to the idea of clear career paths. Some are in fact pre-empting the 'milk-round' altogether by identifying recruits early on and sponsoring their studies, for instance. Others are successfully communicating their organization's values and realistic career opportunities to potential recruits to ensure that there is a good 'fit' at values level between the individual and what the organization holds dear. This seems to link with research carried out by several headhunters who have noticed a definite trend towards recruits being clearer about their own values and wishing to feel comfortable with the ethos of their organization.

# Managing (great) expectations

Whatever the actual career routes open to people, it seems that many people have still not come to terms with the fact that the world has changed. Many still aspire to vertical promotion and job security and expect the organization to look after them. In many cases these are unrealistic expectations. Some organizations are trying to help people get a more pragmatic view of career development by offering them the chance to take part in personal development or career planning workshops that allow people to take stock of the situation in their organization. Usually people are encouraged to take a realistic look at their strengths and weaknesses against possible options where these are known. Sometimes this involves looking at the new skills or competencies which the organization appears to value and helping people understand how they can acquire these.

Just as importantly, personal development processes involve helping people to understand better what is important to them and what motivates them. The emphasis is usually on helping people achieve more satisfaction of these values in the here and now. So if someone really aspires to promotion, for instance, they are encouraged to understand what promotion means to them, such as more money, greater responsibility, visibility, influence, etc. While not all of these things are possible in the current role, some may be, and the individual is helped to take the initiative in growing their role in the direction that may enhance their job satisfaction as well as their effectiveness.

*Status*

Status remains a sensitive issue for many people. In some cases, organizations are encouraging people to gain status in other ways than through promotion. Examples include being involved in important projects, achieving key targets and winning awards such as for outstanding customer service. In others, status symbols such as company cars are available to a wider group of employees than in the old structure. So a junior employee can be provided with a company car (usually contributing financially for the privilege) and end up driving a smarter car than the managing director. In some cases, people are allowed to choose their own job title. This led someone working for a major pharmaceutical company to describe himself as the 'company intellectual'!

In some organizations, there has been an attempt made to eliminate all external trappings of status, such as providing managers with offices, car parking spaces and other privileges. Perhaps the need to distinguish rank is such a strong part of organizational culture that it is not likely to be eliminated so easily. In one financial services organization, titles were abolished for internal purposes. Managers found a way of signalling rank in a way reminiscent of the armed forces. Rather than wearing uniforms denoting their rank, managers started to wear ties of particular colours denoting their status! For many people the route to social and personal success still lies in advancement to positions of seniority and respect. The broader shift in society's definition of success is maybe beginning, but we are perhaps in a period of transition between displaying our value through what we do and our value speaking for itself through who we are. In the meantime, many people feel that describing themselves as 'team leader' rather than 'manager' does not impress mother-in-law.

## The new 'contract' in practice

What does seem to be happening is that more and more employees are starting to say that 'enough is enough'. In recent years, changes have forced people to take stock of what matters, and frequently they are coming to the conclusion that there are more important things in life than the ongoing pressures and lack of satisfaction. Increasingly key employees are voting with their feet and, as growth returns, this trend is set to continue. In this case, the power balance in the psychological contract will swing away from employers (as is already the case in the semiconductor industry) towards employees, and employers who are already making moves in the direction of meeting employee needs are bound to be at an advantage over those who discount them.

So even if the new psychological contract has yet to be crystallized, there are some clear signs about what each party to the contract seems to be asking of the other. Employers seem to be expecting that people will:

- take responsibility for managing their own career
- be adaptable and willing to learn new skills and work processes
- be loyal and committed
- be dispensable when they are surplus to requirements.

From the employee's point of view, the main components seem to be:

> If I accept that my employer cannot guarantee me a job for life, I expect to become more employable in exchange for job security. If I accept that career development is my responsibility, I expect my organization to support me with this in return for my loyalty. If I accept that career development is likely to be at the same level, I expect my enhanced skills and contribution to be recognized and appropriately rewarded. If the organization wishes me to become multi-skilled, I must be supported rather than penalized as I learn.

From the organization's point of view, the new psychological contract is likely to prove far more challenging to implement than the old one. The essence of such a contract lies in building common ground between organizations and employees in today's insecure employment environment. If organizations are going to be able to cope with an increasingly adversarial competitive environment, they will need their employees working with them rather than against them. A psychological contract which is based on power struggles and cynical contempt of the other party is bound to cause difficulties. A contract which attempts to fairly reconcile mutual interests is likely to be the foundation for a prosperous future. Any employer who goes beyond the basic contract, by offering employees, for example, the opportunity for improved job satisfaction, is likely to receive greater commitment in return.

# 13 *Career management – what works in the new structures?*

*Providing a framework to enable employees to map their own future within the organization*

One of the main areas of difficulty for organizations is planning for the resourcing of key positions over time. Career management involves a range of formal and informal planning and implementation processes which are used for the purposes of employee 'stock-taking', talent spotting, grooming for key positions, executive development and resourcing. They are also applied for succession planning purposes and to ensure the retention of key personnel. In this chapter we will be considering what forms of career planning may be appropriate to lean organizations. We will start by looking at conventional career management.

## Conventional career management

Many large organizations use sophisticated formal career management processes that attract potential recruits with the implicit promise of plenty of career development opportunities. Nestlé, for instance, has maintained careful succession planning linked to a hierarchical structure despite structural changes affecting their competitors. Organized career management is most frequently carried out in large organizations. International organizations, for instance, usually have dedicated teams looking after the interests of people on expatriate assignments.

Career management is a way that the organization looks after its longer-term staffing interests. Not surprisingly, perhaps, career planning is usually predominantly geared to the needs of the organization, with individual aspirations addressed where possible. In organizations that offer clear career ladders, employees will often tolerate difficult or unpleasant assignments for a time if they believe the experience is part of a carefully planned career path which will lead to promotion. However, even when this is the case, the 'development assignment' can backfire and the employee may leave the organization.

At the other extreme, some forms of career planning are built largely round the employees' interests. Some organizations, especially small 'people'-based companies such as consultancies and others where having a 'star' performer is vital to the business, gear their career planning activities to the needs of the star performers in question. This can cause problems for the organization in that planning and resourcing new areas of business is difficult when the business is built around the needs of the people in place. Presumably, a balance between these two approaches is called for, with a bias towards the organization's interests since it is greater than the sum of its parts.

## The elements of career management

Career management involves developing and implementing processes which allow organizational resourcing needs to be met through the appropriate recruitment and development of individuals. Formal career management tends to take place mainly in large centralized organizations and is usually the responsibility of Human Resource professionals in partnership with line management. Career management takes care of organizational requirements through recruitment processes, the assessment of potential, succession planning, fast-track schemes, executive development, manpower planning, specific assignments, expatriate policies, etc. In an ideal world, these processes also allow individual career development needs to be met. Career management also encompasses career planning for individuals. This often involves personal growth processes, career counselling, psychometric profiling, mentoring, skills portfolios and learning logs, etc.

Career planning usually involves analysing the organization's strategic plan, together with its operational plans, and working out the requirements of the plan in terms of changes in the number of types of certain jobs, changes in the knowledge, skills and attitudes required and areas of the organization which may no longer be required. From this the implications for career management can be drawn. For this process to be carried out effectively, a large amount of up-to-date data is required on business needs, the organizational structure and personnel. From the analysis of the data in relation to the strategic plan, some conclusions can be drawn about areas of staffing that need to be strengthened.

### Advantages of centralized career management

One advantage of a centralized approach is that when an individual is ready for a move, whether vertically or sideways, pressure can be brought to bear on line managers to release them. A centralized approach also allows for the creation of what Andrew Mayo (1991) describes as career 'bridges' that enable people to move from one function or type of role to another as part of their broader development. Where personnel data are up-to-date and used actively, career management can result in the effective development of staff in whole areas of business as well as ensuring that future executives are making appropriate progress through the organization. Some form of succession planning is important if organizations are going to minimize the need to 'buy in' skilled staff for certain roles, having failed to recognize and develop the potential of their own staff.

### Difficulties of conventional career management

• *Gathering data*

While, on the surface of things, career management should be relatively straightforward, the reality is often very different, even in stable times. Obtaining data about people is notoriously difficult. Sources include appraisal data, which can be misleading and incomplete. In large organizations, particularly those arranged along decentralized, federal lines, each operation may develop its own system for describing skills and recording data. Synthesizing data centrally then proves difficult, especially since it is often out of date.

• *Data can be out of date*

Assessments of potential are another area of difficulty in this respect. People who are labelled 'high-flyers' at the start of their careers often retain the label despite mediocre performance or an actual lack of real aptitude for a senior position. As with any human process, obtaining objective data about people can be very difficult. Typically, joint career planning processes take place between line managers and employees during appraisals and sometimes during specific development discussions. Line managers vary tremendously in their ability to assess performance and potential. Even assessment centres, though relatively less subjective, tend to produce firm judgements on individuals which are perhaps valid only for a time. Assessments of individuals tend to stick.

• *'Secret' processes*

In conventional career planning many related processes are often 'secret'. In one company, an annual review and assessment process of the top third of the management population is known as the 'Management Development Review' (MDR). In MDR meetings, line managers and personnel staff review the performance levels, potential, and readiness for a move of members of the target population. The people under discussion are not party to the conversations. Information taken into account can include performance ratings (sometimes offset where it is known that the person's line manager has a specific bias), general impressions and hearsay. Though hardly a 'scientific' approach, decisions taken can fundamentally shape individual career opportunities within the business. The dominant philosophy behind such processes is that the organization manages individual careers.

*The effect of change*

Of course, few organizations could have foreseen some of the huge competitive pressures that have produced major strategy shifts and structural changes such as decentralization and delayering. Flatter structures in particular have had a significant effect on career management systems such as succession planning. In cases where management layers have been removed, the jobs for which 'successors' have been groomed have disappeared. Similarly, the increasing trend towards a 'core' workforce which is multi-skilled and flexible forces the issue about which people are really key to the organization's future.

• *Succession planning is difficult*

So great have been the changes that in many cases conventional succession planning has not worked. In some cases, the needs of the business have changed so much that potential 'successors' prove not to have the relevant skillset. Career succession plans that apply to a small minority of employees are becoming less appropriate.

Nevertheless, organizations perceive the need for resource and development plans. Some organizations have responded to global competition by developing a federal structure with semi-autonomous units operating worldwide. Such structures tend to rely on voluntary sharing of information about people across business units. This does not always work well. Often line managers are willing to trade skilled employees but there is rarely a systematic way of doing this, resulting in lost opportunities all round. For people in the remaining headquarters functions, coordination becomes difficult due to lack of shared information. The increasing frequency of mergers, acquisitions, joint-ventures and other organizational forms adds to the difficulties of devising a coherent career management system which meets organizational and individual needs.

In response to the difficulties of planning, many organizations have abandoned their career management processes altogether and tell employees that they are responsible for managing their careers. The changing psychological contract implies that as employees start to take the career self-management message seriously, especially when their loyalty to the organization has diminished, the implications for the organization can be serious. Similarly, where they exist, career management processes which seem to be only in the organization's interest are unlikely to motivate the majority of staff. Where the organization's needs shift, increasingly the needs of employees must be taken into account.

• *International assignments*

Difficulties relating to career management are compounded in international organizations, which may require employees to spend periods of time overseas in sometimes 'difficult' locations. Whereas in the past international assignments were recognized as a means of furthering careers, with flatter organization structures there is less likelihood that assignments will lead to vertical progression. Indeed, many assignments appear to be longer than in the past and are often offered on local, rather than expatriate, terms. Consequently, individuals may find that they have actually missed out on career opportunities while they are away from their home base and that their international experience is not used by their organization when they return.

Similarly, many European employees are part of dual-career families. In such circumstances, international assignments put considerable strains on the couple, whether the partner gives up their job to accompany the employee or not. In many cases employees now refuse international assignments unless they have considerable career benefits. This trend amongst certain groups of employees is forcing some companies to address the issues seriously, whereas when people are desperate for jobs organizations can apparently afford to ignore employee needs.

## Towards a new form of career management

Of course many organizations have continued to use conventional career planning approaches throughout the recession and are successfully managing to resource positions despite many structural changes. A consistent feature of such organizations is that they have strong centralized approaches, unified policies and a mechanism that works for moving people about. Indeed, few organizations have abandoned their attempts at career planning for the elite altogether, but many are looking for a new form of career planning more suited to their new structures.

### Career Path Appreciation

One of the more interesting tools of conventional career management is known as Career Path Appreciation (CPA). This assumes that employees' career paths can be assessed and mapped out to assist HR professionals to plan development along those paths. The aim is to produce mutual benefit to both employee and employer by ensuring that enough 'stretch' is built into jobs so that employees are neither under- nor overwhelmed.

The CPA is a one-to-one 'guided conversation' (Stamp and Stamp, 1993) which allows the employee to gain additional insight into their own capabilities and into how they are likely to grow in the future. A key area assessed by this approach is individual judgement – an essential ingredient, particularly when organizations are seeking to empower their staff. The emphasis in this process is on achieving employee well-being. However, CPA can appear deterministic since the individual's rate of development may not follow the predicted curve for a number of reasons, including the ever-changing nature of working arrangements.

### Flexible working

The major trend towards flexible working includes variations on the themes of part-time working, fixed-term contracts, job-share arrangements, working from home or teleworking. It has been estimated that by the year 2001, part-time workers, the majority of whom will be women, will account for nearly a third of the whole UK economy. Recent research carried out by Christina Evans at Roffey Park (1997) suggests that people who work part-time are thought to be less ambitious and may therefore not be the subject of much development planning.

Judi Marshall (1989) feels that we need to think about careers in a different way. For many women, balancing family and work demands has required developing alternative career paths. Marshall believes that women's career development tends to follow a less linear route than men's, and may involve more experimentation and periods of standstill. Ironically, the very flexibility and adaptability shown by many women is increasingly called for by organizations, but women's careers may not be benefiting from this since they may be less visible within the organization if they are working part-time.

Career Path Appreciation may be useful when individual development patterns are synchronized with the organizational plan, but Christina Evans believes that both employers and employees may potentially lose out. She calls for organizations to '... create a climate in which individuals are able to develop in line with their own model of success' (Evans, 1997).

### Career counselling

Conventional processes often have the benefit of letting people know that they are valued by their organization. When people believe that they have a future in the company, and they like the sound of the options available to them, they often develop a greater commitment to the organization and wait for the plans to be materialized. The downside of this is that individuals may adopt a reactive approach to their own development since they believe that they will be looked after. The danger of being open about plans is that these may be impossible to fulfil other than in the immediate short term, and disappointment can be extremely demotivating.

In some organizations career planning is so secret that even the subjects of the planning are unaware of it. Of course, the reason may be that organizations do not wish to arouse expectations that may not be fulfilled, but there may be dangers in not sharing career plans with the individuals concerned. When I started conducting research into the careers of high-flyers I asked organization heads to single out exceptional people whom they wanted to retain at all costs. Several of the identified individuals were astonished to be so described since no one had ever indicated that they were so well thought of. One or two were already so dissatisfied that they were contemplating leaving. Ironically, some of the same individuals moved on to other organizations within two years.

One large fast-moving consumer goods (FMCG) organization had a number of career planning processes in place in its separate organizations but there was little cross-fertilization of personnel apart from specific projects. Following a major restructuring worldwide, the organization was better able to assess its human resource needs and in the process of change there were some job losses. The development of new career processes was underpinned by competencies, supported by a new appraisal process and a suite of training programmes related to each competency area. Most challenging was the development of new succession policies which would take the needs of a truly global business into account.

The period of change produced some turnover among people whom the company had identified as having high potential. Although clear career routes had not yet been mapped out, the decision was taken to introduce career counselling for key employees so that the organization could at least understand their needs. This was taken so seriously that members of the board were trained in career counselling and each now has a caseload of 'clients'. The message of value which this conveys to people receiving career counselling is very important in keeping them committed to the organization.

Career counselling is increasingly seen as a strategic element of organization development, rather than being offered only to the privileged few, or to those who are at a point of career transition, including redundancy. It is a means of enabling employees to express their job and developmental interests, and to gain a realistic view of their current competencies and potential and the chance to understand the requirements of different jobs, together with a feel for realistic opportunities. Typical career counselling activities include some or all of the following:

- development centres
- psychological assessment
- career workshops
- one-to-one career conversations
- computer-assisted careers counselling
- career planning courses
- self-help materials
- mentoring.

## Partner development in a consultancy

The UK base of a major international consultancy firm is trying to meet both organizational and employee needs through its career management policies. In the past, career progression was conventionally via a clearly defined hierarchy up to partner level. Most people aspired to being partners. This was partly because when people were recruited they were usually told 'We don't recruit people without the potential to be a partner', and partly because there was no viable alternative route to status, money and other rewards. In recent years, the firm had tried to professionalize its processes for selecting staff for promotion to principal level, the step below partner. In common with many other consultancies, the firm operated an 'up or out' policy by which people who were not considered to have the potential to reach partner would be required to leave to make way for younger people.

However, changes in the nature of the business meant that the loss of personnel with specific expertise at the point of what was potentially their greatest contribution was proving damaging to the business. The firm now needed to retain and motivate employees who knew that they had no prospects of promotion to partner status. The firm had also found that several of the people who did achieve partner status failed to deliver as expected. The assessment processes appeared to identify the right skills, but when in position, new partners' lack of experience proved unhelpful.

Recognizing that the firm needed to safeguard its interests but also take employees' needs into account, the Human Resources team designed a process which seemed to integrate both. It was decided that all prospective candidates for partnership roles would be invited to attend a development centre about two years before they became eligible for consideration for partnership. During the centre, candidates are assessed against competencies required for partnership, including their potential ability to lead the business.

Following the centre, candidates receive feedback and counselling about probable career options. Those who are unlikely to become partners are encouraged to continue to develop their specialist or people management responsibilities. All the centre participants are assigned a mentor from within the business and helped to create a development plan which will allow them to be exposed to the types of experience that will equip them for future roles.

After two years, the smaller number of candidates go through a very focused assessment centre, following which several become partners. There is still a tendency for unsuccessful candidates to leave at this stage, though this is now a much smaller number than before. Development within the company has allowed the firm to ensure high levels of client management, offer a broader portfolio of services, secure appropriate appointments at senior levels and offer a wider range of career opportunities to employees.

### Behavioural criteria

There is an increasing recognition that changes in the competitive environment are likely to be ongoing, even though they cannot be exactly predicted. The implications of ongoing change on the requirements of the workforce, including the kind of leaders that will be needed, are perhaps less easy to deduce. There seems to be broad agreement, however, that many of the key success factors for the future are likely to be behavioural. The elements of skilled behaviour which an organization believes to be important in delivering business goals are often described as 'competencies'.

Competencies can offer a number of advantages in that they can help people to describe effective behaviour in the same language and thus improve communication about performance. It helps when they are simple, owned by the line and reflect what is really needed in the organization as it moves forward. They can be used systematically to provide clarity of focus for assessment of performance, for development, reward and career planning purposes. They can also provide bridges for people at any organizational level who are willing to help themselves to new career opportunities.

According to advertisements for professional, technical and managerial appointments, the areas of competence which organizations are typically looking for include team skills, flexibility, the ability to learn quickly, good communication and project management skills and being customer-focused. People with these skills are also expected to be able to demonstrate good business acumen, no matter where they are placed in the hierarchy. Above all they must be able to tolerate or even thrive on change. Many organizations are moving away from rigid job descriptions with personnel specifications that call for a range of qualities. Increasingly, role descriptions underpinned by competencies and other forms of behavioural criteria are being introduced to provide a framework for recruitment and career management as well as development purposes.

## Helping people to help themselves

New forms of career planning are likely to include practical support for individuals to be able to manage their own careers. At BP, for instance, support is available through a pilot independent helpline to give staff access to confidential career advice (Daly, 1996). David McGill, BP Chemical's head of individual learning and development, believes that intermediary organizations have an important role to play in the career management process. Managers at BP also help people to become less dependent on the organization for guidance by offering 'roadmaps' signposting possible career routes. Many companies are also introducing Personal Development Policies to enable employees justifiably to seek support for development.

## Job rotation in the financial services

In one major financial services organization, the customer services operation numbered nearly 2000 employees distributed across three divisions, the majority in clerical roles. The customer service operation delayered in 1993, removing numbers of gradual steps up the hierarchy from clerical level to manager. In the previous structure, there was very little career movement across the three divisions other than through vertical progression. This meant that people who might have aspired to junior management roles were frustrated and, had it not been for a poor job market, many would have left the organization.

Recognizing the effects of the changes on employee morale and performance, several team leaders, including former managers, formed a working group to see if they could find ways of offering an alternative form of career progression to clerical staff. They first came up with the idea of a form of job rotation which was intended to encourage some mobility, at least in attitudes, among staff. To support the introduction of the job rotation scheme, they devised competencies which were intended to ensure that people could do the jobs to which they were rotated. The team leaders based these competencies on the types of job then carried out, interpreted some of the organizational changes into competencies and identified a set of core competencies for all customer service staff.

One of the problems in experimenting with job rotation and other development opportunities is that employees may be resistant to a job change even though they are dissatisfied where they are. They may see no advantage to themselves or may not believe that they have the skills to do a job in another part of the business. To help break down this confidence barrier, the line managers devised a self-assessment tool based on the competencies, with the help of management development specialists.

This was intended to help people to understand their strengths and weaknesses, what interests and motivates them and in which jobs these needs might be best met. The competencies were also used to profile jobs so that a comprehensive picture emerged of what specialist skills and knowledge were required in certain jobs. The mysteries about barriers between jobs started to disappear. Surprises were in store for some individuals who were able to see for the first time that twenty years' experience in one division does not preclude a move to a different type of job in a different division.

The tool was cleverly devised to help employees gradually to understand that the gaps between their current jobs and their ideal jobs might not be so great. Employees themselves analysed the gaps in terms of knowledge, experience and skills. Team leaders were trained to hold career counselling discussions. In this way, the competency-based scheme started to bring about much greater flexibility and job satisfaction in the operation. Organizational and individual needs were clearly being met.

The rotation scheme started in a small way, with twenty participants from across the operation. It has since become a regular feature of the organization and in most cases, employees find the rotation helpful since they expand their knowledge of the business but are sure of a return to their own job if they want it. The scheme has given rise to other forms of development, including special assignments, project work, and secondment for some employees. The fact that line managers saw the need to address career issues and were able to work as a team on them made a difference to the climate within the operation since it became apparent to staff that organizational values statements about teamwork did produce benefits when acted upon.

## Career management in Sun Microsystems, UK

Some of the most innovative thinking about career management is coming from the computer industry. As an industry, the computer sector is perhaps unusually aware that success is directly linked to high-calibre employees. Employees tend to know their own worth and move around the industry if their needs are not satisfied. In many companies in this sector, employee morale is the subject of board-level attention.

Sun Microsystems is one of the leading providers of network computer solutions. The secret of its success comes from hiring and retaining the right people. A relatively young organization (it was founded in 1982), Sun employs 15 600 people worldwide, of whom around 1500 are employed in the UK. Within this highly competitive marketplace, Sun has seen its attrition rates fall from around 12 per cent in 1990/91 to around 5 per cent in 1996, a figure well below the norm for the industry, despite the introduction of flatter structures. So how has Sun managed to retain and motivate employees?

One element is Sun's enviable reputation for the way it manages its business, which includes the way it manages and develops people. Employees comment that Sun is an organization which is a 'fun place to work; a place where you can learn'. The culture is business-like but informal. The senior management team reinforce cultural values through their own management style. In addition, investing in employees is given a high priority.

Since restructuring in 1992, the European operation consists of four levels between team players and directors, despite its continued business growth. The company does carry out some conventional succession planning relating to a few critical positions and the highest flyers. However, the career management philosophy within Sun recognizes that most employees, especially if they are performing well, are important to the future of the business. Career management should therefore be as open and shared a process as possible, available to a broad cadre of people, with the emphasis on enabling people to fulfil their potential within the company.

One important development has been the introduction of a programme called *Manage Your Career in Sun*. The programme, which is attended on a voluntary basis, has now been attended by around 50 per cent of the workforce in the UK. It was designed to help individuals to help themselves with respect to career development. It aims to help individuals to focus within their current job role, as well as to consider longer-term goals. The programme enables employees to understand their own aspirations and to explore practical ways in which they can achieve them. The point of the programme is not to discuss a range of prescribed future options, but to help individuals become aware of the benefits of continuing discussion about future development needs and aspirations during quarterly appraisal reviews.

The programme seems to be helping people to take responsibility for managing their career, but in a way that is supported openly by the company. It is one of a series of processes that make the career self-management message achievable by most employees. Job rotation is a common feature, and business growth has led to the creation of a number of non-traditional development moves. Employees believe there to be opportunities for moves within related Sun companies because there is evidence that moves are not only possible but actually happen. They know that the way to have opportunities is to be proactive and create them. Line managers play an important role in supporting people as they build up knowledge and experience relating to future job moves.

The fact that status within Sun is not linked to job titles or grades has reinforced the 'can do' culture in which employees know that they can to a large extent create their own opportunities. Sun also believes that the asset known as 'human resource' needs continuous investment and therefore spends approximately 7 per cent of payroll on training and development. Sun supports employees who are obtaining business-related qualifications, providing not only financial assistance but also time off for study as appropriate.

Employee development issues in Sun are not regarded as the sole responsibility of HR but as a joint effort between specialists and line management. A Staff Development Team has been set up to consider organizational development issues such as skills planning for the future needs of the business. Consisting of line and HR representatives from across the European business, the team approach is resulting in a real sense of ownership of future development policy and initiatives.

Helping people to help themselves involves being willing to share information with them. Employees generally feel that they have a good picture of what is going on in the company and how to make things happen. Employee communications are given high priority, with a varied range of media used to encourage two-way participation. In addition to company-wide communications, some departments run their own conferences, which are sometimes used specifically as training events. This combination of a supportive culture, good communications and providing people with the tools they require to manage their own development seems to be paying off for Sun.

## Open job posting

In one UK-based financial services organization, career management processes used to be focused entirely on the organization's needs. A combination of tough competitive factors led to a complete restructuring, including the introduction of flatter structures in 1993. This caused the company to recognize that its previous methods of planning for executive development and resourcing key posts were becoming increasingly inappropriate.

Employees generally knew what career routes were available to them and when they would be eligible for 'career checkpoints', such as being considered for inclusion in the internal 'high-flyer' programme. People were so used to being approached about specific opportunities that few had considered moving out of their area of specialization. Those who did had to overcome obstacles to sideways moves, including the perception that only those who were failing in their current role would contemplate such a move.

The previous emphasis was on developing most people up functional or business hierarchies. However, when crisis struck, the organization was left exposed when it was unable to fill new positions internally as people were too specialized, and at the same time new recruits lacked experience of the business. The time they needed to acquire relevant learning represented lost opportunities for the business.

One response to the situation was a scaling down of formal planning processes and the introduction of electronic job posting, open to all. When the system was first introduced there were a number of problems. As expected, large numbers of 'inappropriate' applications occurred for interesting-sounding jobs. The system was under suspicion by employees who doubted how open and fair it really was. In many cases, there were already candidates lined up for roles and the open posting of the job seemed a mere formality.

The organization attempted to address these issues by introducing a competency-based job and skill profiling system so that each job role could be described in ways which made sense across the business. The appraisal system used the same competencies and a range of initiatives was introduced to help people gain a realistic sense of their own skill levels. These included development centres, personal learning logs and continuous professional development. Increasingly people were able to be more selective about what they applied for, but with a higher chance of success.

At the same time, people were able to see that their experience did not restrict them to the original career route they had been following. Competency profiling led to some surprising moves, with IT specialists moving to Marketing roles, for instance. Both the organization and the individuals seem to benefit from this broadening of skills and experience. The organization also learned that it was important to be honest when there were preferred candidates for positions. In some cases other candidates still managed to win the role rather than the preferred candidate, but at least everyone was aware of what they were up against. In this case, by appearing to take some risks and give up some control of the planning process, and at the same time helping people to be responsible, the company has created more of a partnership approach to career development; this has had a positive impact on morale.

## Personal development portfolios

Once employees start to take career self-management seriously, it is important that they are able to develop the skills and experience which will move them forward. Many organizations, especially those which are aspiring to Investors in People status, are encouraging people to develop skills portfolios. These can then be accredited towards academic or business qualifications if the organization has clarified linkages between in-company training and formal qualifications. NVQs seem to be meeting a mixed response, but some organizations are encouraging all their employees to achieve an NVQ in the relevant professional area, such as retailing.

Skills portfolios are important because they start to build up a sense of progress for the individual which can be very motivating and can increase that person's employability inside and outside the organization. Encouraging people to develop their portfolios without giving them the time to build their skills is contradictory. Organizations like Standard Life are equipping multimedia learning resource centres that make it possible for people to learn at different times. Work-related learning is regarded as a legitimate business activity. Learning linked to longer-term development takes place out of work hours since the facilities are available even at weekends. More information about some of the innovative ways of supporting development at Standard Life can be found in Chapter 15.

### Career banding

Some organizations are encouraging the development of multi-functional and flexible employees by introducing career banding. This approach involves reducing the number of job classifications while expanding the 'band width', or scope and responsibilities of the job. In many cases, organizations are renaming jobs as 'roles' in recognition of the broader remit. In Honda UK, each role is clearly described and has clear boundaries. However, around the boundaries of each role is a 'fuzzy' area which represents an area of development opportunity for personal growth, according to Ken Keir, Director and General Manager, Cars (Figure 13.1).

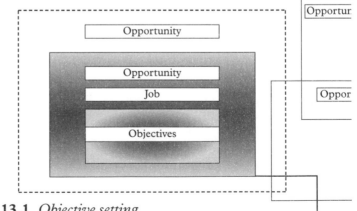

**Figure 13.1** *Objective setting*

Banding produces generic job titles such as 'head of ' and 'team member'. This change of emphasis should allow employees much greater development flexibility than was possible in schemes which gave high status and reward only to those in managerial positions. Banding should therefore help make lateral moves not only possible but desirable. In many organizations, the finely tuned job grading structure works against sideways moves because where the new job is classified at a lower grade than the employee's current role, the lower salary is a direct disincentive to moving. Broader pay bands should allow those pay differences to be 'fudged' so that employees do not lose out in either pay or status.

## Specialist or generalist career routes?

In conventionally structured organizations, the tendency is to be promoted up areas of functional specialism such as engineering or finance. Typically, except in areas where the highly technical nature of the product means that only specialists have the credibility to run the business, the most prestigious roles have usually been managerial. In many cases this has meant that successful specialists have to move into management roles if they wish to progress within the same organization. In the 1996 Roffey Park research we found that the trend towards management careers is still strong. More senior people in organizations tended to talk of developing their career in terms of management responsibilities, compared with more junior people who saw themselves as specialists.

In some cases shifting from a specialist to a managerial role works well. In others, management responsibilities may not be best suited to the individual, who is often obliged to step back from direct involvement in the area of specialization. The classic example is that of an extremely successful salesperson who consistently achieves individual sales targets. When this person is promoted to sales manager and has the challenge of motivating a team of others to achieve the sales, a different set of skills is called for. If the person fails at their new role this can produce a double loss. The individual is unable to contribute in the way the organization needs and at the same time may be unable to return to their area of specialization if their professional knowledge in a fast-moving field is outdated and therefore obsolete.

Some organizations have tried to avoid these difficulties by providing technical ladders as well as managerial ladders. These routes usually allow technical specialists to achieve considerable career development within their function, together with the pay and status usually accorded to managers. The danger is that people who remain within one area of expertise may be unaware of the changing needs of the business. Technical specialists often have a quasi-vocational attachment to their projects and may resist managerial pressure to trim costs or to abandon systems which are not needed by the business. There is considerable scope for misunderstanding between managers and technical specialists about the potential value of certain projects if they do not speak the same (business) language.

Flatter structures call for people who can be business-focused as well as being experts in their fields. In many cases, an understanding of business needs can best be gained by moving into a range of positions around the business. This implies a generalist rather than pure specialist route. Increasingly organizations are looking for employees to be versatile and customer-focused, whatever their specialism.

## Career tracks

The challenge, then, is to create honoured and influential specialists who can play to their technical strengths but who are also business leaders. This may involve a deliberate programme of development, perhaps involving being coached and mentored, so that specialists can acquire a broader business perspective. Training in the skills of internal consultancy can also help. Perhaps talking of career 'ladders' is unhelpful in such circumstances. Career 'tracks' might be more appropriate.

Equally, for those who would welcome the opportunity to develop people management skills, the challenge is to enable people to retain credibility with respect to their technical knowledge so that they can step back into a purely technical role if need be. One large consultancy treats people management and staff development responsibilities as elements of general progression up a largely functional career route. As such, people responsibility is seen as strictly temporary and only one part of the development process. Individual consultants gradually acquire the skills and experience which equip them for larger responsibilities, such as running part of the business as partner. Perhaps those who, because of their career history or the options available to them, have little chance of taking on managerial roles can find outlets for their people development skills by acting as mentors to others.

For people with professional standing, being able to maintain their professional status may be as important as developing their career via the management route. It is important where possible for professional links to be maintained through involvement in selected projects, speaking at conferences or in other ways keeping abreast of the field. Career ladders which rigidly separate job components into either technical or managerial are unhelpful since they force a choice. More imaginative role designs which build in various components may be more satisfying for the individual and more effective for the organization.

# Conclusion

Career planning is perhaps one of the most important and challenging areas for any organization, just as career development often is for individuals. The fact that planning processes during periods of ongoing change are difficult does not remove the need for effort in this direction.

Almost every organization has a direct stake in developing its workforce. Some organizations make their money by buying up businesses and winding them up and selling off assets. Even in these circumstances, a skilled workforce literally adds value to the business. Some organizations prefer to buy in talent when they need it rather than developing their own talent. This may be fine in businesses that do not rely on any loyalty from their staff and are willing to pay high salaries as a means of attracting people. The difficulty in such organizations can be securing any commitment to major change efforts that can produce longer-term benefits to the business.

The development of talent is key to securing the type of knowledge, experience and skills required for an organization to work efficiently and to cope with future challenges. On the whole, most organizations seem to prefer growing their own talent where possible since this offers many advantages. This is where a degree of planning is important.

Conventional processes are only as good as the information they are based on. If that information is incomplete, out of date, biased or poorly managed, the result can be inappropriate resourcing decisions. In many organizations, planning is left to the discretion of individual business units. In flatter structures, the need for people to develop business experience may call for cross-business unit experience. Leaving such moves to the goodwill of interested parties can be a mistake. Someone, somewhere probably needs to be managing information and coordinating moves in the broader interests of the organization.

With flatter structures, career planning may need to encompass a wider group of people than those who were the subject of conventional processes. When promotion opportunities are relatively rare, it is all the more important that the processes for selecting people for promotion appear fair and open. There is no inherent contradiction between 'secret' and 'open' processes; they simply need to be signposted for what they are. The organization is entitled to protect its interests, and this may mean giving privileged development to a few. On the other hand, most organizations recognize that career development has an effect on morale and performance. They tell employees to manage their careers. The more enlightened employers will aim to make it possible for a wider group of people to be able to manage their careers in a way which meets the needs of the individual. The shared nature of more open processes should ensure that both sets of needs are met.

Thus as forms of organization and career continue to evolve we are likely to see a wider range of planning forms and models of career management. A standard solution to the challenge of resourcing for the future may be elusive. Most likely to be effective in the longer term are those processes that are underpinned by a clear sense of what is needed in the organization and clear strategies for developing those skills. These may involve taking an innovative approach to job design and forms of employment and challenging conventional ideas about how work needs to be carried out.

Career development cannot be regarded as an afterthought but must be an integral part of the business strategy. Perhaps the best that an organization can hope for is to gain the reputation of being an excellent employer. When as a result an organization can attract the best candidates and also has a large internal pool from which key positions can be filled, the challenge then is one of choice, rather than shortfall.

According to the new psychological contract, career development is likely to mean growth of skills, responsibilities and challenge rather than vertical promotion. What does this mean in practical terms and what is the link between development and job satisfaction? In this chapter we will look at what development at the same level might look like and consider some of the issues relating to people whose career development in conventional terms has come to a halt. How can the 'plateaued performer' be mobilized to higher levels of output and motivation?

## Attitudes towards development

For many people, career development is seen as vertical progression up a hierarchy, something to be aspired to, a mark of success. Development, on the other hand, is seen as something that should already have happened. Senior managers in particular often believe that their experience has equipped them with all they need to know, and they may feel vulnerable about admitting that they need development. Development is often linked in people's minds with a problem, something that needs to be put right.

The same attitude is reflected in a remark from a senior line manager in a manufacturing company. He was a strong supporter of a new training programme whose aim was to help managers become more effective coaches. The difficulty he had in selling the need for the programme internally was that coaching in that organization was something given only to the least able employee. He suggested renaming the programme 'Maximizing employee potential' in order to attract delegates. Attitudes such as this are hard to shift.

Yet the need for development has never been stronger. If the pundits are to be believed, the nature of organized work is undergoing a profound change in response to ever-increasing competitive pressures. In addition to trends towards multiskilling, teamworking and project working, the nature of employment is in a state of flux. Full-time employment as the norm is being challenged by the increase in part-time and other kinds of flexible employment. The shift is under way towards employing core workers who offer the flexibility, skills, knowledge and experience required by the organization, while 'peripheral' activities are outsourced. Organizations will need new skills and behaviours from their workforce.

Another, perhaps less noticeable, shift is the increase in the numbers of employees who have taken the new career messages to heart and who have taken responsibility for self-development. These are people who recognize that their primary loyalty is to themselves. Even when their organizations are enduring turbulent times, people who have a strong sense of what is important to them and are confident in their own employability are not worried about losing their jobs. If a job does not offer them challenge, variety, stimulus and learning, they leave. In fact, many European organizations are now actively recruiting people on the basis of the 'development package' in addition to the usual terms and conditions.

All of these and other changes also have a bearing on what the critical success factors for 'new' careers will be. Development is directly in the interests of employees. The ingredients of a successful career in the past may not equip people for success in the future, and development may be key to economic survival for individuals and organizations. The challenge for managers is to mobilize development in their teams such that people develop the skills and experience they and the organization will need in the future. In this chapter we will look at some of the different forms of development available and at how to create a situation where people want to develop. If it is true that 'you can take a horse to water but you can't make it drink', this chapter focuses on how to make the horse sufficiently thirsty that it wants to drink!

## The link between development and satisfaction

Of course, many people are strongly motivated to develop, and find development in itself satisfying. This became apparent in my research into career development in flatter structures. When I started to research these issues in 1994, I spoke with 200 people from different sectors of the UK economy. In 1996 we went back to the people who had first helped us with our research. As might be expected, many of the people had left their jobs and it was difficult to find out whether they had left voluntarily or otherwise. From what we could tell, most of the leavers had been dissatisfied with their promotion prospects and felt that there was no scope for growth in their old role.

We found that the 'survivors' fell into three groups. One group had been promoted. In fact 21 per cent had been promoted despite working in organizations that claimed to have flatter structures. They did not necessarily feel loyal to their organizations. If anything, most people in this group were planning to leave at the earliest opportunity. Some of the people who had been promoted talked about feeling exposed, under pressure from peers and much more vulnerable than in their old roles. Another group were in the same job, at the same level as in 1994, though demands on them had grown. They experienced more stress, hard work and frustration about their career prospects. Most people in this group were actively looking for employment elsewhere.

The most satisfied group, and the people most likely to claim that their careers had developed, were people who were at the same organizational level as in 1994, but whose roles had grown. Most people in this group had no immediate plans to escape from their organization. Perhaps this 'same level, broader role' group is typical of the kind of career model which flatter structures lend themselves to: well-motivated and satisfied employees who gain an experience of progression through learning and expanding experience and responsibilities rather than being promoted. How sustainable this model of career development is in the long term, especially if people's enhanced performance is not rewarded financially, is questionable, but development in itself seems sufficiently stimulating to keep people motivated in the short term.

Many people of course will not see things this way. Some people will continue to aspire to promotion up a hierarchy and will be unlikely to value sideways moves unless they are a temporary means to a greater end. Managers of such people can be under tremendous pressure to keep them motivated and committed to the organization, especially if those people are viewed as 'high-flyers'. There can be a strong temptation to imply that progression is possible, whether or not this is the case. When the implied promotion fails to materialize, the frustrated individual may choose not to hang around waiting.

### Age and promotion – a new elite?

On the other hand, our research suggests that many people who are achieving significant promotions are relatively young. In one motor distributorship, the trend is to appoint new managing directors who are in their late twenties or early thirties. In a major FMCG company, it is commonly said that in the past, if you had not achieved a senior management position by forty, you were unlikely to do so. Now the age of 'making it' was felt to be thirty. In many cases we found that people were promoted to significant responsibility without having gradually acquired experience of managing people along the way. Typically, some of the young executives we interviewed felt that managing groups of employees who were usually much older than themselves was a challenge in itself.

Often, the critical time for career sorting is when the delayering first occurs. Some people have the chance to break out of the junior ranks and are promoted to team leader, for example. Other, more senior, people are effectively downgraded and are also team leaders. On the whole older workers, particularly in management ranks, have been phased out. The resulting 'team leader' level then consists of relatively young individuals who will potentially occupy these roles for years. The resulting congestion at the next level down the hierarchy may be reminiscent of the generations born just after the 'baby boomers' who found that promotions had been achieved at an early age by people who are now in their late forties. The gap between management levels can seem unbridgeable to those on the lower levels. Often the only way of breaking out of a seeming impasse is to leave and join another organization at a higher level.

### Development within new career routes

While conventional career routes still seem to be with us, a set of career routes seem to be emerging which lend themselves more easily to flatter organization structures. Flatter structures will probably result in many people remaining at the same hierarchical level for much longer than would have been the case in the old graduated hierarchy. These new routes involve development at the same level, or ceasing to think about status linked with level. This kind of thinking frees up people who would like to try a new area of work within their organization but are prevented from doing so because of the stigma attached to sideways or downwards moves. If people are likely to stay at the same level for longer, by implication, the roles they are doing need to satisfy them. Development is one of the key ingredients in enriching roles and making them more satisfying to the individual.

### Career route 1 – same level, more specialist

In the UK civil service, the traditional career route has involved a number of postings to different parts of the department for which the individual works, or to other parts of the civil service. This has meant that people have acquired good generalist perspectives but few 'professional' qualifications or areas of special expertise. Increasingly, employees are opting to step out of the posting system in order to develop proficiency in areas of special interest, such as strategy or personnel. As such, roles become more fulfilling for those who choose this route.

### Career route 2 – same role, broader responsibilities

Another route may include staying in the same role for longer but broadening the scope of the role. This seems to be the most common route. One facilities manager working for a major utility based in the south-east of England found that her responsibilities expanded beyond a single plant to taking on facilities management for a division and then a region within the company. She enjoys the extra responsibility and visibility. She feels slightly exploited by the company since her responsibilities are broader than those of many of her colleagues (all of whom are men) who are at the next level in the hierarchy. She is not paid extra for the increased scope of her role but she receives a lot of support, encouragement and recognition from her line manager. She describes herself as being broadly satisfied with her role.

Another option is to expand specialists' awareness of the business and the needs of their (internal) customers by encouraging secondments to client departments. Several companies arrange secondments for their staff to external customers and suppliers.

One company in particular has successfully run such a scheme for nine years. Engineers from the company are seconded for up to three years, then return to a guaranteed role in this mainly project-based organization. Secondees return with a much greater awareness of business issues, which makes them more employable internally. They also have an excellent understanding of their client's needs. In effect, by looking after the development needs of their employees, this company also cleverly locks in their clients with the scheme.

*Career route 3 – same level, broader responsibilities*

When jobs are organized functionally or departmentally, a common way of expanding people's experience is through project work, especially if this involves their working crossfunctionally, with new people, or both. For project work to be truly developmental it helps if the project is of great potential importance to the business and involves people in overcoming a number of challenges before they succeed. The results of the project should be highly visible within the organization.

Another option is for the individual to take a more generalist track, acquiring skills, knowledge and experience in several lateral moves. As we have seen, some organizations are actively encouraging sideways moves by introducing job rotation, incentivizing sideways moves, repositioning sideways moves as promotion and making experience of several areas a prerequisite for vertical promotion.

## An antidote to plateauing?

Is it inevitable that employees will plateau in their roles, with all the drawbacks which plateauing can bring, such as loss of commitment and job satisfaction? Research carried out in the States by Hall (1996) suggests that plateaued employees can continue to be highly productive in certain circumstances. Certain job characteristics appear to be important. Employees working in a project-based structure, with plenty of job variety and complexity, find more intrinsic job rewards and recognition than those in other career paths. Thus a structure which offers more recognition, challenge, involvement in their work and psychological success is likely to result in greater employee motivation. Similarly, jobs which offer a degree of autonomy are likely to lead employees to feel responsible for the successes and failures which result from their work. Jobs which have the potential of being enriched also seem to help people find their own motivation.

## Case: career development in the UK secondary education system

The state education system in the UK has long been clearly graduated, with teachers' roles being graded at certain levels. In the past a secondary school teacher might expect to progress beyond the basic grade over time and at some stage might take on responsibilities for managing a subject department, such as languages, or a pastoral responsibility, such as head of year. Whilst these more senior positions were obviously in relatively short supply, there were often a number of intermediate responsibilities which teachers would usually take on willingly to support the school and its activities.

Prior to education reforms, local education authorities had a much greater role with respect to staffing and staff development. This at least ensured some consistency across local schools. Schools were allocated a number of 'points' which then determined the number of teaching posts and positions of responsibility to which they were entitled.

Revisions in the system of secondary education have led to a much greater management focus, with schools effectively operating as small businesses, responsible not just for improving academic outputs but also for managing within budgets which the schools control themselves. Teaching posts are clearly graded, with a few 'responsibility allowances' which allow teachers to see a small reflection in their pay for additional work but do not usually lead to promotion. The influence of local education authorities, which used to ensure that career development possibilities for teachers could be considered across the authority, has waned.

The impact of some of these changes on teachers' careers is now being felt. Now that schools are themselves responsible for determining how they allocate positions of responsibility, some have preferred to reduce the number of senior posts, since these are most expensive on the salary bill. Thus for many teachers, promotion is unlikely. At the same time, changes in the national education system have significantly increased teachers' workloads. The impact of the National Curriculum, compulsory testing of pupils at different ages and many other pressures are producing an increase in stress- related disorders amongst many teaching staff. Teaching is now considered to be so stressful as an occupation that only 3 per cent of teachers retire at sixty.

At the same time, because of the need to save the costs of allowing teachers in their fifties to take early retirement, the Education Secretary is proposing to ensure that compulsory retirement takes place at sixty and not before. The likelihood for many teachers is that people in their thirties and forties will have increased competition for fewer positions, while mature teachers who would willingly have relinquished those positions are forced to continue working until they are sixty. Despite the relatively equal numbers of men and women in secondary education, men significantly outnumber women in positions of responsibility. Women rarely manage to achieve promotion beyond middle management.

Joan Hudson, an experienced secondary school teacher working in Suffolk, has been a head of year for several years. In her early forties, Joan has been a professional teacher throughout her career and, in common with many others, she has in the past found it necessary to move schools in order to achieve promotion. Joan feels that the changes in the education system have made it more important than ever to achieve promotion:

> It gives you credibility amongst the kids and other members of staff. They view you with a different form of respect, especially the younger ones.

Above all, though, it is a mark of achievement in a field where an individual teacher's achievements are relatively hidden from others since the teacher tends to work alone with a class. Promotion therefore has a bearing on self-esteem.

In the absence of promotion, what else is available which offers a sense of challenge? Joan has taken on a number of special responsibilities for the school. She administers the school's timetable on a daily basis, arranging cover for absent colleagues. These responsibilities bring her into daily contact with all her colleagues, the education authority and other agencies. Her responsibilities as year head give her a perspective which is truly crossfunctional. For Joan, A-level teaching of her favourite subject offers both stimulus and personal development. It is an opportunity to step out of the routine. Recognition in teaching can be notoriously difficult to come by and results are often long-term. So when children in her year group achieve something she feels a vicarious satisfaction:

... it gives you a sense of having done your job properly.

Joan enjoys her job and feels loyal to the school, yet being ambitious to achieve what she feels capable of, how much will 'broadening' opportunities meet her needs in the long term?

## What might it be useful to develop?

Of course, the answer to this is: 'It depends'; it depends on a range of factors such as the individual's starting point in terms of motivation, strengths and weaknesses, and what their job requirements, career aspirations and likely options are. At the start of a career or when an individual is in a new role the development needs may be obvious – some information here, technical training there, a professional qualification are typical elements. In addition to purely job-related issues, 'it depends' on what their organization is looking for them to develop. Is it a broader business perspective which will give them a more commercial focus? Is it greater understanding of the financial dynamics of the business, or 'strategic thinking'? Often organizations are pretty vague about what skills they need people to develop to help the organization achieve its goals.

It is beneficial when organizations develop criteria around the kinds of behaviours that will help the organization. Typically, these involve teamworking and leadership. This leaves development of the bulk of the workforce less open to chance, especially when the desired elements are reinforced through training and other development processes. In some organizations, the attempt to define elements of future competence goes further. Competency statements are developed for each level in the organization, job profiles are created and the competencies are then used to select and develop staff. It is vitally important that these competencies are considered credible by employees or they will be little use in focusing development. People need to understand why certain skills are valued and consider them relevant if they are to go to the effort of developing them.

## What is developmental?

Development implies a change from one state to another, in which learning and growth have probably taken place. What people find to be developmental has been much researched. Some of the common strands to the research suggest that challenge, which is within the scope of the individual, allows the person to stretch beyond their current level of skill, understanding, etc. to another level. A 'stretch' may therefore seem risky since there may be new factors that can affect the outcome of the activity.

Challenge takes many forms. In some cases, it may involve doing new things, juggling a range of new responsibilities, dealing with new people, a variety of people and situations which cause the individual to operate in different ways. Other challenges are to be found in the level of difficulty – problems to be solved, difficult people to be dealt with, scarce resources to be marshalled, setbacks to be overcome. Challenge is all the greater when the nature of the activity is important, the outcome unpredictable and when the results will be known to important others. According to some, the amount of development which is likely to take place is in direct proportion to the number of challenge elements present in the activity.

What people believe to be an acceptable challenge depends on a number of factors, such as how much they feel in control of what is happening to them. If they feel in control and believe themselves to be active agents, rather than passive agents, they are more likely to be willing to take risks, especially if they have faith in their own abilities. On the other hand, if people lack confidence in their abilities, or are extremely sensitive to the opinions of others, they are less likely to wish to take on a challenge. Research from the States suggests that control does seem to matter. Those who have it are not only more satisfied with their careers, they are usually also more successful in conventional extrinsic terms, such as salary, promotions and job level (Judge and Cheung, 1993). What is an appropriate challenge for one person may be a threatening experience for another.

*Overcoming difficulties*

The Center for Creative Leadership has produced some excellent research in the area of development. Amongst other things they discovered that people grow as a result of hardship, as long as they learn from the experience. They also found that people are strongly influenced by role models, both positive and negative. A very bad boss (who perhaps causes hardship) often helps a person identify the kind of leader they would prefer to be by providing a counter-example. Training can also help, since it can expose people to new ideas and techniques. Often the biggest developmental benefit of training comes from the networking and sharing of ideas amongst fellow delegates.

## Off-the-job development

Off-the-job experiences are often ignored by organizations as a source of development since they are strictly the business of the individual. Yet these are often indicators of individual motivation and talents which may not have been picked up in any development centre. Off-the-job activities are often where the frustrated talents of employees are put to good use. Leading scout troops, being involved in community affairs and running small businesses are often outlets for under-used leadership and entrepreneurial skills.

The challenge is to offer those same talents an outlet inside the organization. The chief executive officer of a major US automobile manufacturer was told by a consultant investigating the slump in employee morale which was adversely affecting production:

> You have the most dynamic workforce in the US. They are running businesses, they are highly committed to what they are doing and they give 150 per cent to what they do. The problem is that they are not doing it for this business. This is what happens when they leave the factory at the end of their shifts.

## On-the-job development

Perhaps the biggest source of potential development is on the job. This is where the role of the line manager is vital in creating opportunities for development and also in removing barriers to development. Johnson and Indvik (1992) suggested that more help should be given to employees to encourage them to be more entrepreneurial. They found that most people tend to adopt a passive stance when it comes to developing their 'mental capital'. The effect is that employees are highly susceptible to cultural conditioning at work. This can depress their ability to perform, especially in times of change when the dominant reaction to delayering, for example, is likely to be negative.

This can be a delicate balancing act for managers. On the one hand, research suggests that if people are strongly self-motivated they are likely to have high levels of self-control and may resent heavy-handed attempts to help them to develop. On the other hand, lack of intervention and encouragement may be interpreted as a lack of interest on the part of the manager. Creating specific development assignments can be difficult in lean organizations. The alternatives include thinking about how developmental challenges can be built into every role so that development takes place continuously. The art therefore is engaging people in developing themselves.

### Creating development opportunities

Part of this may involve asking people what they find motivating, and helping them to develop aspects of their job which are satisfying to them. Raising awareness amongst team members about developmental aspects of roles can help. Here are a few suggestions about how to engage the members of your team in developing on the job.

1 Discuss the changes in the organization; what do the changes mean for the way the team works, what new skills will be needed, which competencies apply?

2 Brainstorm all the ways the team can think of in which people can develop within the organization.

3 Analyse the development suggestions. Do they break down into certain categories, such as short-term, small-scale challenges, major projects, training, etc.?

4 Identify development needs for each team member, including the manager. These will usually be known from appraisals, development discussions, development centre feedback, 360 degree feedback, etc. Alternatively use competencies or value statements about what the organization considers important.

5 Build up a matrix of development options, graded into size or nature of challenge, against the development needs of team members. Map across the matrix to identify what might be useful starting points for each individual. Your matrix should help you identify development options for different individuals. Two people who both need to develop their leadership ability may be able to do this in the ways which best suit them.

6 Set up learning groups. Some of the biggest stimulus to development occurs when people realize that they are learning. This awareness may be accidental, or it may be designed into team processes so that learning becomes a practical business resource. Often people who attend courses on strategic leadership talk of

the day-to-day difficulties of making time to think. As they develop their ability to think and act strategically, they are able to make more conscious choices about how they use their time. They are better able to take the helicopter view and understand what needs to happen. In a sense, they learn to learn in a way which allows them to shape their destiny, rather than just being tossed about by conflicting currents of activity.

Some organizations have recognized the business value of learning. ICL, for example, has encouraged staff to set up learning groups as part of a self-managed approach to adult learning. The process of setting learning goals, linked with support and challenge from a group of peers, seems a powerful force for encouraging people to implement their learning plans. When people see that development is not only possible but satisfying, they need little encouragement to continue with their development.

## Energizing the plateaued performer

Many people may have been ambitious in the traditional sense but have reached the point when there is no longer an opportunity to progress up the hierarchy. This may have nothing to do with the person's skill or potential value to the organization. It may simply reflect the fact that few organizations, even relatively hierarchical ones, have senior positions for the majority of employees. As such, career plateaux have long been a structural reality.

In the past, plateauing tended to occur when people were in their forties, by which time they had usually achieved gradual progression and the signs of success that went with progression. Coming to terms with the end of the upward career climb is no doubt easier when the first phase of one's career is over. The difficulty caused by flatter structures is that structural plateaux are occurring to many people at an earlier age and are therefore likely to last longer.

This kind of structural gridlock may result in some loss of motivation when the employee becomes aware that career progression has come to an end. Even though flatter structures are becoming commonplace in the West, few employees seem to have adjusted their career expectations accordingly. What causes most dissatisfaction is the perceived gap between employees' career expectations and their actual work experiences. Recent research at

Roffey Park found that many employees whose careers have stalled are actively looking for other jobs, even though they claim to be loyal to their current employer.

Managers have the challenge of retaining and motivating people who may be critical to the organization's success and represent the 'engine' of the operation, but whose own ambition is not being satisfied within their current organization. Structural plateauing may not adversely affect people's motivation as long as they feel that they are growing within their jobs. This element of growth, or its absence, when the job itself becomes routine, is known as content plateauing. Another form of plateauing exists when people reach a salary plateau, having reached the maximum on their pay grade. Any element of plateauing can cause problems for some people and not for others, depending on their individual circumstances and motivation.

## Salary plateauing

Research carried out in Canada amongst a group of 900 engineers suggests that salary plateauing can compound the effects of other forms of plateauing. If an individual is a high performer and the reward system does not reflect this, the individual may develop a sense of being treated unfairly. If in reality it is unlikely that his salary will increase if he stays in his present position, the individual may be tempted to try for a management position if this releases the salary bottleneck. Alternatively, the authors suggest that people's perception of a salary plateau may lead to a downturn in performance.

> According to the theory of equity, it is probable that they adopt behaviours aimed at re-balancing the perceived disparity, either by decreasing their performance, their involvement on company premises, their job involvement or by thinking about quitting their present employment. (Tremblay *et al.*, 1996)

The impact of salary plateauing is explored in more detail in Chapter 16.

## Content plateauing

Not everybody is ambitious and frustrated by the lack of promotion opportunities in flatter structures. Indeed, some people may prefer to do a nine-to-five job which allows them to concentrate on other parts of their life. They may be doing their job adequately, but without the 110 per cent dedication that most employers look for.

Research suggests that this may be a natural tendency since many people's performance tends to decline in as little as two years after taking up a new role. This is typically when an individual's initial energy and enthusiasm linked with learning tend to settle down or decline. Beverley L. Kaye (1993) refers to this as 'content' plateauing. It occurs when an individual does a job that is no longer challenging and that they know perhaps too well. There are few opportunities for the individual to broaden their experience beyond their role and work becomes boring as well as stressful. For managers, the challenges of gaining a 'supercharged' performance from such individuals can be daunting.

## The plateaued expert

There may be many different reasons for content plateauing and different ways in which people can be helped to find renewed or enhanced motivation in their work. In some cases, people are genuinely interested in their work and may have an area of expertise which makes them feel important. Typically such employees tend to stay for a long time with the same employer and may lack external marketability as a result. They may not in fact be motivated by promotion within the organization as much as by gaining the recognition of their professional peers outside the organization. As long as their expertise is valued within the organization, specialists are usually motivated to pursue their own interests within the context of their job.

Problems occur, however, when the organization's needs change and the employee's area of expertise becomes progressively obsolete or irrelevant. Often the demands of the job call on specialists to demonstrate an understanding of the needs of both internal and external business clients. The individual who presents themselves first and foremost as a specialist, rather than a business person, may be seen as out of touch. Typically, specialists are unwilling to change jobs since they have developed their career on a single path of knowledge and skill. Amongst Human Resource professionals, for instance, the least mobile group appear to be compensation and benefits specialists who have built up a wealth of expertise in this area and are reluctant to abandon their power base.

The challenge for the manager at this stage is to recognize whether the person could make a more valuable contribution elsewhere in the organization, or be able to develop a more valued form of expertise, and to help them make the necessary transition. If the individual's self-esteem is tied up in their knowledge of that particular specialist area, making the transition may not be easy for them or the organization. If the individual is believed capable of making the transition, the manager may be able to phase the new responsibilities such that the employee has time to acquire some relevant expertise in the new area and be able to avoid failing in their own eyes.

People are often able and willing to change. What is lacking is simply information. Candid feedback, both positive and negative, can help the employee understand what may need to change. Explaining new projects carefully and providing learning resources can help. These can include peer coaching, especially when peers work together in project groups or along the customer–supplier chain. Training and skill-upgrading opportunities can help employees to see how their skills can be used in their current and future roles. People may need to be rewarded as they acquire new skills and experience. One company offers a small non-pensionable bonus to employees who are willing to take a lateral job move to a more valuable area for the company. Another company encourages employees to remain actively involved with their professional body even though they may now be engaged on other kinds of work.

## Plateauing as a 'fine art'

Another form of content plateauing occurs when the employee has managed to boil their contribution down to a fine art. The manager is aware that the individual is capable of higher output, but the employee's skills are underused even though performance targets are being met. Often individuals are motivated by a desire to avoid stress and maintain a satisfying life outside work, linked with a reluctance to change. Whilst it is not unreasonable for employees to seek to maintain a balance between work and other parts of their life, the speed of change calls on many full-time employees to give more than in the past, just to keep abreast of developments. 'Just' giving 100 per cent does not seem enough any more.

## Case: the director of operations

In a major international travel business which is experiencing huge competitive pressures, there is intense pressure on all employees to produce high levels of performance. Martin A, director of operations, has worked for the same business for nearly twenty years. In his mid-forties, he achieved rapid promotion relatively easily in the 'boom' days of travel in the early 1980s and has been in his current role for almost four years. Martin sees that there are few further promotion opportunities, especially now that the organization has delayered and there are fewer positions above him. To some extent he would be reluctant now to move out of his niche and take on higher responsibilities anyway.

As is customary for anyone at director level in that organization, Martin has always received 'good' performance ratings. He is highly visible within the business and his business standing is respected. He always takes part in executive development programmes and other business-related initiatives which involve being amongst his peers. However, he is rarely to be seen taking responsibility for any change initiative and is more likely to express scepticism at those who do.

He enjoys the opportunities to play golf with clients, takes an active interest in his children's university careers and generally enjoys life. He has developed the art of delegating and believes in a clear desk policy – for himself. His subordinates grumble that he actually dumps work on them, and that he expects them to work all hours when he himself leaves at the end of office hours. He accuses them of incompetence rather than supporting them or taking a bigger share of the load. He has perfected the fine art of managing his own workload down to very manageable proportions, even though this is at the expense of his team.

In this case, Martin A has no vested interest in giving more since there appear to be few sanctions for not doing so. In fact he has continued to enjoy all the status perks of the more hierarchical structure and is able to manipulate his team, using the new cultural directives about teamwork and customer service as points of criticism.

The turning point came for Martin A when he was approached and asked if he would like to be a mentor to a more junior person who was taking part in a development programme. The management development professional who was responsible for the mentoring programme introduced a selection procedure for mentors which required that mentors display many of the new skills and attitudes. Martin, unlike many of his peers, failed the procedure and the shock caused him initially to rubbish the process. However, the feedback process caused him to want to take stock. Whilst there have been no overnight changes, Martin has volunteered to lead a business change process and he is leading by example.

The danger of not addressing performance issues such as these is that such behaviour can spread by example, causing bigger problems for the organization. For managers, these people often cause the biggest dilemmas since they cannot be accused of not doing their jobs, yet they are often in positions of significant influence and can provide a negative role model for other employees. It is not so much what these employees do as what they fail to do that can adversely affect their contribution.

What can managers do to stimulate higher levels of performance? Introducing an element of challenge can help. Often people are stimulated to produce higher levels of performance when they are actively involved in developing new products, implementing initiatives and projects or leading highly visible teams. Sometimes employees enjoy the challenge of acting as mentor to other employees. Training for mentors is essential if bad habits are not to be passed on to others as 'the way we do things around here'.

Increasingly, it is at the organizational level that issues relating to plateauing may need to be addressed. Reward systems are being redesigned to recognize employees for experience and knowledge rather than years in the job. Similarly, many organizations are introducing initiatives based around values which encourage employees to develop behaviours more closely linked to helping the organization achieve its goals. These include feedback processes on some of the 'new' behaviours required in flatter structures, such as coaching, teamwork and leadership. Standards and behavioural targets can encourage new ways of working. These cultural initiatives, if applied appropriately, can give people the guidance they need in developing more appropriate performance. Similarly, organizations that want to see these behaviours developed across the workforce should beware of promoting people who do not demonstrate them.

### The powerhouse plateau

These are employees who are actively involved with their job and whose jobs maintain plenty of stimulation and challenge. These people are not necessarily motivated by promotion but by the chance to achieve. They see possibilities for themselves and make things happen. They are usually appreciated and supported by their colleagues and managers. They are strongly loyal to the organization and put themselves out for its good. Since flatter structures call for most employees to remain at the same job level, the ideal form of content plateau should be this high-energy–high-trust relationship between employee and employer. The danger is that such people can be taken for granted and performance can start to suffer.

## Case: the desktop publisher

Judy is an expert typist responsible for desktop publishing in a medium-sized management consultancy. The work is high pressure, with over twenty people requiring Judy to produce perfect proposals and other documentation within short deadlines. On the whole, Judy loves her work and likes many of her colleagues. Her excellent work standards are widely acknowledged and she has twice refused promotion since she does not wish to take on additional responsibility. She is able to keep her family and work lives separate but they are both very important to her.

Unfortunately, as business has expanded, so has Judy's workload. What was barely manageable but a matter of pride for Judy a few years ago, has become an avalanche of work with which she can barely cope. Initially she was reluctant to delegate any of her work since she did not trust her colleagues to produce work to the right standards and she did not have the time to coach them. To some extent she enjoyed the process of prioritizing work so that she was the person who decided which piece of work was handled first. Attempts to speed up the workflow by equipping Judy with a high-powered computer, installed as a surprise during her annual leave, backfired when it took her three weeks to learn the system, adding to her distress.

As time has moved on Judy has learnt to delegate and is still highly productive. She feels threatened, however, by the changing values evident in the organization. The introduction of new staff with different values from the old has left Judy feeling sad and disorientated. She particularly dislikes the more political behaviour of some of her colleagues and feels that increasing management controls on her are undermining her confidence. Though confident of her value to the organization, she is now questioning her commitment to it.

**Plateaux are not static**

It is often assumed that once a career is plateaued, the person will continue to perform at a constant level. Of course, some of the factors we have discussed will have an impact on this and often experience suggests that performance can deteriorate over time. Yet this need not be the case. The manager's task is to spot when performance is about to deteriorate, before it actually happens. The challenge then is to inject new elements into the role so that the person continues to develop as their job grows. Even the best performers will inevitably plateau in terms of career structure at some stage. Keeping people stimulated by their work and feeling that their performance is appreciated may be a means of keeping their motivation high. It has even been known for people whose performance has slowly declined to boost their performance and contribution to superb levels. Even the hardened cynic can become a champion of change given the right opportunity. The challenge for the manager is to work with team members to find or make the right opportunities.

# Strategies for motivating and developing employees

| Employee | Challenges | Required to | Ways of developing and motivating |
|---|---|---|---|
| The high-flyer | coping with potential hostility from other employees<br><br>finding a future outlet for their talents<br><br>being recognized | perform well as well as manage own development<br><br>communicate the organization's values and vision to staff<br><br>develop own successors<br><br>manage people who are often older than self | provide a real job challenge<br><br>encourage risk-taking and innovation<br><br>round out the individual's knowledge of the organization<br><br>enhance their people management skills<br><br>encourage development of problem-solving skills<br><br>recognize and reward their development of subordinates<br><br>offer opportunity for leadership of significant project or business activity. |

| Employee | Challenges | Required to | Ways of developing and motivating |
|---|---|---|---|
| The super executive | leaving operational decisions to others<br><br>developing and communicating a vision<br><br>staying in touch with other levels in the organization<br><br>experiencing a sense of vulnerability<br><br>managing a team of older executives | develop awareness of long-term economic and other trends which may affect the business<br><br>be accessible<br><br>develop listening skills, strategic thinking and acting | expose to external influences and pressures through secondments, study tours, business luncheons at which people from other organizations will be participating; develop opportunities for networking<br><br>encourage attendance at external development courses designed to meet strategic management needs, such as broadening an executive's analytical and decision-making abilities<br><br>assign a senior executive as mentor |
| The victim | may feel marginalized and demotivated<br><br>uncertain about prospects and expecting the worst<br><br>may be blocked by younger bosses<br><br>may be suffering mid-life crisis<br><br>may lack skills or confidence to change course | contribute further to the organization<br><br>possibly re-orientate their contribution to the organization<br><br>learn new skills | clarify roles required in lean organization<br><br>arrange for them to attend a personal development workshop<br><br>give feedback about actual standard of performance and performance required<br><br>recognize and support as appropriate<br><br>stimulate out of complacency<br><br>give people a chance to learn new things<br><br>involve in the development of crossfunctional or team projects<br><br>build in some challenge and 'stretch' to objectives<br><br>expose to new ideas and new issues<br><br>encourage contact with customers, competitors, suppliers |

| Employee | Challenges | Required to | Ways of developing and motivating |
|---|---|---|---|
| The victim (continued) | | | engage them in benchmarking internally and externally |
| | | | consult and involve them in new projects |
| | | | appoint as mentor to others, or provide a mentor for them |
| | | | identify skill deficiencies and offer training as required |
| The winner/ opportunist | may be identified as having high potential but with few outlets for promotion | continue performing well | adopt an enabling management style |
| | | communicate the organization's values to staff, customers and other constituents | arrange for them to attend assessment centres and provide follow-up |
| | may be frustrated with the slow pace of change | | encourage them to develop a personal development plan and support them with it |
| | | manage own development | recognize specific achievements |
| | may take on too many projects if 'unfocused' | | listen to their ideas and encourage them to work with other team members on developing and implementing them |
| | | | build on their initiative and help them develop sound business judgement and risk-assessment skills |
| | | | encourage and enable opportunities for developing cross-business awareness |
| | | | offer opportunity for responsibility |
| | | | delegate stretching tasks |
| | | | provide variety of assignments and a high workload |
| | | | encourage them to network inside and beyond the organization |
| | | | give them the chance to be ambassador for team, on strategic visits to customers, suppliers and competitors |

| Employee | Challenges | Required to | Ways of developing and motivating |
|---|---|---|---|
| The winner/ opportunist (continued) | | | offer management development programme, business school programme or other 'formal' development as appropriate<br><br>provide career counselling<br><br>send on secondments: special, high-profile projects where their development can be accelerated<br><br>make it possible for them to move outside their area of specialism; facilitate moves. |
| Technical specialist into functional manager | letting go of operational work<br><br>resisting the temptation to take over | manage people<br><br>quickly become familiar with tasks, environment, people and responsibilities<br><br>develop new satisfactions e.g. helping others learn<br><br>develop specific skills and knowledge to perform in this role | offer structured induction into the role, with mentoring as appropriate<br><br>provide training in management skills, i.e. interpersonal, communication, delegation and giving direction, using information systems, budgeting, time-management<br><br>provide coaching as appropriate in administrative skills such as budgeting, as well as skills such as political awareness, managing the boss and managing people problems<br><br>encourage to spend time with staff, customers, suppliers and develop sensitivity and credibility required<br><br>provide 360 degree feedback so that development needs can be clarified<br><br>set up peer network of line managers for mutual support on people management challenges |

| Employee | Challenges | Required to | Ways of developing and motivating |
|---|---|---|---|
| The technical/ professional specialist | to add value to the business in a constantly changing environment

to keep up to date with area of specialism

to ensure that their area of specialism does not become obsolete and redundant | develop the ability to think and act like a business person and understand issues from the client's perspective

provide higher quality service, more quickly and cost-effectively | show understanding of value of technical expertise to the business

encourage to broaden beyond original specialism but to further enhance core area of expertise if the organization values this

provide flexible pay packages so that managerial work does not become the only route for progression

reward high-quality work in the field with participation in professional associations

encourage and recognize development of expertise

encourage professional membership and continuous professional development

sponsor for development of further professional qualifications, and/or a business qualification

encourage them to write professional articles

offer secondment to customer or supplier

encourage attendance at specialist conferences as a speaker

expose to cross-business issues to build business acumen

encourage customer contact and opportunities to understand the customer's business and real requirements

provide coaching in technical specialism through others, if need be

provide other forms of coaching and feedback; show that their contribution is valued

train in consultancy skills, interpersonal skills as appropriate |

| Employee | Challenges | Required to | Ways of developing and motivating |
|---|---|---|---|
| The generalist | ensuring the all-round 'multi-skills' and experience to really add value | develop sufficient knowledge that they can quickly 'hit the ground running' | clarify the competencies needed for success as a generalist |
| | making a difference to any part of the organization | have a flexible approach but be good at follow – through | ensure that career opportunities are made known |
| | managing career moves, especially in project-based structures | maintain at least one area of real expertise | facilitate lateral moves every two or three years |
| | | acquire management or team leadership competencies | provide relevant coaching, especially when first joins new function |
| | | | assign a longer-term mentor |
| | | be able to contribute well to teams | tap into their experience – encourage them to share ideas and approaches from other roles within the team |
| | | | reward enhanced experience and 'value-add' competence acquired through generalist experience |
| | | | sponsor to develop professional or business qualifications as appropriate |
| | | | provide incentive payments for keeping up technical skills |
| | | | encourage them to share their cross-business and cross-cultural experience in learning networks |
| | | | provide accelerated training required for new roles |
| | | | offer challenging and exciting projects which offer a stretch |
| | | | encourage them to maintain and build their network |

Whichever stereotype one looks at, certain common themes emerge. Individuals are increasingly required to develop themselves by building their skills, knowledge and expertise. To be really effective, it helps if there is a developmental relationship between employees, their line managers and Human Resource professionals. Managers can learn about career resources that are available within the organization, hold development discussions on a regular basis, and identify development opportunities and experiences. Human Resources professionals can provide the internal facilitation of development moves, build up knowledge and systems which support individual and organizational development and help managers clarify roles and make opportunities. Employees can take greater responsibility for their own careers by assessing their own skills, values, interests and development needs. They can determine long-term goals and short-term development targets, creating a career development plan with their manager which it is up to them to follow through. They can also recognize that career discussions imply no promises or guarantees.

## Conclusion – what is development?

The term 'development' implies a positive step forward towards the future, with better personal well-being and professional growth as the outcomes. Career development no longer implies onwards and upwards for the broad mass of people, and perhaps it never did. Career development is coming to mean developing in the workplace in a way which is personally satisfying. Development can occur when people move sideways, downwards and even out of an organization. It can occur in almost any situation but almost always involves active learning. Development is no longer a series of promotions; it is the ability to create challenge in even mundane tasks and to visualize ongoing challenge and growth in the future.

Real development depends on the individual's needs and their work situation. Consequently, it is all the more important that people are able to grow their jobs in a way which stimulates them, or that they find a role which better fits their needs. In mobilizing development it is often sufficient to provide people with the means to better understand their values, competencies and interests. Once they have a clearer understanding of what is really important to them, and have some ideas of how to achieve their aims, people usually see development as the means of achieving bigger ends rather than as an end in itself.

Ultimately, people who are motivated will usually want to develop; those who are not motivated by the work they do will put their energy and interest into other things. As ever, individuals are responsible for managing their own motivation. Yet development is a business issue. It is firmly at the 'input' end of the work process model. Unless people are able and willing to acquire the skills needed by the organization, outputs are likely to suffer. The kind of situation in which people find themselves will have a huge bearing on whether or not they are motivated. As always, the challenge of looking after the organization's interests by mobilizing development falls to the manager. They can help by ensuring that the work climate, roles and tasks are appropriate to the individuals in the team. The real art of mobilizing development lies in understanding what challenge each individual needs and in helping them to rise to that challenge.

It would be unreasonable to expect any organization to support people development for the sake of it. In the past many organizations demonstrated support for staff development through providing comprehensive training programmes that employees would go through on a 'sheep dip' basis. The difficulty with this approach was that the objectives of the training programmes were often only loosely linked with what the organization as a whole was trying to achieve, and consequently when savings had to be made, training was usually the first thing to be cut since it was seen as a cost. In this chapter we will be looking at a range of ways in which organizations can and do support people development.

## Why should organizations support development?

Examples in this book suggest that organizations are increasingly recognizing that their future success will, to a large extent, depend on how well they develop their current employees and how successfully they attract future employees because they are good developers of people. Knowing that people represent an organization's competitive advantage is one thing. Investing in helping that asset to appreciate is another. There seems to be a kind of corporate schizophrenia that prevents senior managers translating their intellectual understanding of the importance of staff development into policies and practice.

In the UK, government-led initiatives such as Investors in People have tried to encourage organizations to take this message seriously. Judging by the relatively few major organizations who have managed to achieve Investors in People status, putting this message into practice is harder than it seems. After all, developing people calls for an investment perspective rather than a cost-cutting one since the returns are often not immediate. This is where corporate value statements such as 'our people are our greatest asset' are at odds with the pragmatic short-term considerations which dominate many Western businesses.

## How clear are organizations about what they want people to develop?

Many employees are keen to succeed and want to know what they have to do to be considered successful. Many organizations find it difficult to help employees be clear about this since they do not know what skills and behaviours will be needed in the future. Some organizations have a very broad and often ill-defined list of requirements for staff. They are aware that the rapid changes brought about by new technologies require people to be able to adapt to new working practices. They want people to develop a more flexible approach, be able to innovate and continuously find ways to outsmart the competition. If an organization hopes to be successful in the longer term, employees with these skills and approaches will certainly contribute to their future success.

Others try to define specific competencies at different levels of management linked with their vision and mission statements. Many organizations spend time and money painstakingly trying to define competencies which can then be used for job profiling, to assist internal moves, to target development opportunities and ensure that potential is spotted. The danger of producing a 'perfect' scheme is the temptation to leave it unchanged once it has been developed. Almost inevitably, things will move on and competencies need to be reviewed. Competencies devised on behalf of the organization by outside agencies, or by Human Resource professionals, are often not accepted or used by the line management population for whom they were designed. Often the very process of discussing what skills will be required in the future is enough to engage those concerned in developing something that will be useful, rather than perfect.

People are often motivated to develop skills and behaviours that are relevant to their career development. There is often less clarity in flatter structures about possible career routes. There can be confusion about whether to develop as a generalist, because that is what the organization seems to call for, or to become more of a specialist. People often look carefully at who is being promoted and try to work out why. This is often the only 'career guidance' available.

Another source of confusion arises when it becomes apparent that the same sorts of development do not apply across the board. Many organizations encourage people to work in teams, and provide training and other support to encourage this. This causes problems when it is seen that the people who achieve rapid promotion are anything but team players, and that in fact other kinds of approach are called for. There is often muddled thinking attached to 'cultural' development initiatives such as leadership programmes and attempts to ensure that all line managers act as coaches. Sometimes individuals who otherwise make an excellent contribution are unable or unwilling to take on behaviours that they consider inappropriate for them. Should the organization demand change, or should each person's potential contribution and therefore development be judged on an individual basis?

## Organizational support for development

Support for development can come at a variety of levels. Starting with the organization itself, some of the greatest barriers to development lie deeply embedded in the culture of the organization – 'the way we do things around here'. How seriously organizations take the message about supporting development will be reflected in formal systems and processes.

### Development culture checklist

Indicators of a culture in which development is taken seriously include:

- Do managers have developing others as a key results area?
- Are career issues for employees really understood at the top level?
- Is staff development on the board agenda?
- Do senior managers attend and lead training programmes?
- Are people encouraged to or deterred from making sidewards development moves?
- How easy is it for people to develop new skills and acquire new experiences within the same organization?

- Is training the first thing to be cut in difficult times?
- Does the organization prefer to buy in new talent over developing existing employees?

*Blame culture*

Another indicator of how seriously the organization supports development is how innovation and learning are encouraged or discouraged. When people are learning new skills they make mistakes. The blame culture mentality encourages direct reports to be dependent on their managers for specific instructions; in other words it encourages a parent–child relationship when in fact development calls for more of an adult–adult relationship.

The blame culture is often a continuation of hierarchical thinking that seeks to avoid accountability and pass on responsibility for mistakes to others. Unfortunately, it is relatively common and is often to be found in a single manager who is unable or unwilling to delegate appropriately. At an individual level it is demonstrated in the style of the chief executive of a small consultancy group. He appears to give staff a good deal of latitude, then criticizes employees destructively for relatively minor mistakes. Needless to say, an atmosphere of fear and risk aversion surrounds him. He is then critical of staff for not coming up with new ideas!

The degree to which managers encourage people to learn from their mistakes rather than punishing them will to a large extent determine whether people are willing to carry on learning new things. The blame culture is a great deterrent to people being innovative. So in the broader sense support for development leads to the development of a learning culture within an organization, one which involves managers modelling, learning and coaching, and people being prepared to experiment and have feedback on how well they are doing without the need for defensiveness.

*A learning culture*

In fact, learning is a key skill that underpins the development of almost every other skill. Learning to learn in itself is not an easy process, especially for adults who have been in the world of work for many years and who may be tempted to think of learning as a remedial activity. Coaching and training are also viewed by some as activities to be applied to the most needy, rather than seeing development as a dynamic process. In one major organization, a much needed coaching programme had to be entitled 'Executive enhancement' before it found a willing audience.

Some organizations are keen to encourage employees to develop even if there is no immediate pay-back to the company. There are several examples of organizations that offer employees a small development grant which they can use as they wish. Some employees use the money to pursue hobbies such as photography or to have sports coaching. The effect is that employees appreciate the opportunity to learn at the company's expense and are more willing in return to learn new work-related skills.

## Qualifications

How much an organization supports people who wish to take qualification programmes is another key indicator of whether or not it actively supports development.

Typically certain types of professional development are recognized as essential and supported by employers with financial help and time off for studying. These include finance, accountancy and legal qualifications. In some cases the situation is forced on the organization.

In many cases organizations are reluctant to support people who wish to take broader business-related qualifications such as MBAs. Although the official reasons given for not supporting such studies are cost and favouritism, the reality is often that organizations are unwilling to spend money on equipping people with qualifications that may make them more marketable elsewhere. In recent years there has been an increase in the number of organizations supporting people taking MBA and other programmes.

## Accreditation

An increase has also been seen in accrediting employees for training carried on within the organization towards forms of qualifications such as NVQs, GNVQs and qualifications of other professional bodies. The extent to which these are encouraged will reflect the organization's real attitude towards employability. Some organizations actively discourage people from developing accreditation since they fear that people will move once their CVs are in better shape. In other cases supporting employees to develop a range of qualifications is seen as a means of securing ongoing loyalty from them.

## Training

• *Job skill training*

Another key form of practical support is to be found in training. One of the biggest issues in changing organization structures is the confusion over what is required to be effective in a role. Training can help provide clarity of focus and also practical opportunities to develop relevant skills. For greatest effect, training needs to be geared towards the most relevant aspects of the person's role or of their longer-term development. In some organizations there is heavy emphasis on providing training in so-called transferable skills; in others the training is provided only in very job-specific areas such as project management.

• *Culture change*

In some organizations training is provided as part of a wider culture change process brought in to forge a new identity and purpose for the changing organization. This typically involves training staff in customer service skills, or developing managers as leaders. This kind of training is often linked to the organization's values. Other forms of training prepare people for new ways of working. Typically these are offered on a just-in-time basis to relevant individuals or work groups, especially when they concern quality initiatives.

• *New working practices*

Flatter structures also call for people to work increasingly in teams, and training in team meeting and problem-solving skills is frequently provided. The greater workload of most employees means that training in time management and other self-management skills is also of value. Increasingly people at all levels are required to use IT, and in some organizations training in the use of PCs is provided for managers who may no longer have the support of secretaries. Often the gap between levels means that people who previously had several levels of management above them now report directly to directors. For them training is often provided in how to prepare, report to and otherwise communicate with senior managers.

Training has many practical benefits apart from the content of the programme. Often its real value lies in the opportunity it provides for people to network with others from the same organization or other organizations. Individual training based on technology such as multimedia will not have the same advantage. Training, when it is geared to meeting both individual and organizational needs, is a very tangible form of support for development.

### Learning resource centres

Another practical demonstration of support for development is investment in learning resource centres. British Airways, for example, has an open learning centre which caters for flight crew who arrive back in the UK at different times of night and day. Learning materials are available on a wide range of subjects, including languages, and the varied use of media ensures that different learning styles are catered for. Learning is also accredited towards qualifications. Standard Life also provides open access development centres, and a more detailed case study appears later in this chapter. Learning resource centres seem all the more relevant when they are part of a cohesive package of training and learning activities that are linked to the business strategy.

## Support from bosses

As we have already seen elsewhere in this book, one of the most tangible forms of organizational support for development comes from bosses. In the Roffey Park research people were asked if they felt they needed support from anyone to achieve their role successfully. The majority, 88 per cent, said 'yes'. However, when asked if they felt they received the support they needed, only 14 per cent of senior managers were satisfied. Most people stated that they most wanted support from their boss.

### *The manager as leader and shield*

What kind of support do people need from their manager? In times of change the manager can become even more important in providing the kind of shield from the rest of the organization that is essential if people are going to be allowed to experiment and learn. John Whatmore's research (1996) into managing creative groups found that this was a vital aspect of successful leaders. Changing circumstances create much ambiguity, and the manager should act as a leader to their team, providing focus and direction even during periods of instability.

### The manager as coach

In particular, managers who are able to coach and develop their team are able to unlock potential within the organization. Coaching is an underestimated set of skills for which training is often required but not provided. Through effective coaching the manager is able to recognize and encourage those new behaviours that the organization wants to see.

### How managers can help others to develop

1  By watching what they do and advising them.
2  By watching what they do and giving feedback on what was noticed.
3  By offering basic principles on dealing with work problems.
4  By being a hands-on expert: 'I will do it for you and then show you'.
5  By being a model: 'Watch me and learn from me'.
6  By being a technical adviser: encouraging and asking questions.
7  By working on problems with them and learning together.
8  By being a sounding board: encouraging them to talk things through and work out answers for themselves.
9  By setting out clearly the criteria for success in a particular job or task.
10  By encouraging them to develop their own appropriate success criteria.
11  By asking stimulating questions.
12  By placing colleagues in situations where they are working to their strengths.
13  By placing colleagues in situations where they will be helped to develop in their weaker areas.

## Effective delegation

A good coach is also a good delegator when appropriate. Delegation is a strategic activity since it allows employee potential to be realized and frees up resources elsewhere in the organization. According to the well-known model of situational leadership, the skill of delegation lies in judging whether an individual is ready for a particular task (Hersey, 1984). 'Readiness' will depend on a number of things, such as the situation the person is in, the nature of the task and the skill level of the individual for the task. As importantly, the individual's motivation and confidence levels for the task need to be appropriately high.

Judging when an individual is ready for a task is therefore rather an art, and many managers are unable to delegate effectively. Ineffective delegation is evident when managers are unwilling to pass on parts of their job to others. This may be because they have a need to control everything and are unwilling to trust the direct report. Alternatively managers 'dump' work on people who lack the skills, motivation or confidence to carry it out. Whatever the reasons for ineffective delegation, the result is that people are unable to develop.

## Hallmarks of effective delegation

Key activities involve:

- agreeing broad objectives
- recognizing major successes/milestones
- being available but not intrusive
- identifying further challenges for people.

Typical situation when delegation is appropriate:

- when somebody can do the task and is able to provide their own support and feedback mechanisms, e.g. through customer feedback, peer support.

Characteristics of effective delegation:

- communication is mostly initiated by the other person
- takes little of your time
- the other person makes the decisions – you are 'hands off'.

# Support from other people

Other people can supply support for development. People look for support from their colleagues, often because their line manager has such a wide span of control that their support is unlikely to be forthcoming.

## Mentoring and peer mentoring

Many of the people who helped with the Roffey Park research talk of increasing their range of contacts amongst peers elsewhere in the organization for coaching and mentoring purposes since support from their bosses is often lacking. Other people always receive the support they want from sources outside the workplace, mainly friends and family. In some cases people are provided with external mentors, but this is usually restricted to senior people, in fact there seems to be a growth of peer mentoring networks establishing themselves inside organizations. These are often prompted by some training but prove to be continuing sources of support for the individuals who are part of those sets.

## Support or control?

When does support become control of development? Take personal development planning, for instance. Many organizations have adopted this approach as part of the answer to people managing their own careers. On the one hand, people should be able to keep the contents of these plans secret and it should be a voluntary activity if the spirit of development is that people manage their own careers. On the other hand, many organizations require people to inform them of the contents of their personal development plan and then do nothing with the information. There is a potential contradiction in what the organization is trying to achieve. If the organization needs to know the content of the plan so that this can be fed into broader processes, this should be apparent from the outset to avoid mixed messages. In the Standard Life case study that follows there is an example of the dilemmas that well-meaning attempts to support individual development can cause if they are misinterpreted.

Another example is where 360 degree feedback processes are initially introduced as part of development processes to help people understand the need to change and what specific changes would be useful in their own behaviours. As long as the feedback is confidential to the individual, they can choose to do nothing with the information. However, if people do act on such feedback it is usually because they feel committed to making the change. Increasingly, organizations are integrating 360 degree processes into appraisals and many plan ultimately to integrate them into reward schemes. There is a fine line to be drawn between encouraging development and mandating it.

One of the simplest, least complicated ways of supporting development can be to provide line managers and individuals who are interested in developing with the tools to develop. In some cases these may be as simple as structured self-assessment instruments, questionnaires and interview formats, that enable development discussions to take place in an informed way. Standard Life has placed a special emphasis on providing people with the means to develop themselves within the organization. In that organization, development is considered to be intimately linked to its long-term business success.

## Supporting development at Standard Life

Standard Life is the largest mutual life assurance company in Europe, employing 7500 people in operations in the UK, Republic of Ireland, Canada, Spain and Germany. Its head office is in Edinburgh and its products include life assurance, pensions, health insurance and investment. Having been in business for over a century, Standard Life has achieved a solid reputation for performance and reliability and has amassed firm financial resources. The company is managed by a board whose background is mainly actuarial, a profession which has the reputation of being risk averse.

In 1990, business was booming but increased competition from new and existing sources such as banks, building societies and retail organizations put pressure on distribution. Other changes in the operating environment, such as the ever-increasing impact of technology, the burden of regulation and other shifts, caused the company to take stock. Whilst there was no real pressure to change the way the business was run since it was clearly successful, Standard Life decided to seek the views of customers about the company.

Some strong messages emerged. Customers' expectations about what they wanted clearly differed from what was being offered. While customers liked the company's financial strength and investment performance, they considered that the service they received was not sufficiently customer-focused. After reviewing their position, Standard Life developed a forward strategy. The company introduced 'Total Customer Satisfaction' (TCS) as a means of retaining their market lead. TCS consists of three elements:

- customers
- processes
- people.

Standard Life decided to act on customer issues first and to develop operating principles around the people issues. The People Operating Principle was devised as follows:

> We will train and develop all staff to realize their full potential to serve our customers.

From 1990, staffing levels started to rise in response to the changing economy. By 1994 staff numbered 6500. Promotions were plentiful, with many internal moves and much informal development. Careers were managed paternalistically. The company safeguarded its interests by managing careers for the business, with intervention at the individual level mainly restricted to senior management. The company operated a no-redundancy policy.

One of the elements of the 'People' component of TCS was the introduction of the Career Management department. The department started to survey staff attitudes about their careers, building on the company-wide staff attitude survey that takes place every two years. 'Listening lunches' were introduced and feedback came from many other sources. What emerged was that problems with retention were starting to cause concern. People were leaving because they did not feel they were being developed. Internal vacancies were opened up in order to have a more equitable system. The early effect of this was a large number of unrealistic applications, which only added to concerns about development within the company.

It became obvious that for the business to retain its lead, it would have to remain successful at selecting, developing and retaining key people. It was recognized that attending to people's development needs was a business issue, since without the right staff and attitudes, customers were not receiving the right level of service. It was also recognized that it was unrealistic to expect people to become responsible for managing their careers overnight. Telling people that they were responsible for their careers and doing nothing to support them would not be appropriate. Thanks to the feedback, the Career Management team knew that any new processes would have to recognize and reconcile the needs of the business much more obviously with the aspirations of employees.

## The Partnership Principle

Therefore the triarchal Partnership Principle was established, balancing the needs of the individual with management and organizational needs (Figure 15.1). As in the Thresher example, the Standard Life team knew that evolving this principle into reality would take time. A key ingredient in winning the right to take this approach lay in securing the support of the senior management community, and ensuring that the General Manager of Personnel was clearly associated and linked to the Career Management team. They planned the phases of this evolution as follows:

1992–94   Aligning the company to the way forward
1994–96   Mobilizing the company
1996–     Acceleration in partnership.

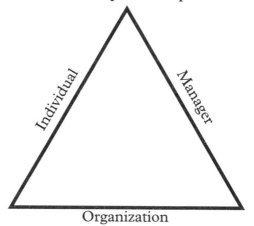

**Figure 15.1** *Triarchal partnership – paternalism to autonomy*

The Partnership Principle is based on:

- different needs are recognized and reconciled
- the individual has ownership
- managers support and coach
- the organization supplies the framework and the resources to make it happen.

In a little more detail, each partner had responsibilities as follows:

- *The individual* is responsible for their own employability. This means that the individual is expected to own their self-development and continued learning. The individual is also expected to articulate their aspirations.
- *Management* is the fulcrum of the partnership. Managers have to make the tough decisions and balance the day-to-day requirements of mobilizing employees and aligning their needs. They are the reconcilers of the two sets of aspirations (those of the organization and the individual). Managers have the responsibility of providing TCS practices of coaching, support and guidance.
- *The organization* is responsible for putting responsive frameworks in place to ensure that the needs of the individual are recognized and that money is invested in tools and resources which enable them to work. These frameworks would underpin all aspects of the career lifespan:
  - recruitment and selection
  - performance planning
  - individual development planning
  - internal vacancy advertising
  - redeployment.

*Benchmarking*

In the early phase of the Career Management initiatives, the team undertook some specific information gathering. They carried out internal benchmarking studies and discovered that although there was plenty of good practice at the local and corporate level, there was no cohesion, vision or consistency between different activities. External benchmarking then took place with companies like Sears and Peugeot Talbot. The team were searching for what could complement, enhance or replace current arrangements. They discovered that in reality, with respect to career management, the organization had all the information and therefore the power. Managers were reasonably well trained but needed more, and there was nothing in place to help people to take ownership of their careers.

## Recommendations

The team believe strongly that people will be motivated to develop if development meets their needs. They recommended providing the means to help people to help themselves. Following a feasibility study, the team recommended a suite of self-development tools. They recognized from the outset that focusing on only one part of the partnership (the individual) would be unlikely to produce well-motivated and committed employees. They knew that support would have to come from managers, many of whom did not espouse an enabling style of management. They also saw that with the real-life pressures under which employees work, telling them to manage their own development on top of everything else might be counterproductive. They recognized that the company might need to invest to make the 'self-development' message a reality.

## Partnership Principle in practice: 1 – Self-development tools

One of the first tools developed was a PC-based tool called 'Horizons'. This is a self-assessment tool, available to individuals and owned by them. The organization does not require people to divulge information. It is designed to help individuals to understand themselves better, to know what motivates them and to gain a realistic sense of their strengths and weaknesses. The individual works through a series of questionnaires which look at:

- work values
- transferable skills
- occupational interests
- learning styles
- personality and temperament types.

By better understanding some of these aspects of themselves, employees are able to make clear choices about the type of role which might suit them, their training and development needs, and the kind of learning process which might be most helpful for them. They also have a clearer understanding of what gives them most job satisfaction. All of this adds up to a rich range of insights. On the strength of completing Horizons many people are able to put together a personal development plan which they are encouraged to share with their manager, a coach (not necessarily the manager) and a peer. People are thus encouraged to look for development resources beyond their immediate reporting relationship. Another benefit of introducing the tool has been the drop in 'unrealistic' applications for internal vacancies, since people are better able to judge where their particular talents might best fit.

Another tool, the 'Personal Recognition Portfolio' complements Horizons. This guides individuals in how to market themselves. It is a central folder for containing personal information, including feedback on performance and development. People are encouraged to include in their portfolio internal and external training certificates, other qualifications, their Horizons self-assessment and a note about external achievements. Again, this remains the responsibility of the individual to update and the organization makes no attempt to acquire the information.

### Partnership Principle in practice: 2 – Development tools for managers

One tool which slightly backfired was known as XXEN (short for Kaizen). This was a PC-based structured questionnaire which helps the individual to create a detailed CV. It explores the individual's skills, experience, knowledge and competencies with respect to long- and short-term development planning. This time individuals were expected to share the information with their managers. The idea was that managers could then load the information into the database for matching against possible opportunities within the organization.

However, staff loathed the instrument; they found it too complex and felt threatened by the idea of revealing their plans and aspirations to their managers, especially at a time of change. The team accepted that the tool was not well marketed and withdrew it. There are no plans to re-introduce it at this time.

A key tool in activating the Partnership Principle is the 'Professional Development Interview'. Managers are often very skilled technically, but have not in the past been required to be people developers. This tool is based on the assumption that many managers will lack the time, the skill or the inclination to coach their team members. It is designed to enable managers to build a coaching relationship with team members with the help of a structured interview. The Professional Development Interview provides managers with a toolkit which helps them to understand motivation and learning styles. As a result of asking the right questions managers learn how individuals within their team prefer to be rewarded and criticized. The toolkit provides a way of talking to staff that is consistent across the organization. It encourages and facilitates a flexible and responsive style of management.

In training managers to adopt new practices, the Career Management team have been careful to avoid a 'sheep dip' approach. Training is offered specifically to role model managers, who are then taught to train others. The power of line role models removes residual cynicism amongst their peers about the value of coaching.

### Partnership Principle in practice: 3 – Organizational resources

Standard Life has carried through its commitment to provide resources for development. One such resource, piloted in 1996, is the 'Open Access Development Centre' (OADC). This is a centrally located resource which is open to any employee. It is open from 8 a.m. until 9 p.m. during the week and is also available at the weekend. The centre is fully staffed and has a comprehensive set of development resources. These include:

*   training materials such as videos, books and journals
*   computer-based training packages
*   open-learning packages
*   self-development resources
*   multimedia learning materials.

Using their knowledge of their preferred learning styles, employees can select relevant learning media for their purposes. Learning groups meet in the OADC, and there is also scope for working alone or with the help of staff.

The OADC is underpinned by the development of role competencies, which form an element of cohesion between all the career processes. The competencies support corporate initiatives and are directly relevant to job needs. Training in computer skills and languages is available to anyone who needs it. If development is considered an essential job element, the employee is encouraged to attend the OADC during working hours and learning is given some priority.

However, the company is keen to encourage a learning community. If an individual wishes to take up a new area of interest, develop their portfolio for the longer term or even learn a non-work-specific activity such as languages, the facilities are available for them to do this out of working hours. Take-up of the facilities has been impressive, and now further OADCs have opened at two other major sites and two satellite sites to make it as easy as possible for all employees to have access to them. The initial investment of £170 000 is being recouped from savings on formal training programmes.

## Key learning point

A key learning point for the team during 1994–96 was that supporting infra-structures and communication were critical to the success of the programme. Not enough focus was perhaps given to this, and 1998 will see more work being done in this field and this learning key point keenly incorporated.

## Management style and Contribution Management

Attitude survey results suggested that a culture of empowerment was developing. However, these changes were not in isolation. A common problem when culture change is under way is that managers' behaviour does not reflect company rhetoric. To avoid this, workshops on empowerment, visioning and coaching were piloted on the executive, who support the principles. Over 600 managers have now been trained and are implementing these practices. The evolution towards coaching management styles is having an effect, and the Manager as Coach has become a key leadership practice on which managers are measured.

Another key part of the organizational framework is the reinforcement of the new culture through the pay system. A system of Contribution Management has been piloted for a year and introduced to replace the performance management system from November 1996. The new system is intended to be flexible and responsive and is based on contribution as a whole, not just on performance. Thus people are asked to consider how they can contribute and grow the company and be responsible for continuous 'personnel' development.

Contribution Management discussions take place quarterly and managers have a pot of money to allocate for specific contributions. Jobs are allocated to several 'development' bands, each underpinned by a maximum of nine core competencies. Training for all Contribution Managers is provided by licensed trainers and coaches from the line. All staff have also received a half-day training programme so that they understand the system.

## Future developments

As the Partnership Principle unfolds in practice, obvious next steps emerge. Standard Life will develop crossfunctional career paths and skills streams based on job communities. Career bridges based on role rather than function will also be clarified, making it easier for people to move laterally or vertically through job communities. The company is also keen to accredit learning through named awards and is working with several Lead Bodies to develop these. The use of technology to support development will expand, with the competencies database available via the Intranet. New self-assessment instruments, such as Horizons 2 and further OADCs, are planned.

## Benefits

Standard Life is moving closer to the ideal of providing training when, where and in the way most appropriate to individuals. The tangible demonstrations of the Partnership Principle have resulted in a significant drop in staff turnover, producing cost savings in recruitment. People are now better able to take much greater ownership of their own development, leading to more satisfying and stimulating career routes. Even while individuals are making themselves more employable, their loyalty to the organization appears to be undiminished, and in many cases is actually stronger. By investing in developing people, Standard Life is developing its culture in a way which will equip it for future changes.

Some of the main sources of discontent in changing organizations revolve around the reward systems in use. In particular, people who are dissatisfied with their career development are more likely to consider that the organization's reward scheme and leadership are inappropriate. When people are reasonably happy with their jobs, the reward scheme is seen as less of a problem. In flatter structures which offer career challenges for many, reward schemes are topical. The difficulty is knowing what needs to change and what the organization wishes to reward. In this chapter we will explore some of the issues relating to reward systems in these changing times and look at some new approaches to rewarding employees.

Reward schemes are used for a variety of purposes apart from reward. They are used, for instance, to incentivize particular types of performance, such as increased sales, and to punish those who appear to be underperforming. Reward schemes are especially important since they are a powerful means of teaching employees what is actually valued in the organization. The financial value attached to particular aspects of performance usually outweighs any company rhetoric. So if the organization encourages teamwork but continues to award significant bonuses to lone contributors, teamwork is less likely to be taken seriously.

## Hierarchical pay schemes

In times gone by, when organizations had relatively stable hierarchical structures, pay schemes were relatively clear cut. Job evaluation was used to decide how much each job was worth in terms of its contribution to the organization. Jobs were defined and allocated according to a clear set of job grades, each of which had a salary range. In some organizations there would be as many as twenty grades. Only certain grades and types of job would be eligible for a bonus, and the majority of staff would be on some form of fixed pay, which made managing the salary pot relatively straightforward. In the past, pay was often linked to seniority, with more or less automatic increases achieved year by year regardless of the individual's performance.

Progression usually involved vertical promotion through the grades, with 'high-flyers' often jumping a grade or two. Promotion meant not only more status but more money as well. Being promoted was often the only way of earning more money or breaking though a pay ceiling for a grade. In some cases, eligibility for promotion was based on age and experience rather than performance. HR specialists often appeared to have power in negotiations about pay and promotion since they were the organization's gatekeepers and saying 'no' was part of the job.

In an attempt to move towards a performance culture, many organizations over the past two decades introduced pay schemes intended to reflect performance in the job more than the job grade itself. Performance-based pay has been relatively well established for a number of years in the UK .

## What is performance?

The question of what constitutes performance or output continues to be debated. In some cases only output, or achievement against agreed targets, is taken into account. In other cases there is an increasing interest in the inputs or *how* targets have been accomplished. To support this approach there is usually an emphasis on competencies. In some organizations, a range of other cultural and behavioural elements which are meant to help the organization achieve its business strategy are taken into account. These may include, for instance, how managers operate the corporate values on leadership or how they demonstrate customer service.

Performance-based schemes need to be responsive to the business drivers, the changing technology, the new skills needed and the fact that to be successful in a new environment, people need to do different things. Broadly speaking, any reward system needs to reflect these key drivers for future organizational success.

What, for instance, are the critical roles, tasks and skills that should be rewarded? What are the critical indicators of business success in the short and medium term? Will teamwork be more critical to achieving business goals than individual performance, or will there be differences across the system? Is having one system the only way of thinking about a revised system?

## What is appropriate to a flatter structure?

Since many organizations have now restructured and delayered significantly, traditional job evaluation-based pay structures often seem outdated and inappropriate. With flatter structures, the reduced number of management levels usually means that people's job responsibilities have grown way beyond the original job description. Typically, the job environment includes large teams often managed remotely, new processes crossing and removing traditional functions and the need to create new and different relationships with a changing customer base. Allocating a 'pricing' value to a job in such changing circumstances seems restrictive.

While vertical promotion may be less possible for most people, pay systems may still be a means of providing people with a real sense of progression. Above all, reward systems need to be able to motivate, or at least not demotivate, employees when promotion opportunities are fewer. At the same time, no system can allow its costs to escalate out of control. The challenge therefore is to find a flexible and tailored alternative, or set of alternatives, which allows for a better match between organizational needs and constraints and employee needs.

Because organizations can no longer guarantee vertical promotion they are actively looking for ways to promote and introduce the idea of lateral careers. However, fixed grading schemes often deter people from making 'sideways' moves since they will actually lose pay in the bargain. Increasingly the link with pay is being disentangled from seniority. Many organizations are introducing broad banding, where a small number of wide salary bands encompass many varied roles. This should make job enrichment and lateral moves easier, as long as moves towards empowered ways of working are introduced alongside. In practice, the process of introducing broad bands is fraught with difficulty. Often the rationale for grouping together certain roles does not make sense for the job holder if jobs appear to be simply pushed together into one category.

Increasingly, variable pay is being applied to a wider range of staff than those who were conventionally incentivized to achieve targets, such as sales staff. Though bonuses send out fairly tough messages about what is required, typically the new areas of incentivization include 'soft' areas such as making creative suggestions, receiving positive feedback from customers and demonstrating leadership. When introducing variable pay in place of a wholly fixed pay system, what is rewarded as 'core' to the job may assume a lesser importance in the mind of the job holder than any aspect of the job that is singled out for variable pay. Therefore if individual bottom-line performance is the basis of the bonus, employees are likely to put their efforts into this, perhaps at the expense of other things the organization is trying to achieve in the longer term.

## The changing demands on employees

Organizations are demanding more from their staff. Not only are they expecting more in terms of output, in other words performance, there is now an increasing emphasis on the input or how people do their jobs. Many organizations recognize the importance of such 'inputs' as an employee's drive to provide customer satisfaction, their ability to work in a team and to develop others. They want people to be keen and willing to take on broader responsibilities, learn new skills and develop wider competencies. In addition, technology is bringing about a more fundamental change, switching the nature of the way work is carried out from directive tasks to process-driven activities. The increased use of technology calls for greater teamwork with broader, more flexible roles that demand a more versatile management style.

Yet if organizations require this level of flexibility of employees, reward systems in themselves may need to be flexible. Job grading needs to support these initiatives rather than work against them. For this to work, organizations need to introduce grading, reward and development systems which are in line with these needs and fully linked up with future opportunities. Not surprisingly, many organizations are now under great pressure to change their pay systems. They need flexible schemes which still evaluate relative contribution but which also allow assessment of competence and skill progression. A number of experimental reward schemes are under way. One clear trend is the move towards individual-based pay rather than job-based pay. This reflects the growing recognition that people and their skills and intellect are the real capital of organizations. Competence-based pay, based on the ability to meet individual targets, takes the notion of performance-based pay in a particular direction.

## Competence-based reward systems

Competence-based pay (CBP) is also known as knowledge- or skills-based pay. CBP is person-based rather than job-based, and works on the basis of rewarding the skills an individual possesses and actually uses. The completion of a training unit relating to a particular competency or skills unit usually results in a pay increase. Though CBP is usually available in manufacturing environments and up until now has rarely applied to managerial jobs, research carried out in the UK by the CBI found that 45 per cent of UK firms are considering linking rewards to competencies. Competence-based pay seems appropriate in flat organizations with few management levels, since it provides a larger scope for the growth of individual roles.

Where competencies are taken into account there is sometimes an element of personal development built into the target so that employees can see continuous development as part of their responsibility. The downside of such schemes is that they often fail to reflect cross-organizational teamworking, quality and other sought-after business goals. At the time when many early competency models were developed, appraisal schemes measured only the output side of performance. There were numerous examples of individuals or teams achieving all their targets but these were frequently achieved at the expense of other departments or the organization as a whole.

The difficulty with competency-based schemes is that they tend to be very complex. They rely on having identified the correct competencies in the first place, on having forms of assessment that really reveal these, and having assessors with the skill and ability to make appropriate judgements about the demonstrated competencies. Sometimes 360 degree mechanisms are used as a means of collecting 'objective' data about an individual. While such feedback can be helpful for development purposes, it becomes problematic for both the givers and the receiver of feedback if it is linked to pay. Some organizations try to integrate competency, performance and labour market considerations together in their reward system. Often these systems fail.

Competencies are inputs, they are a quick way of thinking of people in their roles and looking at key requirements and gaps in the way people meet these requirements. However, when it comes to performance there may be external environmental factors to take into consideration. Competencies are only part of a very varied picture. Pay is one thing but the opportunity to develop is another. People need to be helped to develop their competencies and be rewarded for performance.

# Job families

In federated organizations, it is difficult to devise a reward scheme that offers a company-wide grade structure along with local autonomy. Several companies have attempted to move away from set grading schemes but are struggling to find a more responsive alternative. ICL has introduced the notion of 'job families', which aims to tie all the new roles and rewards into other aspects of HR processes such as recruiting, training, organization, management style and internal communication. They wanted to introduce a flexible system which could meet both business and employee needs in changing times.

In the past ICL was a highly integrated company with a hierarchical grade structure based on job evaluation. The principle of performance-related pay was well established. In a period of rapid technological change, with markets diversifying and new competitors, the company has had to develop new ways of working. ICL recognize that people in a service environment are the products. They understand that skills and the ways these are used will be competitive differentiators. They are aware that the company is moving from one, relatively well-known, steady state to a state where change is likely to be an ongoing feature. They recognize that the reward system needs to be part of a holistic set of parallel processes that are critical in releasing people's potential and value. The job family approach is a response to this.

In ICL, job families, which are now called 'professional communities', have been established that link to the business drivers that relate in each business. They have established the capabilities and behaviours required by investigating and modelling the business processes. The required capabilities are then established and combined into roles. The key performance measures are then directly cascaded from the measures of business performance. The rationale for rewarding is based on rewarding today's performance and paying the going rate for the skills. Unlike the approach of benchmarking competitors and customers against what they did, this approach is intended to set the agenda by focusing on the skills and behaviours needed for tomorrow. They are focusing on 'total pay', which includes both benefits and pay as well as taking into account employees' perception of the package.

Job families are intended to help managers understand how people add value to the business by measuring the value of the inputs, such as skills and capabilities, against the outputs for each type of role. Although deciding on performance is inevitably a subjective process, the approach offers managers a set of tools with which they can make more objective judgements. The approach can be challenging for some, since people's progress will depend in future more on increasing their personal capability than on grade. Since it is envisaged that this is a dynamic, rather than a fixed, process, people will be able to slide down, as well as go up the slope since the value needed in the future may not be the same as in the past.

Job families reflect the corporate strategy but also take into account the different markets for skills. There is no attempt to standardize every job family into a single company structure for pay. They provide a broad role description, define the three key levels at which the role is to be performed and the capabilities required at each level. There are different measures of success for each job family. These measures have to be adaptive for different sorts of people. Having one set of measures imposed across the business would probably work counter to the needs of some parts of the business. What is needed is not one set of rules but a methodology that different businesses can adapt to what is key for them. The notion of individual value and capability is crucial, with increased value reflected in earnings. Since it is recognized that employee inputs and outputs have both changed, the need to create an employment environment that meets employee and business needs is a prime consideration.

Consequently, potential applications of job families extend beyond remuneration. The approach applies to career development, and people are encouraged to develop their career routes breadthwise. It also allows for more strategic recruitment since the company recognizes that a range of roles is needed, rather than a single set of 'ideal' competencies. Assessment and development centres help employees to see if they have the capabilities for new roles. In managing performance, managers must have the right skill set so that employees are appropriately focused into roles, developed and managed. The approach also applies to appraisals since the key performance indicators for each job family derive from the business drivers and are then built into role processes. This makes the process more responsive to the changing business environment.

## Team-based pay

Many organizations are now trying to encourage teamworking and want to see this reflected in their pay schemes. Many employers have misgivings about the effectiveness of individual performance-related pay schemes. A recent CBI survey found that one in seven organizations expected to introduce team rewards below senior management level before the end of the century. Team-based pay schemes provide financial rewards to individual employees working within a formally established team. Payments are linked to team performance or the achievement of agreed team objectives.

Team-based pay gets a good press. According to its supporters there is mounting evidence that in the new delayered organization team pay can help to reinforce teamworking arrangements and encourage more effective team performance. But while team rewards may offer some important advantages, their implementation is by no means easy and can be a high-risk strategy. Experience suggests that improving team performance cannot be left to the reward system alone. The quality of teamwork depends on a whole range of factors, including the organization culture, management style and performance management systems.

Team pay looks good in theory but has not yet been proved to be effective for white-collar workers. Research carried out by the Institute of Personnel and Development (IPD) (1996) has shown that team pay is often more talked about than practised. One of the drawbacks of the wider spread of team pay is that every scheme is unique. It is not possible simply to adopt some broad recommendations from other organizations, nor are such schemes easy to design or manage.

Part of the difficulty lies in defining a team. Typically there may be several types of team operating within an organization. There is usually a top management team providing direction within the organization. Then there are work teams which are self-contained and permanent, with a focus on achieving common objectives. In addition there are project teams that are brought together to complete a specific task and that are disbanded once it is completed. Then there are *ad hoc* teams set up to deal with specific problems: these are usually short-lived and operate as a task force.

The IPD found that team pay works best if teams stand alone with agreed targets and standards, have autonomy, are composed of people whose work is interdependent, are stable, are well-established and make good use of complementary skills. Similarly, they need to be composed of flexible, multi-skilled team players who are capable of expressing a different point of view, if it is for the good of the whole. Before team pay is considered it is necessary to ensure that basic pay is right.

Some companies see little need for team incentives, while others recognize that flexible working with individuals sharing responsibility implies greater pay equality. Pay strategies for team-working are diverging. There are companies that are devising incentives such as coupled team and individual bonuses, while others are flattening pay differentials and putting little emphasis on incentives. Hierarchical pay structures are not appropriate for teamworking. It is difficult to foster team spirit if individuals are concentrating on promotion.

There are three basic elements to a reward package that includes teamworking. First, there is the individual element, the basic salary but varied in relation to performance or skills/competence. Second, there is a team element related to the achievement of team targets, and third, an organizational element related to business performance measured as profit or added value. These may be in the form of cash or shares. The drawback to team pay can be that individuals may feel that their specific contribution is diminished. Teams may also compel people to conform to oppressive group norms. This may result in low output that is sufficient only to gain a reasonable reward.

## Recognition

Herzberg's theory distinguishes between so-called 'maintenance' factors, or hygiene factors, and real motivators. Thus money is sometimes thought to be a motivator, and it certainly appears to be for some people, at least at some stages of their career. However, money is just as likely to demotivate. Take the example of someone who is told by their manger that they are going to get a 10 per cent pay rise in recognition of superb performance. The employee will no doubt be very pleased unless he/she finds out that other members of the team are going to get a 15 per cent pay rise. In flatter structures, money alone does not seem to be a key factor in enhancing motivation, except in circumstances where it is seen as an alternative form of career development with the idea of staged or rapid progression being maintained through pay.

Similarly, once the employee has grown used to the level of pay, no matter how large the initial rise, money in itself ceases to be motivating, although losing money continues to be demotivating. There are numerous examples of people whose jobs have been effectively downgraded during delayering, and so have their pay and benefits. The 'running sore' effect of such organizational decisions can cause people to see themselves as victims. Almost inevitably, loyalty to the organization can be adversely affected.

In practice it is probably unrealistic to expect any pay structure to provide all the answers to the question of how to motivate people. In theory, pay structures are really just elaborate ways of recognizing people and providing a fair exchange for their labours – an actual income. An arguably more important means of motivating people is often underestimated since it does not lie in one system-wide approach. Recognition by other people of what an individual or team has achieved can be very reinforcing, confidence-building and supportive. As such it can form part of an individual's 'psychological' income or what makes coming to work really worthwhile. Given the need for people to work in new ways, including in teams, formal recognition processes are a means of encouraging people to focus on what the organization really needs, both in the long and short term.

Some organizations are introducing or reviving corporate recognition schemes. It seems that these rarely have the effect of motivating people but do appear to reward individuals and teams for outstanding performance. The danger can be that employees perceive such schemes to be a cheap way of rewarding employees rather than an adequate recognition of value added. An engineer in a multinational communications organization was part of a team working on a new product. When the time approached for the product launch, consultants were brought in to identify an appropriate name. After £50 000 had been spent and a satisfactory name had still not been identified, the project team were finally asked for their ideas. The engineer in question had his suggestion adopted. He did not appreciate the company's gesture of recognition – a bottle of champagne at Christmas.

Although recognition schemes can have a vital part to play in reinforcing the organization's vision, the onus for providing ongoing recognition generally falls on the line manager. Generally employees are used to receiving recognition in the form of criticism when things go wrong. When recognition of improved performance is part of the manager's toolkit, the team respond with improved performance. It is part of the virtuous cycle of motivation that builds confidence and releases potential. One line manager in a pharmaceutical company supported an employee who had previously been an adequate rather than an outstanding performer as he took on a new role. With her coaching and recognition as his performance improved, the employee grew in confidence. Within weeks, the individual was able to achieve a significant sale in a difficult market.

Recognition seems to work best when it is timely and specific. Peer feedback can be as motivating and reinforcing as that given by a manager. In 3M a 'thank you' scheme allows any colleague to send a small token of recognition to any other colleague. Ideally, the individual should have some say in how he or she is recognized, to ensure that the form of recognition has some financial or intrinsic value to the recipient. There should also be some element of unpredictability about formal recognition schemes so that they do not become 'formula' and stale.

## How do people want to be rewarded?

In the Roffey Park research, people were asked which forms of reward they found most motivating. Most employees considered that the chance for personal achievement and job satisfaction motivated them most. Another important aspect of this was having those achievements recognized by others, especially bosses. By and large, intrinsic rewards such as job satisfaction, outweighed extrinsic rewards such as money every time. Of course, some people are motivated by money. As might be expected, there was an age relationship – people below the age of thirty were more likely to be motivated by the prospect of more money.

This contrasts sharply with what happens in practice, with most organizations relying on their pay scheme to both motivate and reward employees. For while organizations try to ensure that their scheme is tailored to rewarding the kind of performance the organization needs, there is often less effort put into thinking about how people may prefer to be rewarded. Some of the more imaginative schemes try to be responsive to employee requests. So the past few years have seen the introduction of extrinsic rewards such as:

- profit (gain) sharing
- flexible benefits
- bonuses payable in terms of extra leave rather than pay
- bonuses payable towards prestigious qualifications
- deferred incentives
- extending private health schemes to all employees and their families
- longer holidays
- sponsored holidays
- 'free' family holidays in company-owned cottages
- enhanced early retirement.

### Psychological income

Less attention is often paid to the range of intrinsic rewards or 'psychological income' that may be truly motivating. This is more complex since it involves understanding what motivates any one person. Perhaps the person best placed to do this is the individual's manager, but this is not always the case. For many people, the chance to travel and variety in their work are important features. For someone who is a keen specialist in their area, attending a conference in their specialist area or representing the company as an industry expert can enhance their prestige inside and beyond the organization. For someone else, the opportunity to take on a new job challenge or learn a new skill can be very motivating. Non-financial incentives such as having greater autonomy in one's role, or being able to achieve a better balance between work and home life, can be genuinely and continuously rewarding. Discussions with individuals about their own package can help both parties understand what is an appropriate and motivating reward.

### Valuing contribution

While bonus-related and performance-related pay can reinforce the results that distinguish the most 'successful' employees from the rest, rewarding performance should involve rewarding quality as well as bottom-line contribution. This is where an organization needs to be clear that different types of contribution are required in order to achieve the bottom-line results of the 'stars'. This seems to be increasingly in line with what many employees are asking for.

When people were asked how they would wish their reward system to be amended, the overwhelming majority thought that any new scheme should take personal achievement and development into account. The difference that any individual makes needs to be reflected, and recognition by line managers was a vital ingredient. Very few people favoured team bonuses, preferring individual achievement to stand out. This could cause difficulties for companies planning to introduce such rewards. More and more organizations are starting to recognize this and talk in terms of 'value' and 'contribution' management rather than 'performance' management.

It seems that the more impersonal and corporate the scheme, the less employees find financial reward motivating. It is as if there are too many external factors that have a bearing on the pay decision, reducing the importance of individual achievement. It is really important that people can see the link between what they have achieved and what they are paid. Producing excellent performance then becomes a matter of individual pride and motivation. However, no matter how rigid the pay system appears to be, the importance of recognizing the unique contribution of each individual is obvious. This is where line managers and peers have such an important role to play. If an organization is able to revise its reward systems, it may be useful to ask employees to identify the important considerations that need to be taken into account.

The more employees feel a sense of involvement and ownership of the scheme, the more they are likely to find it motivating. The more choice, flexibility but clarity that can be built in, the better. The key to any reward scheme is ensuring that it gets people motivated, rather than 'turned off'. People need to know that they are valued by their employer and learn to value themselves. When people feel valued and confident, they are more likely than not to release their potential to the benefit of the organization. When this happens, the virtuous cycle of motivation is under way.

# 17    *Conclusion*

Looking back over the past few years of rapid organizational change, the pendulum swings between different types of organization structure are evident, with shifts from regional to central structures and back again – networked, matrix, project-based and other organization forms waiting to be superseded by yet different patterns. Through many of these trends there is arguably a more persistent trend – a dominant tendency towards the lean organization. It is unlikely that the days of stability and high staffing levels will come back as business growth returns. Technology makes possible new products and business opportunities as well as enabling new ways of working.

Perhaps more than ever before, the increasingly competitive global marketplace is numbering the days of the stand-alone organization which is able to invent and sell its products to a grateful world. In days gone by, organizations were able to contain threats and capitalize on opportunities in a hostile trading environment by becoming bigger than the competition. Nowadays, organization strategies are more likely to be driven by the need for flexibility and partnering arrangements. Mergers, acquisitions, strategic alliances, or joint ventures as means of gaining and maintaining market penetration and supremacy are now commonplace. The days of the 'fat' organization with ample staffing levels and the separation of strategy from implementation are probably over.

So if lean organizations are here to stay, what are the implications for employees? Currently the negative effects seem to outweigh the benefits. This is particularly the case when the change process itself is badly handled or appears to be imposed from outside the organization. Much has been written about the stressful effects of feeling that one has little control over one's working environment. The British Civil Service is perhaps a case in point. In such circumstances it is all too easy to understand how employees can perceive themselves to be victims rather than the fully functional, high-performing individuals their organizations want them to be. The damaging cocktail of negative ingredients, namely lack of career development, poor leadership and inappropriate rewards, perhaps reflects the deeper malaise experienced by employees in organizations in transition. Overwork, continuing role confusion, and lack of resources add to the problem.

## The future of lean organizations

So are lean organizations doomed to extinction because the effects on employees are not sustainable? Alternatively is it just a matter of time before people adjust to the new realities? Is pressure that is seen as stressful today likely to be accepted as the norm and cease to be stressful? Since any structure will determine to some extent how people behave, how can lean organization structures support the achievement of organizational goals rather than work against them?

We are moving into an era when it no longer makes sense to be 'lean and mean'. Employers no longer have the whip hand in dictating conditions in many sectors. In the age of the 'knowledge' or 'information' worker, organizations are increasingly dependent on the goodwill, loyalty and commitment of employees; just telling people to 'put up and shut up' is not good enough. In every sector organizations that have realized this are struggling to become the employer of choice. Achieving that status is neither simple nor easy. It relies on a range of cultural factors and organizational intentions being appropriate.

The knowledge worker is becoming more selective. In years gone by, organizations could rely on competitive salaries and blue-chip reputations to attract the best candidates. Now, potential employees are looking much more closely at the fit between their needs and those of the organization. This is not just a fit in terms of the basic package. As messages about new career forms percolate through society, people are considering more obviously what development opportunities they will have in the new organization. At a more basic level, as we emerge from the so-called 'caring nineties' few people opt to join organizations with a reputation for ruthless exploitation of staff, no matter how good the package appears to be.

## Becoming a lean and clean organization

So what does it take to become a 'lean and clean' organization? First, a recognition that employees matter and that how they feel makes a difference to how they perform and therefore to the bottom line. It is not a question of being soft-hearted; it makes sound business sense. Peoples' motivation can be the vital missing component in the business effectiveness jigsaw. How can organizations realistically target to achieve improved employee motivation? Given that motivation is so individual, perhaps the best way forward is to put employee needs on the business agenda. Broadly speaking, this means addressing three employee-related questions that are implicit and therefore do not often get answered:

- What is my role?
- Where do I fit in?
- What is my future?

## Developing future directions

To be able to answer these questions at an individual level, an organization needs to have answers at the corporate level. There has to be a balance between short-termism and building for the future. There also has to be a partnership approach to developing the future with employees, rather than viewing people as dispensable overheads. People who perceive that their organization views them this way are likely to lose commitment to the organization. It is a matter of people feeling valued. As one UK civil servant said: 'I look forward to the day when the government treats staff as valued employees, not the butt of their public spending strategy.'

So answering the question 'What is my role?' at the organizational level requires a clear business strategy and future direction that is well-communicated and understood by staff. People do not have to like the direction, but at least if they are aware of it, they have a choice about their next steps. The vision, mission and strategic purpose of the organization need therefore to be clearly communicated, and its successes and strengths celebrated. Employees need to know that what they are doing makes a difference. Educating, informing and involving people in the change process lead to true empowerment.

Communication should not be a one-off activity but a multiple set of relationships and processes where the power of influential individuals to model desirable behaviours that reinforce the vision should not be underestimated. Clear, honest communication on a regular basis is critical in building trust internally and generating true confidence in the future. Leaders who are able and willing to 'walk the talk' are vital to gaining employee commitment to change and to building up a climate of trust. As one film industry employee put it: 'We need a consistent and positive management to motivate change.' Without this, people are unlikely to be willing to innovate and otherwise take the risks that are implicit in learning. A stultified culture is unlikely to equip an organization for the next millennium.

## Creating a change-oriented culture

Being clear about what kind of culture will help the organization achieve its vision is the first step towards changing those aspects of the culture that work against the vision and strengthening those that are working for it. Given that, as ever, the future is full of unknowns, a culture that is receptive and responsive to change is at least an insurance against disaster. If problems occur, a responsive culture enables the organization to adapt quickly and change course. Going beyond responsiveness to a culture which positively embraces change and is continuously developing new ideas is perhaps a key to future competitiveness. Organizations with such a culture are likely to be those that, being in the forefront of economic effectiveness, give others something to respond to.

So in creating a change-oriented culture, organizations must be clear about what in the status quo may need to be challenged, since any change upsets vested interests. This may include removing systems and processes that reinforce behaviours more appropriate to the organization as it was, rather than the organization which is emerging. Understanding what gets in the way of the new culture is important. In the words of a famous cartoon character: 'You can observe a lot, just by watching.' However, a willingness to act on that understanding is even more important. Cultural 'irritants', such as reserved parking for managers, office size and other status issues, may need to be addressed. Managers who cannot adapt to a more empowered culture may need to be helped into other roles since they are squandering the organization's potential in its current workforce. Planning around future resources, including people, is essential if recruitment is to be truly strategic and reinforce the new culture.

Working in teams and being able to recognize interdependencies will be increasingly important. Similarly, in change-orientated cultures, leadership will be a vital factor in organizational survival. Leadership does not have to be vested in a few individuals or roles, but it does need to be somewhere in the organization, providing focus and coherence for the future. Leaders can help people develop a positive and pragmatic approach to the future, as well as ensure that the organization is well matched to its competitive environment. Leaders are at the key interface between the organization and other stakeholders, such as shareholders, who may have different and shorter-term requirements of the organization. Without a longer-term investment perspective on staffing, it is unlikely that organizations will be able to build up and retain their key resource, people, in years to come. Leaders may need to be courageous and politically skilled to act as the honest broker between conflicting interests. Lack of leadership or inappropriate leadership merely produces drift or demoralization.

An important aspect of preparing for the future is developing a culture in which learning is valued and rewarded. Developing a multi-skilled and motivated workforce takes time and investment. Ensuring that the skills being developed are going to be helpful to the organization as it moves forward involves aligning business and people development strategies. Thus any business plan should be overtly linked to individual developmental objectives. Self-development should be encouraged and supported. Structured programmes for personal learning should be provided. Learning, and the development of all the other behaviours that organizations are calling for, should be recognized and rewarded, as well as the results achieved.

While individuals may be responsible for managing their own motivation, increasingly the challenge for organizations is to eliminate many of the common demotivators and to create an environment in which people are likely to be motivated. Many of the common irritants are to be found in Human Resource systems which are out of 'sync' with the lean organization. Processes such as performance appraisal should be adjusted in the light of what 'performance' really means in the lean organization. Is it just the 'what' of bottom-line performance or also the 'how'? Should appraisal merely reflect on past performance or focus also on development for the future? The need for coordination and consistency in practices has never been greater.

Similarly, some of the main sources of dissatisfaction for employees are the ways in which they are rewarded. In the long term, if people are going to have fewer opportunities for vertical promotion, pay schemes may have to be decoupled from hierarchical levels so that individual contribution can be truly reflected in pay. If people are being encouraged to learn new skills, develop their careers sideways and in other ways contribute more to the organization, the difference they make should be evident to the individuals and their managers. My research suggests that reward schemes which reflect individual development, achievement and performance are more likely to motivate people than standard performance-related pay schemes. This is where personnel specialists, working in partnership with line management, have a particular role to play. Through aligning all aspects of the human resource cycle to the business needs, which involves taking employees' needs into account, personnel specialists can help people answer the questions 'Where do I fit in?' and 'What is my future?'

These are perhaps the toughest questions to answer since they imply that the answers are fixed, while in reality yet more change may be on its way. At a basic level, helping people to be clear about their role and how they can add value to the organization is a way of activating their energies. Helping them to see what skills and competencies might be helpful in the future gives them the choice about developing them or not. Roles should allow individuals room to grow. Developing assessment processes and learning resources can be useful.

Workforce loyalty is a big factor in finding creative futures but it cannot be mandated: loyalty has to be two-way. Helping people to become more employable is perhaps a tangible way of demonstrating commitment to the workforce. People need to be able to feel that their good work today will help them secure a good future. Similarly, given the ongoing uncertainty of the nature of employment, perhaps the biggest proof of commitment to staff is offering continued employment. This may involve not overhiring when times are good but getting the best out of the existing workforce. Downsizing can then be achieved gradually by attrition. Enabling people to consider new career tracks and making these possible within the organization is a good way of activating potential and removing bottlenecks productively.

Careers are the key area where a partnership between the orga-nization and the individual is required. Many people will need to manage their careers more actively than in the past. This will involve becoming aware of current strengths and weaknesses, iden-tifying the skills to develop and possible development options, and taking responsibility for making these happen. No doubt some people will continue to lead an apparently privileged existence on the careers front, but increasingly the people who are proactive, make themselves visible as well as doing an excellent job are those who seem to have all the 'luck'. In changing times, perhaps more than ever, the old formula:

Luck = preparation meeting opportunity

may hold true. Organizations, too, cannot afford to wash their hands of the career development issue. It remains one of the main sources of dissatisfaction. Imaginative and employee-friendly systems may need to be set up to ensure that people are able to adjust their career expectations and can then develop satisfying, challenging and rewarding roles for themselves.

Providing support for development, whether on the job or off the job, or by offering training, will be vital if people are to gain the skills and the motivation to carry out new and more complex roles. This support can take many forms, as we have seen. Perhaps one of the most telling forms is allowing employees to acquire new skills in work time, rather than requiring them to learn in their own time. One major multinational takes this issue so seriously that a major recruitment campaign has been launched to recruit dozens of new graduates. The idea is to build a bit of slack back into the system so that others may develop beyond their role.

Above all, creating a less pressured work environment may seem a pipe-dream but it is probably management's greatest challenge. What needs to stop being done, in order that more important things can be achieved? Just 'working smarter' is not enough. It is unreasonable to expect employees to continue to pay with their well-being and health for corporate greed. That is where down-sizing takes on the status of 'dumbsizing'. Leanness may not be sustainable and some 'fat' may need to be put back into the system. Giving people a say in their own personal and business futures is not running the risk of anarchy. It is recognizing that people are unlikely to put all their motivation into their work if they feel that they are exploited, undervalued or that what they do is the base-line, with ever higher targets to be achieved tomorrow.

Perhaps in order to prepare for the future we need to learn from the recent past. In the days when certain products were in short supply, organizations could afford to be arrogantly indifferent to the needs of their customers. With increased competition and customer choice, organizations have mostly stopped taking their customers for granted. Many have learnt painful lessons from their balance sheets about the perils of doing this and have managed to adapt their service to customer requirements in the nick of time. Perhaps the early warning signs are now flashing on the employee front. The skilled, knowledge workers of today and tomorrow can manage their own motivation, but they may do this in organizations other than yours unless their needs are taken into account. Treating employees as valued customers is perhaps the best way of ensuring that they are motivated to 'fire on all cylinders'.

# References and further reading

Abrahams, B. (1996). Life after downsizing. *Marketing*, 30 May.

Ashridge Management Index (1996). Rich but are they happy? *Accountancy Age*, March, 8.

Bagnall, S. (1996). An appetite to keep customers satisfied. *The Times*, 10 February.

Bardwick, J. M. (1986). *The Plateauing Trap*. American Management Association.

Belbin, M. (1981). *Management Teams: Why They Succeed or Fail*. Heinemann.

Bennis, W. (1989). *On Becoming a Leader*. Addison-Wesley.

Bennis, W. and Nanus, B. (1985). *Leaders*. Harper and Row.

Bridges, W. (1995). *Jobshift*. Nicholas Brealey Publishing.

Caulkin, S. (1995). The New Avengers. *Management Today*, November, 48–52.

Clemmer, J. and McNeil, A. (1990). *Leadership Skills for Every Manager*. Piatkus.

Cooper, C. (1994). Presentees: new slaves of the office who run on fear. *Sunday Times*, 16 October.

Cranfield HR Research Centre. *Research into the Financial Services Industry*.

Daly, N. (1996). Career planning shifts gear. *Personnel Today*, 2 July, 15.

De Woot, P. (1992). *Towards a European Management Model*. EFMD Forum.

Depree, M. (1993). *Leadership Jazz: The Art of Conducting Business Through Leadership, Followership, Teamwork, Voice, Touch*. Dell.

DFEE. *Labour Market & Skill Trends 1996/1997*. Skills and Enterprise Network.

Doherty, N. and Horstead, J. (1995). Helping survivors to stay on board. *People Management,* 1, 26–9.

Drew, S. (1994). BPR in financial services: factors for success. *Long Range Planning,* 27, 32.

Drucker, P. F. (1989). *The New Realities.* Harper and Row.

Evans, C. (1997). *Managing the Flexible Workforce: A Sourcebook for Change.* Roffey Park Management Institute.

Evans, T. (1996). Recognising and rewarding individual roles and competencies. Paper presented at the Business Intelligence Conference: Developing Your Company's Human Capital, June 1996.

Gelder, M. G., ed. (1996). *Oxford Textbook of Psychiatry.* Oxford University Press.

Gretton, I. (1995). Taking the lead in leadership. *Professional Manager,* January, 20–2.

Hall, D. T. (1985) Project work as an antidote to career planning in the declining engineering organization. *Human Resource Management,* 24 (3), 271–92.

Hall, D. T. (1996). *The Career is Dead – Long live the Career.* Jossey-Bass.

Handy, C. (1978). *Gods of Management: How They Worked and Why They Fail.* Sovereign Press.

Hastings, M. O. W. (1996). *Flexibility and Fairness.* Institute of Management Research Report.

Heard, R. (1996). A soupcon of loyalty. *International Forum,* 3.

Hersey, P. (1984). *The Situational Leader.* Center for Leadership Studies.

Herzberg, F. (1966). *Work and the Nature of Man.* World Publishing Co.

Holbeche, L. (1994). *Career Development in Flatter Structures: Raising the Issues.* Roffey Park Management Institute.

Holbeche, L. (1994). London Underground case study. In *Career Development in Flatter Structures, Research Report 1.* Roffey Park Management Institute.

Holbeche. L. (1995) *Career Development in Flatter Structures: Organizational Practices.* Roffey Park Management Institute.

Holbeche, L. (1997). *Career Development: The Impact of Flatter Structures on Careers.* Butterworth-Heinemann.

Institute of Personnel and Development (1996). *The IPD Guide on Team Reward.* Institute of Personnel and Development.

IRS Employment Trends: Pay and Benefits Bulletin (1996). *Team Reward: Part One.* No. 604, PABB 2–5.

ISR International Survey Research (ISR) (1995). *Employee Satisfaction: Tracking European Trends.* International Survey Research Ltd.

Jacobson, B. and Kaye, B. (1993). Balancing act. *Training and Development*, February, 24–7.

Johnson, P. R. and Indvik, J. (1992). The mindfull use of mental capital in career development. *International Journal of Career Development*, **4**, 8.

Judge,T., Bretz, R. D. Jr, Kennedy, D. J. and Bloom, M. C. (1996). People as sculptors vs. sculpture: test of a dispositional model of career. Paper presented at American Academy Of Management Conference, Cincinnati, August 1996.

Judge, L. and Cheung, M.-Y. (1993). *Equal Opportunities in Management, Education and Development.* Research Project.

Kotter, J. P. (1995). Leading change: why transformation efforts fail. *Harvard Business Review*, **73** (2), 59–67.

Kouzes, J. M. and Posner, B. Z. (1993). *Credibility: How Leaders Gain and Lose It, Why People Demand It.* Jossey Bass.

Kransdorff, A. (1995). Succession planning in a fast changing world. *Training Officer*, **31** (2), 52–3.

Kubler-Rosse, E. (1989). *On Death and Dying.* Routledge.

Laabs, J. J. (1996). Downshifters: workers are scaling back. *Personnel Journal*, March, 62, 64, 66, 68, 70, 72, 74, 76.

Levin, I. (1991). *Stepford Wives.* Bantam.

Levine, S. and Crom, M. (1994). *The Leader in You.* Simon and Schuster.

Lewin, K. (1958). *Group Decisions and Social Change. Readings in Social Psychology.* Holt, Rhinehart & Winston.

Lifo, copyright Lifo Associates (1988). Division of Stuart Atkins, Allan Katcher International Inc.

Lombardo, M. and Eichinger, R. (1989). *Eighty-eight Assignments for Development in Place: Enhancing the Developmental Challenge of Existing Jobs.* Center for Creative Leadership.

MacLachlan, R. (1995). Flatter structures create problems of their own. *People Management*, 23 March, 16.

Marshall, J. (1989). Revisioning career concepts: a feminist invitation. In *Handbook of Career Theory* (M. B. Arthur, D. T. Hall and B. S. Laurence, eds) 275–91. Cambridge University Press.

Maslow, A. (1943). A theory of of human motivation. *Psychological Review*, **50**, 370–96.

Mayo, A. (1991). *Managing Careers.* IPM.

McAdams, J. L. (1996). *The Reward Plan Advantage.* Jossey Bass.

McCall, M. W. J. R., Lombards, M. M. and Morrison, A. M. (1988). *The Lessons of Experience*. Lexington Books.

McKenna, S. (1995). The cultural transferability of business and organisational re-engineering: examples from Southeast Asia. *The TQM Magazine*, 7, 21–16.

MORI Survey (1995). (Commissioned by *Security Gazette and Control Risks*.)

Moss Kanter, R. (1994). Change in the global economy: an interview with Rosabeth Moss Kanter. *European Management Journal*, 12 (1), 1–9.

*Myers Briggs Type Indicator* (1987). Oxford Psychologists Press Ltd.

Personnel Today survey quoted in: Whatever happened to leisure?, *Management Today*, May 1996.

Post, F. (1989). Beware of your stakeholders. *Journal of Management Development*, 8, 28–35.

Ratiu, I. (1983). Thinking internationally: a comparison of how international executives learn. *International Studies of Man and Organisation*, xiii, (1–2), 139–50.

Research International research quoted in *Loyalty*, May 1996.

Roach, S. S. (1996). quoted in *The Independent*, 12 May.

Schein, E. H. (1996). Career anchors revisited: implications for career development in the 21st century. *The Academy of Management Executive*, X, 80–89.

Stamp, G. and Stamp, C. (1993). Wellbeing at work: aligning purposes, people, strategies and structures. *The International Journal of Career Management*, 5 (whole issue).

*Strength Deployment Inventory* (1994). Personal Strengths Publishing Inc.

Swierczek, F. and Hirsch, G. (1994). Joint ventures in Asia and multicultural management. *European Management Journal*, 12, 197–209.

Terazono, E. (1994). Japanese companies squeeze their white collar workers. *The Financial Times*, 23 May, 12.

Tremblay, M., Wils, T. and Lacombe, M. (1996). Structural, content and salary plateaus: their influence on engineers' attitudes. Research paper 96/2. Department of Industrial Relations, University of Quebec.

Unruh, J. A. (1993). Change begins and 'Square Zero'. *Directors and Boards*, 17, 55.

Waitley, D. (1995). *Empires of the Mind*. Nicholas Brealey Publishing.

Waterman, R. (1994). *The Frontiers of Excellence*. Nicholas Brealey Publishing.

Whatmore, J. (1996). *Managing Creative Groups*. Roffey Park Management Institute.

Wickens, P. (1995). *The Ascendant Organisation*. Macmillan Press.

Yarwood, V. (1993). The new style of leaders: what does it take to be No.1? *Management*, **35** (September), 32–8.

# Index

3